BEYOND PITCAIRN

Harvestime
Books   *Books for Happier Homes*

HB—301

BEYOND PITCAIRN
by the Editor of Harvestime Books

Harvestime Books
Altamont, TN 37301 USA

Printed in the United States of America

Cover Painting: John Steel

Inside Sketches and Maps: The Author

BEYOND PITCAIRN

About the Cover: January 23, 1790 dawned bright and beautiful as the H.M.S. Bounty sailed eastward. Toward the middle of the day, the men on board discovered where their captain had been taking them. Pitcairn Island loomed large before them. Yes, they had reached their new home, but what the future held, none could know.

Contents

A list of maps in this book will be found on pages 236-238

To The South Pacific

Out in the Pacific there is an island that time forgot.

A little over two hundred years into the past will bring us to it. For there we shall find one of the most fascinating adventures of all time.

Far out in the Pacific Ocean, on the outer edge of the Tuamotu Archipelago, at Latitude 25⁰5' S., and Longitude 130⁰5' W, is a green paradise known as Pitcairn Island. About two miles long and one mile wide, it is ringed with a rugged coast of cliffs, and within their protecting care is nestled rich, fertile soil, and the mild climate and lush tropical fruit that makes the South Pacific Isles so famous.

But there is more to this little island than its location or its climate. For here is to be found the rendezvous of one of the most amazing stories in all sailing history.

Our story actually begins on July 2, 1767, when a midshipman climbed the ship's masthead of the Swallow and called out, "Land ahoy!" He had sighted a previously unknown island. Philip Carteret, captain of this British sailing ship in the midst of a voyage around the world, carefully checked through his charts and not finding the island listed, recorded its longitude and latitude and named it in honor of the midshipman that first spotted it. He wrote down the name, "Pitcairn," and in his ship's log he said that it was about three thousand miles west of Chile. "It was like a great rock rising from the sea," he wrote, "about five miles round, apparently uninhabited, with trees on it, and a stream of water running down one side. The surf breaking upon the rocks rendered landing difficult. After examining it from the ship, I called it 'Pitcairn Island,' in honor of my midshipman, and sailed on."

What Captain Philip Carteret wrote in his log actually told a lot. The island was uninhabited and it had water and soil. If he had not mentioned this, the little island probably would never have entered history in the surprising way that it did.

But now, let us go on with the story. It is the year 1777, and the British government is planning to send an expedition to the South Pacific. Early explorers of the Pacific, such as William Dampier and George Anson, had brought back to Europe fascinating tales of the South Pacific islands and its peoples. One food that they particularly mentioned was the breadfruit. Later, Captain Cook, following his trans-world voyage, also commented on the breadfruit plant, told of its very fine qualities and declared that it was the staple diet of the Pacific islanders and that they were able to obtain it for eight months out of the year.

In 1777 the Royal Society of Arts in London, England, offered a gold medal to whoever should succeed in transplanting the breadfruit to the West Indies in order to help feed the workers on the sugar plantations there. King George III, recently defeated in a war to retain possession of the American Colonies, now had the opportunity to give his thoughts to some other part of the world. And so the British Admiralty was given permission to fit out a ship that would win the gold medal. Its destination was Tahiti. There it was to collect a supply of young plants of the breadfruit and carry them to the West Indies in the Gulf of Mexico.

It was recognized that this would be a unique voyage, and the attention of all Europe was upon it. One of the best merchant ships obtainable was purchased by the Naval Board for this purpose—the Bethia. It was renamed the Bounty, and Lieutenant William Bligh was given command of the vessel.

Bligh was a short man, small-featured, about thirty-three years old. Naval historians tell us he was not a man to inspire love. He is variously described as irritable, truculent, overbearing, and a driver rather than a leader of men. But in those days,

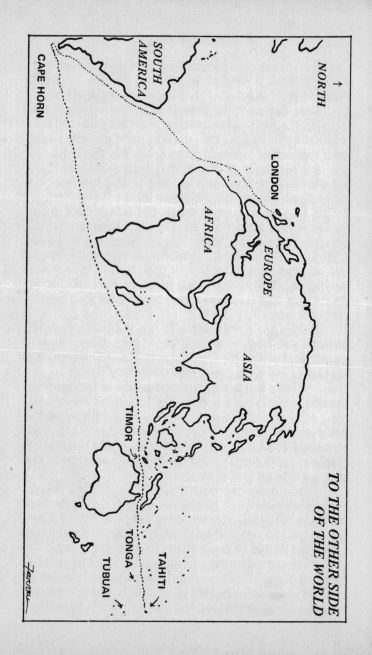

TO THE OTHER SIDE OF THE WORLD

such qualities would not rule him out, for he knew how to command the men that manned the ships.

Forty-five men between the ages of seventeen and forty were signed on as crewmen. Instead of exploring new lands or engaging in conquest, this expedition was designed to promote good will and to exchange colonial benefits, and therefore the crew was carefully selected.

As the officer second-in-command, twenty-two year old Fletcher Christian was chosen. Christian was a man highly regarded in the admiralty, and was generally conceded to be one who would rise high in naval rank. He had earlier been a particular friend of Captain Bligh, and so by special request he was asked to join the ship's company as its chief officer. He had accompanied Bligh on two earlier voyages, and was highly regarded by him.

But something went wrong this time. Something had happened to Bligh.

The three midshipmen were Peter Heywood, Edward Young and George Stewart. They also were looking forward to higher positions in the British Navy. But little did either of them know that only one would ever return to England again. This was Peter Heywood, and his story of pardon from execution, as a result of his sister's devotion and prayers, is something of an epoch in British naval history. Of the rest of the crew, little is known until we learn of them later in the unfolding of the story of the Bounty.

Later in the afternoon of the twenty-third of December, 1787, the Bounty weighed anchor and slowly headed down the River Thames. One of the best-known voyages in the history of England had begun.

Crossing the Atlantic and traveling down the coast of South America, the Bounty headed toward the Horn,—the southern tip of the continent—planning to round it and sail into the Pacific. But at the Horn it encountered such fierce storms that Bligh feared that the ship might be lost. In his later report, this part of the voyage is quoted from his log: "Repeated gales seem now to become more violent, the squalls so excessively severe that I dare scarce show any canvas to it.

The motion of the ship is so very quick and falls so steep between the seas that it is impossible to stand without man ropes across the decks."

So fierce did the weather become that Bligh was forced to turn back,—and head east—and sail more than three quarters of the way around the world in the other direction, by way of Africa, through the Indian Ocean and past Australia. He was not to drop anchor in Tahiti until October 26, 1788. In ten months he had sailed over twenty-seven thousand miles.

And what those months and miles had brought to all concerned was something of a nightmare.

Lack of food, close quarters, poor water, difficult conditions, bad weather and seemingly endless months put a severe strain on the nerves and temper of everyone on board. But the breaking point was the quarter-deck tactics of Bligh combined with the short rations he gave the men.

The problem was that Bligh was not only the Master of the ship, he was also the Purser—its treasurer. It was later said that his excessive economy with the food brought on most of the problems. It has been suggested that the short allowances doled out to his own advantage.

A ringleader in the growing resentment was Matthew Quintal. He smoldered with resentment for he was the first to be "logged" by Bligh for reported insolence and contempt, and given two dozen lashes. James Morrison, a fellow shipmate, later declared before the Court of Enquiry, upon his return to England, that all that Quintal had done was to complain about the unnecessary cutting down of the regular food allowances.

On another occasion, Bligh ordered a supply of cheese to be brought up on deck and aired. When the cooper (the one in charge of the barrels) opened one of the casks, Bligh declared that two of the cheeses were missing. "They must have been stolen," he thundered.

Quietly the cooper reminded him that the cask had been opened while the ship was still lying in the Thames River, and that by order of Mr. Samuel, the clerk, the cheeses had been sent to Captain Bligh's home. At this, Fletcher Christian stepped forward and politely gave supporting evidence to this fact.

Cutting short all further discussion, Bligh ordered the cheese ration stopped from both officers and men until the man who had taken the cheeses returned them. Speaking violently to the cooper, he swore at him and declared he would be flogged if anything further was said about the incident.

After ten months of this—the ship finally laid anchor in Matavai Lagoon. A nightmare was behind them and what appeared to their weary eyes to be paradise lay before them. They had arrived at the warm and friendly land of Tahiti.

We are told that the natives of the island showered hospitality upon Captain Bligh and the crew of the Bounty. Gone were the routine and the strain of ship life. Now there was work to do on the island, preparing breadfruit plants for shipment to the West Indies. And there was time for relaxation. And especially so, since we are told that Nelson, the ship's botanist, and Brown, the gardener, did most of the slipping and potting of the 1,015 breadfruit plants that were gradually taken on board the ship and stored in the hold in a special room earlier prepared to receive them.

No one knows why the captain decided to remain so long in Tahiti—from October 26, 1788 to April 4, 1789—but it did little to lessen the final clash of wills.

When the day came to depart, it was hard to say goodby. But at last the men boarded the ship again and bade farewell to their happy life of many months. None aboard had any idea that within twenty-three days a mutiny would take place—a mutiny that would affect every man on board for the remainder of his life.

Slowly the ship was towed out into the sea by large native canoes, and then, setting sail, the ship slowly headed west toward the Indian Ocean. All prepared for another long, wearisome journey. And it was quick to begin. Two or three days after embarking, Captain Bligh confiscated all the food that had been given as presents to the crewmen by their many friends back in Tahiti. To this Christian objected. Bligh immediately retorted with an outpouring of foul and sarcastic language. To this, Christian replied, "Sir, your abuse is so bad that I cannot do my duty with any pleasure."

Christian had been warned by Bligh not to use arms against the natives, and so, two weeks later, when the Bounty stopped at the island of Anamooka for water and were repulsed by unfriendly natives, Christian returned to the ship without firing on them. At this, Bligh swore at him and called him a coward for not attacking them. The breach between the two men was widening.

Three days later, while still in the Tonga group of islands, the episode occurred that was the direct forerunner of the mutiny. On the afternoon of the 27th of April, Bligh came up on the quarter-deck and discovered that some coconuts were missing from a pile stored between the guns. In a storm of anger, he declared they had been stolen—and with the knowledge of the other ship's officers. To this, they replied that they had not seen anyone touch them. (These were Bligh's own coconuts; the officers and men had theirs in their own rooms below deck).

Turning to Christian, Bligh ordered him to go below and search the officers' quarters and bring up every coconut to be found. "How many coconuts do you have in your cabin?" he roared at Christian.

"I really do not know, sir," replied Christian, "but I hope you do not think me guilty of stealing yours." "Yes," Bligh snapped, with an oath, "I do think so,—you are all thieves alike! You will steal my yams next. I will flog you, and make you jump overboard before we reach Endeavor Straits!" He then turned to Mr. Samuel, the ship's clerk (who later reported the incident at the official inquiry back in England), and demanded that he stop "the villains' grog" and give them only half a pound of yams for food the next day. Then turning to the men he declared that if any more nuts were missing he would reduce the rations to a quarter pound.

The effect of all this was terrific on Fletcher Christian. There was a growing question in his mind as to what effect all this would have on his service record upon returning to England. What lay ahead? Such thoughts as these were in his mind as evening drew on. He did not know that he was only twenty-four hours from the end of his naval career.

2

Mutiny On The Bounty

The "Great Enquiry" was destined to become the talk of all England. Indeed, it would become the naval hearing of the decade. Months of careful deliberation and many witnesses were to open up before the British Empire the story of the mutiny on the Bounty.

The Enquiry was to bring London the closest it had ever come to the South Pacific.

But that was to come later. Just now we must return to the Bounty. Of the events that were to rapidly bring the mutiny to a head, John Fryer, the ship's master, was to later give the clearest picture. You can read it in the official "Report of Enquiry" that resulted from this naval hearing.

Fryer tells us that Bligh's "Passions were apt to ebb as swiftly as they flowed. An hour or so after he had abused Christian on the afternoon of the 27th, he sent him an invitation to sup with him that very evening. Christian, however, excused himself on the pretense of being unwell. The other officers agreed among themselves not to sup with the Commander should he ask them."

By the time the sun began to set on a shoreless horizon the next afternoon, a plan of action was forming in Christian's mind. The calm waters of the Pacific brought no peace to his heart. For he intended to leave the ship that evening. Desertion was his objective. He now saw in Bligh an enemy, and he felt that all hope of future promotion had been destroyed by what had been taking place. What report Bligh might later bring against him back in England, he knew not, but he was sure it would not be good.

Quietly that evening he received from the boatswain, the carpenter, and two midshipmen,—the men who were acquainted with his plans,—some supplies to trade with natives for food, when he should later land on some shore. As soon as the opportunity afforded, he planned to be lowered in a boat and leave.

But there seemed to be more activity than the usual that night, and he would have to wait. He must not be seen departing. And so the night deepened, and he retired for sleep. But he had had little of it, when he was called to take over his watch. As the quiet waters lapped against the side of the ship, he leaned against the railing with Matthew Quintal, and he looked beyond the waters to the far distance. Matthew knew what he was planning, and suddenly turning to him, he urged him not to try to leave the ship—but rather to seize it, for there were others of the ship's crew who had been abused by "Old Breadfruit," as some of them privately called him.

Immediately Christian acted. He called Isaac Martin, Charles Churchill, and Matthew Thompson, all of whom had tasted "the cat" (the whiplash), and he suggested a plan to them. Alexander Smith also supported it, and he called William McCoy and John Williams who also favored the plot, for they had all received harsh treatment. The next hour brought a dramatic turn of events.

Christian, accompanied by three others, took the captain by surprise while he was sleeping in his cabin. Dragging him from his bed, they overpowered him and tied his hands. Out on the deck a small boat was lowered and Bligh and the eighteen men who chose to remain with him were forced into it. Provisions were given them and they were set adrift.

The little boat carrying these nineteen men drifted west, past the New Hebrides, New Guinea and Australia, the long distance to Timor, a Dutch settlement off the coast of Southern Asia. Their sufferings had been intense. Eventually they returned to England, there to give a full report on the mutiny.

As Fletcher Christian turned his ship into the dark night and left the little boat behind him, he had to decide where to go. Most of the men remaining on the Bounty wanted to return to Tahiti, but Christian well-knew that this would be too dangerous. He told them that in time a British naval ship should come in search for them, and Tahiti was not the place to be living at that time. So he headed for the island of Tubuai, but there he found a lack of livestock as well as unfriendly natives. Finally, at the insistence of his men, he turned the ship toward Tahiti.

Tahiti is the largest of a little group of 14 islands that lie in the South Pacific. As the mutineers neared it, they could see massive volcanos rising from its interior, and an outer coral reef completely encircling it. Landing on the reef, they went ashore in smaller boats. For many of them it was a return to "paradise"—coconuts, sugar cane, tropical fruits, and women. From the rugged interior, with its waterfalls and rapid streams cutting through steep mountains, to the belt of fertile soil near the shore, the Englishmen found much to enjoy.

As soon as they arrived on shore, sixteen of the mutineers voted to remain in Tahiti. But the other eight decided to cast their lot with Christian—for he was determined to sail away shortly.

In the wild orgies of madness that were to follow on this island after Christian and his eight had departed, two of the sixteen were killed by the natives because of their thievery and adulteries. The other fourteen were later caught by a searching party sent out from England. Placed in chains by Captain Edwards of the Pandora, the party set out for Britain. During the passage, four were drowned when the ship struck a coral reef. Only ten returned to England, there to stand trial. By its verdict, three were executed.

Peter Heywood, one of those pardoned, had written his mother from Tahiti, after the mutiny. In it, he told of Christian's final request: "Gentlemen, I will carry you and land you wherever you please. I desire none to stay with me, but I have one favour to request, that you grant me the ship, tie the fore-

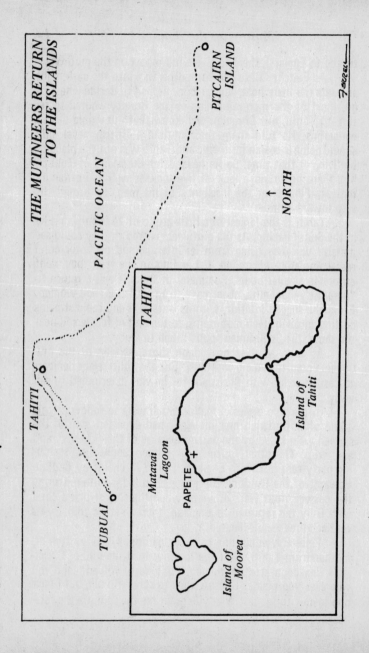

THE MUTINEERS RETURN
TO THE ISLANDS

PACIFIC OCEAN

PITCAIRN
ISLAND

NORTH

TAHITI

TUBUAI

TAHITI

Matavai
Lagoon

PAPETE

Island of
Tahiti

Island of
Moorea

sail, and give me a few gallons of water, and leave me to run before the wind, and I shall land upon the first island the ship drives to. I have done such an act that I cannot stay at Otheiti [Tahiti]. I will never live where I may be carried home to be a disgrace to my family."

At this, Edward Young, one of the midshipmen, and seven others stepped up to him and said, "We shall never leave you, Mr. Christian, go where you will."

The men who remained with Christian were John Williams, William Brown, Isaac Martin, John Mills, William McCoy, Matthew Quintal, Edward Young, and Alexander Smith who later changed his name to John Adams.

On the final night in Tahiti, Christian spent the evening on shore with the crewmates he was leaving behind. Heywood wrote of this: "we had spent some two hours together, when Christian arose and it was with difficulty that we spoke to each other. It was a sad farewell. He stepped into a canoe and we saw him no more, for in the morning the ship was gone." The night of the 21st of September, 1789, was the last that civilization ever saw of Fletcher Christian.

With the eight that elected to remain with him, Christian sailed north to another part of the island, and there the crew stayed long enough to marry Tahitian wives and take on provisions for a lengthy voyage. Mi'Mitti, the noble daughter of an important chief, married Christian. Brown, the ship's gardener, loaded the hold with plants from fruit trees. The other men brought chickens and goats on board. Also, six young Tahitian men were taken on as additional crewmen.

And then the Bounty sailed away into oblivion. Christian had had access back in England to the latest naval records, and very likely copies of the most recent annotated maps were in the chart room of the Bounty, which was a ship of the British navy. Christian had no doubt read of the discovery of the uninhabited island with water and good soil that lay a thousand miles east of him. For it appears that he sailed directly to it. On the morning of January 23, 1790, Pitcairn Island was sighted by the men on the Bounty.

Dropping anchor in a small cove, later to be known as

Bounty Bay, they slowly unloaded the ship, carrying everything up the 200-foot high cliff to the Edge,—from which
one can see the landing place and Bounty Bay. They found
that the island did, indeed, contain water, wood, good soil as
well as some fruit trees. Every movable thing was taken to
shore and up the cliff. The Bounty was completely stripped,
even to the planks from her sides, and then the hull was set on
fire. The ship that had been their home for two years was no
more.

        Christian divided the settlement into sections and soon
all were busily engaged in building homes, clearing land for
gardens and setting out trees. Salt was obtained from the sea
and an abundance of fish was available. Life in their new little
world took on the routine of daily living. The continents
around them were the scene of continual discontent, greed,
strife and misery. Could the brave new settlement escape the
heritage of their forebears?

        One day while rummaging through his sea chest, Chris-
tian discovered, deep beneath the spare clothing, the Bible that
his mother had placed there years before. As he held it in his
hands, he recalled how she would read to him from it when he
was a child at her knees. He well knew that she felt that this
was the best gift she could give him. One day, he took it to
a cave on the mountainside and there began reading in it.
Many were the hours that he spent there. And then another
began coming to the cave with him. It was Alexander Smith,
who had by now changed his name to John Adams. As the
days passed into weeks, Christian's book brought a wonderful
peace into Adams' life. For he was finding what Christian had
found not long before—that his sins could be forgiven through
the forgiving grace of Jesus Christ.

        But in spite of this, the next five years became a night-
mare for the small colony. Williams, McCoy and Quintal had
always been heavy drinkers, and now finding it not available
they began experimenting with native plants. McCoy had been
brought up in a distillery, and fevered with a desire for his old
way of life, discovered that he could make an alcoholic drink
from the roots of the native tee plant. One day, Williams' wife

fell from the cliffs and died while trying to gather eggs from the nests of sea birds. Shortly thereafter, Williams while half drunk went down to the home of one of the Tahitian men, Talalu, and took his wife. In a rage, Talalu, uniting the other Tahitian men with him, began a warfare that took the lives of Williams, Martin, Brown and Mills. Fletcher Christian was taken unawares while working in his garden and killed. John Adams, though shot in the shoulder, managed to escape, while Edward Young was successfully hidden by his wife. The four remaining Englishmen, and the widows of the men who had been murdered, realized that they had but a short time unless something was done immediately. In a sudden attack they slew all the Tahitian men.

But McCoy and Quintal were still alive and well, and now every imaginable vice was practiced by them. Treachery and aggression raged and no one felt his life secure. Some of the women in desperation tried to get away from the island on a raft, but this they were not permitted to do. The future of the little colony seemed dark.

One day, in a drunken depression, the distiller McCoy made his way down to the rocks by the water's edge, and there fastening a large stone to his body, picked it up and jumped into the ocean. Thus a sad but miserable life ended.

Then Quintal's wife died in an accident and he demanded another, but no one on the island wanted to become the wife of a drunk who earlier in an angry stupor had bitten off his wife's ear upon learning that she had brought in a smaller than usual catch of fish. Finally Quintal demanded that either Adams or Young give him one of their wives, or he would kill them. Having no doubt that he intended to do this, they made him drunk with his own liquor, overpowered him, and dispatched him with an ax.

And now the community settled down to the peace it had been seeking for years. Never again was the use of alcoholic beverages allowed on the island. It was outlawed. The year was 1798. Eight years had passed since the mutineers had first landed on Pitcairn. Adams and Young were now the sole survivors of fifteen men who had come to the island, and

thirty-six-year-old Adams was to see Young succumb to an
attack of asthma two years later. For the first time an islander
had died by a natural death.

An island paradise, far off in the Pacific. And yet when
people came to live there, they brought the vices and immoral-
ity of the rest of the world with them. Passion, strife, drunken-
ness and bloodshed were the result.

Is there no answer? Is there nothing that can keep man
from destroying himself?

But then came the discoveries at Pitcairn.

3

Discovery At Pitcairn

It seemed that there was no hope. The past was following them too closely. Liquor and passion were bringing the lawlessness of civilization to this once-peaceful island.

Of all the men once on the island, John Adams now stood alone. What was he to do? The future seemed dark and bleak. There must be an answer.

With eleven women and twenty-three children on the island, sons and daughters of his companions, Adams began to realize that he had a great responsibility to lead them into a better way of life. Going down one day to Christian's Cave, he lay down and spent some time gazing out across his island home and over the waters that stretched to the great beyond. He thought over the experiences of the past, and recalled the many happy times when Christian had read to him from the Bible and they had talked about how the island might have a better way of life.

But while he was thinking on these things, he fell asleep. In his own words, he describes what followed: "I had a dream that changed my whole life. There seemed to be standing beside me an angel who spoke to me, warning me of my past life, and then he called me to repent and go down and train the children in the way of Christian's Bible." With this, he awoke and he seemed to feel the very presence of God about him. Kneeling there, he asked his Creator for forgiveness for the sins of a lifetime.

From that day on, he carried with him a deep and abiding repentance for his former way of life, and he tried not only to live on a higher level himself, but he also determined that he

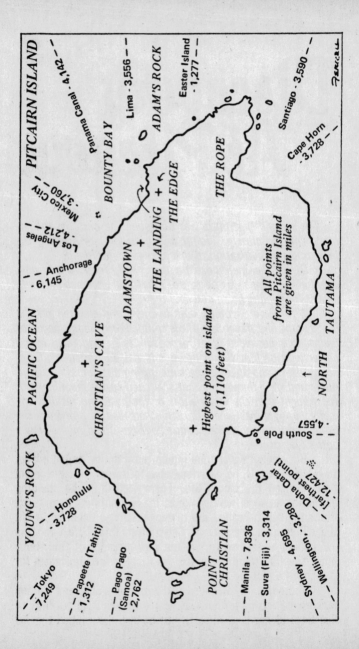

PITCAIRN ISLAND

YOUNG'S ROCK

PACIFIC OCEAN

Tokyo - 7,249
Papeete (Tahiti) - 1,312
Pago Pago (Samoa) - 2,762
Honolulu - 3,728

Anchorage - 6,145
Los Angeles - 4,212
Mexico City - 3,760
Panama Canal - 4,142
Lima - 3,556

BOUNTY BAY

ADAM'S ROCK

Easter Island - 1,277

CHRISTIAN'S CAVE

ADAMSTOWN

THE LANDING

THE EDGE

+ Highest point on island (1,110 feet)

All points from Pitcairn Island are given in miles

THE ROPE

Santiago - 3,590
Cape Horn - 3,728

NORTH TAUTAMA

South Pole - 4,557

POINT CHRISTIAN

Manila - 7,836
Suva (Fiji) - 3,314
Sydney - 4,695
Wellington - 3,280
Doha Qatar (farthest point) - 12,427

must help those young people learn of God as well. It was now the year 1800.

John Adams had four children of his own, but he was very much attached to Fletcher Christian's eldest son. This boy had been the first to be born on the island, and because he was born on a Thursday in October, his father had named him Thursday October Christian. By now Thursday was ten years of age. Adams told him of the dream and Thursday asked that he might learn to read his father's Bible. Digging it out of the old sea chest, they went with it frequently to the cave and there in the quietness of this shady den, they learned to read.

Sorry for his past life and zealous for the honor of God, this tough old sailor became a softened man and began to teach the minds of the younger people about him the love and fear of God. He prayed for them and conducted morning and evening worship, a custom that is still practiced on the island.

As the families of the island gathered morning and evening and studied the Word of God together, they grew strong in its messages. A depth of character and a firmness to do the right began to mark their bearing. A wonderful peace came into their lives, and with thankfulness of heart they determined never to return to the old ways of life.

From the Bible they learned their duty to be kind and helpful to one another. And they learned the importance of obedience to the will of God as revealed in His Word. Repeatedly, they found in Scripture that when the people of God did not obey His moral law, the results were always disastrous. Together, from the written Word, they found that which other civilizations of our time have yet to learn,—that God means what He says, and that He sent His Son to enable man to obey all that He says. And that those who refuse obedience, will always suffer.

When it was suggested that a small school building be built, the five older boys—Thursday Christian, his brother Charles, Daniel McCoy, George Young, and Matthew Quintal—quickly set to work and soon with the help of the younger boys their first school house was completed.

At first the daily program consisted of study from the one Bible. These were happy times for all. On one occasion, Adams asked Arthur Quintal and Robert Young to prepare a plot of ground for some yams. When the ground was plowed, he offered them a little gunpowder. They both declined and said they would rather have some extra lessons out of the Bible, a request which he happily fulfilled.

Adams diligently sought to teach his people the importance of prayer—prayer for protection, prayer for guidance and the prayer of thanksgiving. On one occasion when he and some of the women went out fishing on the south side of the island, the surf broke their canoe. It was impossible to scale the cliffs, and so gathering them together he offered a simple prayer for strength to swim to a distant point. All having reached it safely, they shared the story with the others at home. It was experiences such as this, combined with the daily study and prayer, that day by day strengthened and ennobled this quiet people of the Pitcairn.

Alone, Adams began every day with earnest prayer to God that he might guide his people aright. He had had no formal schooling, and as both pastor and teacher of the entire settlement, he felt his need of divine help. And it was given, day by day, as he needed it.

He was attentive to the needs of all. If any were ill, he went and prayed with them. Consistently, he asked God for help and then went forward and did what he knew to be right. On this island where looseness of morals and indifference to religion had once prevailed, a wonderful new way of life was being discovered. The sordid round of crime and treachery that had marred its early history were becoming only a memory, as a younger generation of a strange blood-mixture was growing to maturity, under the influence of the book that Adams had opened before them—the Book of God.

On September 17, 1814, quite by accident, two British frigates, the "Briton" and the "Tagus," arrived at Pitcairn. They were searching for a pirate ship, the "Essex," which had been seizing English whalers. Headed for Valparaiso from the Marquesas Islands, they suddenly came in sight of land that they were not expecting, for by an error in reckoning, they thought Pitcairn to be 200 miles distant. Adams recognized the flags and well knew that captains in command of British naval ships were not given to sentiment. Calling Thursday, he requested him to go out and meet the captains. So, accompanied by eighteen-year-old George Young, Thursday paddled out in a small canoe to the side of the "Briton." Captain Staines was astonished to hear Thursday call out in good English, "Won't you heave us a rope now?" Arriving on board, the mystery of how English-speaking people happened to be on this little island was quickly explained by the boys. Their deportment and natural, easy manners interested everyone. To the question, "Who are you?" twenty-four-year-old Thursday replied with frankness, "I am Thursday October Christian, son of Fletcher Christian, the mutineer, by a Tahitian mother, and the first born on this island." They then ate lunch with the captain and he observed how they prayed before taking food. When asked, they told him that John Adams had taught them this. To these naval men this was amazing—the simple piety of these young men, living so far from all civilized lands, yet in the vicinity of islands whose peoples were sunken in heathenism and ignorance.

Both Captain Staines and Captain Pipon went ashore and saw the colony and interviewed Adams. He offered to return with them and stand trial in England for his part in the mutiny. Immediately the islanders gathered around and pled that he might remain. Both captains were deeply touched by the scene and resolved not to disturb the colony. Upon their return to England an official report was presented, with the request that Adams not be sought for. Since Bligh was now dead, it was decided that the case should remain closed.

On March 6, 1829, John Adams peacefully passed to his rest at the age of sixty-five. And Thursday October Christian became the recognized leader of the island. With the passing of the years additional vessels stopped at the island and reported on the remarkable way of life to be found there, and the fact that it was directly attributable to the reading of the Bible. New insights from the Word of God will continually be found by those who in humility and prayer search its pages. And this was to be the experience of the faithful Christians on the island of Pitcairn. Coming in at night from their gardens, they would study the Bible to learn more of its treasures.

In 1876, the little group came upon the truth that Jesus is soon to return to this earth for His own. How this cheered their hearts! All they had was the word of God but they knew that as they studied and trusted themselves to it, they would always be guided aright.

Noble stories and wonderful principles were to be found in this Book of books. But the more they studied, the more they learned. In October of 1886, after checking and rechecking, they came upon the truth that Sunday sacredness was not to be found in the Bible. This came as something of a shock to them, as you might imagine, but additional reading confirmed this fact.

Thursday October Christian II (Thursday's son) was the leader of the island at the time. He and Simon Young, the beloved and respected elder of the church, were the first to accept this new Bible truth. And so it was that within a short time the church bell was no longer tolling on Sunday the first day, but on Saturday the seventh day, as it called the people to worship. For each of the families had studied it out for themselves and nearly all on the island had accepted the simple facts it taught about this.

Over the years, a better way of life had opened up before this quiet people who chose to pattern their lives according to the Bible. And as they studied, they learned a simple, Biblical way of life that has become a model for many in other lands.

It is of interest that in 1838 the Pitcairners drafted a constitution for the government of the island. Within it were enlightened laws, far in advance of the rest of the world. For example, as of 1838, every 18-year old might vote, but this did not come to the United States until 1971. England still does not have it. In 1838 women were granted the right to vote on Pitcairn. But not until 1920 in the United States and 1928 in Great Britain were women given equal voting rights.

After the first nine-year orgy of violence on Pitcairn, the island found the Bible and thereafter became a model of moral prosperity for the entire world. During those first years, while John Adams was the leader, his island had no written laws. They were not needed. Later when they began to appear, most of them dealt with crimes by or against animals: chickens digging up yam patches, etc. One important law prohibited liquor on the island. The reign of terror created by McCoy's tee-root (ti-root) whiskey was never to be forgotten. There is a jail on Pitcairn, because the British authorities thought one should be constructed. But none of the islanders can remember when it was last used. At this time, the iron door stands ajar, rusted tight in a half-open position. But no one sees any need to replace it.

In the story of Pitcairn, we find what the Bible can do for men and women. Ever since John Adams and Edward Young dug Fletcher Christian's Bible out of the old sea chest, the Word of God has played an important role in Pitcairn affairs. A recent Bible census noted that there were 247 Bibles on Pitcairn. This is about 3 for every man, woman, and child on the island. The pastor declares that the Bible is the best-read book on the island, and he is probably right.

Would you like to live with the Pitcairners? We both would, I am sure. But though it may not be practical to move there, yet we can have the faith of the Pitcairners. For it is the Word of God hidden in their hearts, and an open Bible before them, that is the real secret of the happiness of this little island in the South Pacific.

The story of Pitcairn has indeed been a fascinating one. It has explained mysteries but has uncovered still more. Now we must travel across the world in order to find the answers we are seeking. This trip will take us to other lands and other places, but this is necessary.

For we must now go back—beyond Pitcairn—to peoples and events of many centuries earlier.

And only then will we understand the mystery of Pitcairn.

4

West OfPompeii

A fleet of oar-powered war galleys commanded by a Roman officer, Gaius Plinius Secundus, was based at the small town of Misenum on the westernmost point of the Bay of Naples when the inferno exploded to the east of them.

This commander is better known in history as the famous scholar and historian, Pliny the Elder.

His nephew, Pliny the Younger, was only eighteen years old when the holocaust came. But in answer to a letter from the historian Tacitus, the young man told how Pliny the Elder had boarded a ship and sailed right into the heart of the destruction.

"On the 24th of August [A.D. 79], about one in the afternoon, my mother desired him to observe a cloud which had appeared of a very unusual size and shape. He had just taken a turn in the sun, and after bathing himself in cold water, and making a light luncheon, [had] gone back to his books.

"He immediately arose and went out upon a rising ground from whence he might get a better sight of this very uncommon appearance. A cloud, from which mountain was uncertain at this distance, was ascending, the form of which I cannot give you a more exact description of than by likening it to a pine tree, for it shot up to a great height in the form of a very tall trunk, which spread itself out at the top into a sort of branches . . It appeared sometimes bright and sometimes dark and spotted, according as it was either more or less impregnated with earth and cinders.

"This phenomenon seemed, to a man of such learning and research as my uncle, extraordinary, and worth further looking into . .

"As he was coming out of the house, he received a note from Rectina, the wife of Bassus, who was in the utmost alarm at the imminent danger which threatened her; for from her villa at the foot of Mount Vesuvius, there was no way to escape except by sea. She earnestly entreated him therefore to come to her assistance. He accordingly . . ordered the galleys to put to sea, and went himself on board with an intention of assisting not only Rectina, but the several towns which lay thickly strewn along the beautiful coast."

The youth had stayed at Misenum with his mother when his famous kinsman set off across the bay to rescue those in danger at Herculaneum and Pompeii. But the elder Pliny never returned from his mission, for going ashore at Stabiae, just south of Pompeii, he was asphyxiated by a smothering blanket of ash and gases and perished in the holocaust.

Meanwhile, his nephew and sister stayed on at Misenum until the next day, when the narrative continues:

"Though it was now morning, the light was exceedingly faint and doubtful; the buildings all around us tottered, and though we stood on open ground, yet as the place was narrow and confined, there was no remaining without imminent danger; we therefore resolved to quit the town.

"A panic-stricken crowd followed us, and . . pressed on us in dense array to drive us forward as we came out. When we had gotten away from the house, we stood still, in the midst of a most dangerous and dreadful scene.

"The chariots, which we had ordered to be drawn out, were so agitated backwards and forwards, though upon the most level ground, that we could not keep them steady, not even by supporting them with large stones. The sea seemed to roll back upon itself, and to be driven from its banks by the convulsive motion of the earth; it is certain at least that the shore was considerably enlarged, and several sea animals were left upon it.

"On the other side, a black and dreadful cloud, broken with rapid, zigzag flashes, revealed behind it variously shaped masses of flame . . Soon afterwards the cloud began to descend and cover the sea. It had already surrounded and concealed the island of Capri and the promontory of Misenum . . I looked back; a dense dark mist seemed to be following us.

" 'Let us turn off the main road,' I said, 'while we can still see. If we should fall down here, we might be pressed to death in the dark by the crowds following us.'

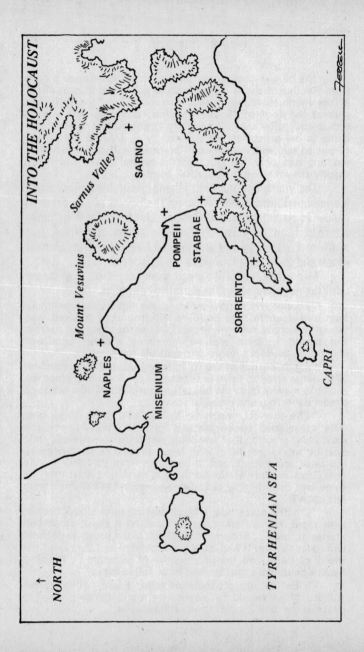

INTO THE HOLOCAUST

NORTH

Mount Vesuvius

Sarnus Valley

SARNO

NAPLES

MISENIUM

POMPEII

STABIAE

SORRENTO

CAPRI

TYRRHENIAN SEA

"We had scarcely sat down when night came upon us,— not such as we have when the sky is cloudy, or when there is no moon, but that of an enclosed room when the lights are out. You might hear the shrieks of women, the screams of children, and the shouts of men; some calling for their children, others for their parents, others for their husbands, and seeking to recognize each other by the voices that replied; one lamenting his own fate, another that of his family; some wishing to die from the very fear of dying; some lifting their hands to the gods; but the greater part convinced that there were no gods at all, and that the final endless night of which we have heard had come to the world . .

"A heavy shower of ashes rained upon us, which we were obliged every now and then to stand up and shake off, otherwise we should have been crushed and buried in the heap."

The young Pliny tells us that they waited there in "the belief that the whole world was dying and I with it," until a yellowish sun finally brought the morning—and revealed a landscape "buried deep in ashes like snowdrifts."

It was the latter part of August, 79 A.D. The end of the world had indeed come—to the inhabitants of Herculaneum and Pompeii.

Founded in 80 B.C., Pompeii was the commercial, agricultural and maritime center of the Sarnus Valley in south-central Italy, and had a population of about twenty thousand. Pompeii had the palatial country estates of many of the wealthy of Rome. Mount Vesuvius had not erupted for several centuries, and no one suspected that the cooling breezes from the Bay of Naples would that summer turn into a fiery, smoking besom of destruction.

We have no record of the death of any Christians at Pompeii when Vesuvius exploded, but of course this is possible. Herod Agrippa I is mentioned in the Bible in Acts 12, when he killed the Apostle James and tried to kill Peter, before he, himself, was killed by an angel (Acts 12:1-3, 19-23). This Herod had three daughters, one of whom was named Drusilla. When she was grown, she married Azizus, king of Edessa. But it was not long until Claudius Felix, the procurator of Judea, asked her to leave her husband and marry him. This she did. During his rule, he came to Caesarea with Drusilla, and the Apostle Paul was brought before them to be examined.

A warning to flee from a terrible doom was given by Paul to both, as he spoke of righteousness, temperance and the judgment to come. Felix was terrified, and answered Paul: "Go thy way for this time; and when I have a convenient season, I will call thee." (Acts 24:24-27).

Felix died a terrible death and left his wife, Drusilla, and her son behind.

Drusilla and the boy were at Pompeii that summer in 79 A.D. when Vesuvius belched fire and ash. Both of them died as the suffocating heat, smoke, and fine dust poured over the city.

The location of both Herculaneum and Pompeii was forgotten in the centuries that followed. In 1738, diggers trying to find antique treasures for the king of Naples accidentally discovered Herculaneum. Pompeii was found ten years later.

On the walls of Pompeii were scribbled curses and vile love notes that give indication of the kind of people destroyed in the eruption that summer.

But beads of sweat broke out on the foreheads of the archeologists as they stepped back from the writing on one wall:

"And three words were found that seem to turn the destruction of Pompeii into a divine judgment—three simple words that even 2,000 years later make us thoughtful: 'Sodom and Gomorrah.' "—*Ivar Lissner, "The Living Past," page 402.*

And yet, one hundred and thirty miles north of the flames and sulphurous rain over Pompeii was to be found yet another Sodom.

5

Roman Holiday

Slowly, the men worked the winches—and an immense section of sand-covered floor arose to the surface of the Colosseum. On it were four wild African lions. As it moved upward, the men could hear the muffled cheers of thousands as they sat in the bleachers awaiting the end.

The men at the winches were slaves brought in from the provinces. They knew that as the massive framework neared the surface, it would become suddenly lighter as the beasts bounded out onto the floor of the vast amphitheater.

Overhead, they knew that more Christians were preparing to die.

The city of Rome, in the years that followed those when Christ walked the dusty lanes of Galilee, was a metropolis unmatched by any other in all history. And yet we must go to Rome in order that we may better understand the mystery of Pitcairn.

But the power of Rome went on for centuries. And as we shall learn, history was made—and changed—at Rome. For Rome was a different kind of place .. in many ways.

The remains of the Colosseum are to be seen in Rome to this day. Shaped like a football stadium, its four stories were 161 feet high, 600 feet long and 500 feet wide. 45,000 spectators could watch as men and beasts fought and died on the vast amphitheater floor.

Jesus taught and suffered and died in the early part of the First Century A.D. By the end of that century the Bible

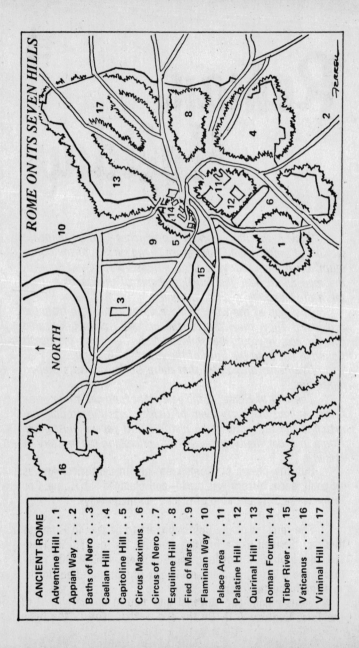

ROME ON ITS SEVEN HILLS

NORTH

ANCIENT ROME
Adventine Hill . . . 1
Appian Way 2
Baths of Nero . . . 3
Caelian Hill 4
Capitoline Hill . . . 5
Circus Maximus . . 6
Circus of Nero . . . 7
Esquiline Hill . . . 8
Fied of Mars 9
Flaminian Way . . 10
Palace Area . . . 11
Palatine Hill . . . 12
Quirinal Hill . . . 13
Roman Forum . . 14
Tiber River 15
Vaticanus 16
Viminal Hill . . . 17

had been finished, as the Apostle John penned his books.

Turning time back, we walk its streets and find about us a metropolis such as the world has not otherwise seen. Many of the free citizens may have been poor, but at their disposal was the luxury of this city that ruled the civilized world. For Rome was a welfare state within itself. Always available was the free food, attendance at the theaters, circuses, amphitheaters, and stadiums. Romans exercised, refreshed, amused and educated themselves in the baths. They enjoyed the shade of a hundred massive colonnades, and walked under decorated porticos that covered many miles of streets,—three miles in the Field of Mars alone.

In the center of town was the Roman Forum, ever busy with business, echoing with oratory and debates. Encircling it were the majestic temples to the gods, the palaces of nobility, the theaters and baths for the masses. Gardens and pleasure places were to be found everywhere.

Marriage, once sacred in ancient Rome, had now become a passing adventure. Amid a heavy overextension of credit, everyone was in debt, and no one wanted children. Abortion of babies had become not only a city-wide pastime, but a publically approved science.

For Rome had become decadent. Expensive silk cloth from the Orient was so common in the Eternal City that men as well as women wore it. Delicate eye makeup, exotic facial cosmetics, and high-heeled shoes were common. Jewelry was in abundance among the middle and upper classes; so much so that the manufacture and sale of imitation "emeralds" and other fine jewels was a thriving business. Rome was not only decadent; it had become artificial.

The luxuries of their homes exceeded the luxuries of their clothing: floors of marble and mosaic; columns of alabaster, many-colored marble, and onyx. On the walls were to be seen brilliant hand-painted murals, or inlays of costly stones. Ceilings were often in gold or plate glass, while beneath them rested tables and divans decorated with ivory, silver, gold or tortoise shell.

By the Fourth Century A.D., there were 856 baths and

1352 public swimming pools in Rome. The Baths of Nero had 1600 marble seats and accommodated 1600 bathers at a time. But there were others that held 3000 bathers each. This was Rome.

Banquets began at four in the afternoon and lasted until late in the night or till the next day. The tables were strewn with flowers and parsley, the air was scented with perfumes. Rare fish, birds and fruit from far-away lands were to be had. Eels and snails, ostrich wings, flamingo tongues, geese livers and songbirds were favorite dishes.

But everything in Rome centered around the Roman holidays. Every century, more were added until fully one-half of each year was dedicated to some festival or other.

The festivals took the people to the races at the Circus Maximus, where forty-four races might be run in two days. Or a holiday might be spent just outside the imperial city viewing the stupendous naval battles that took place on artificial lakes. For each such occasion, enormous boats were constructed and, as the people gazed from the sidelines, massive battles would take place for their amusement. In one contest alone, 19,000 men in ships fought and died together while the people on shore applauded.

But even more popular was the Colosseum:

The arena was an immense wooden floor strewn with sand. Parts of this floor could be lowered and then quickly raised with a change of scene. At brief notice the whole floor could be covered with water. Beneath it, in large rooms, were the wild animals, men and machines that would be used in the fights for that day. No admission was charged. All Rome could come and sit in its thousands of seats, beneath huge canvas awnings, and watch what took place. In one day, under Nero, 400 tigers fought with bulls and elephants; on another day, under Caligula, 400 bears were slain; Claudius made a division of the Praetorian Guard fight panthers.

And this is where the humble Christians were brought to die, for no other crime than that of following the teachings of the Bible and living as Jesus lived.

But the influential Roman Christians lived above all this.

They were able to enjoy the good life. The worst of the world flowed into Rome, for that is what it wanted. And the Church at Rome also wanted that which the world had to offer.

As if there were not already enough at Rome, new deities and gods were imported from everywhere. War captives, returning soldiers and merchants brought in new religions and philosophies from many lands. And they were welcomed by worldly pagans and worldly Christians. Yes, there were faithful Christians in the city who lived and died in the catacombs or in the Colosseum. But it was the worldlings who were the leaders of the Christian Church at Rome. It was they who demanded that all the other churches of Christendom bow to their brand of Christianity.

And, as we shall see, it was the Church at Rome that introduced paganism into the Christian churches everywhere, by requiring that they accept these heathen rituals and beliefs.

But more than just new rituals—it was the Church at Rome that was destined to give to all the world the new Roman holiday.

6

Christening Of Paganism

We have from ancient records the stories of many brave men and women who suffered and died for their faith, rather than yield their allegiance to God and Jesus Christ. One of these was Perpetua. About twenty-six years old, she was married and had an infant child. Seized as a Christian, she was thrown into prison, where her father came and tenderly pled with her to give up Christianity. When she refused, he became angry, beat her and left, declaring she would never see his face again.

Then Perpetua was brought before the Roman pro-consul, Minutius, and was commanded to sacrifice before an idol. A shrine was in a prominent place of the large room, and a statue of a heathen god was standing within it. A small box of incense was handed to her husband and he held it out to her. All she need do was to take a pinch of the fragrant herb and place it on the smoking incense plate that lay before the unspeaking idol. A large number of people had gathered for the occasion, for she was known and liked by many. On one side stood her husband and close friends who pled with her. On the other, stood the Roman pro-consul, Minutius. By his side was a scribe prepared to pen "not guilty" in a record book if she would but offer the incense.

But Perpetua refused the command to sacrifice to idols, for in this way she would have proved to all that she had renounced her faith in Christ.

Taken back to prison, she was again visited by her father

who, sorry for having earlier beaten her, again pled with her. But her only reply was that she must obey God. At the urging of her husband, relatives and friends, the judge himself then went and pled with her.

While awaiting the day of execution in prison, she was joined by another young woman who had also refused to renounce Christianity. Her name was Felicitas.

When the day of execution arrived, they were taken out into the amphitheatre, where wild beasts were turned loose upon them. It was March, A.D. 205.

If faithful, someday you will meet them in heaven. The Bible is worth it; Jesus is worth it; eternity is worth it. Give to God all that you are and have, and obey His Written Word. And you will never be sorry for having done so.

But back in those early centuries, just as today, there were many professed Christians who were not faithful to God and the teachings of the Bible. The last writer of Scripture had laid down his pen, and although many were dying for the Christ of Christianity, there were yet others who decided to follow an easier way. And there were those who decided to gain power and prestige by so doing.

Here is a description of a church service at approximately the time when Perpetua and Felicitas laid down their lives for Christ:

"The daily ritual of Isis, which seems to have been as regular and complicated as that of the Catholic Church, produced an immense effect on the Roman mind. Every day there were two solemn offices, at which white-robed, tonsured priests, with acolytes and assistants of every degree, officiated. The morning litany and sacrifice was an impressive service. The crowd of worshippers thronged the space before the chapel at the early dawn. The priest ascending by a hidden stairs, drew apart the veil of the sanctuary, and offered the holy image to their adoration. He then made the round of the altars, reciting the litany and sprinkling the holy water from the secret spring."—*Samuel Dill, "Roman Society from Nero to Marcus Aurelius," pp. 577-578. London, Macmillan, 1904.*

What you have just read sounds exactly like a Roman Catholic "sacrifice of the mass,"—but instead you have read about the service that gave birth to the later Roman Catholic services: The Egyptian worship of Isis, the "Queen of Heaven," and her infant, Horus, the "Son of the Sacred Heart."

Long robes - "tonsured" heads (cut bald in the center with a ring of hair on the outside, in honor of the Sun god) - in a sacred procession with acolytes (men and boys dressed in robes) - carrying an image of the Mother god and her infant son - as the holy priest recited the "litany" (mystic words spoken in an unknown tongue) - while making signs with his fingers and sprinkling holy water upon the faithful bowed before him as he passed by.

All this was taking place in the Near East, and down in Egypt, years before the local Christian Church at Rome decided to begin copying it.

But it was not long before the worldly Christians at Rome discovered that if they modeled Christianity closely enough after the heathen pattern, they would cease to be persecuted.

And the plan worked. While the true Christians, who loved God and obeyed Bible teachings were thrown to wild animals in the Colosseum, the Christian modernists decided to be more progressive. Blood wasn't worth the price of obedience to God, they decided.

We have already mentioned the tonsure (read Lev 21:5, and Deut 14:1) in honor of the Sun god; and holy water for sprinkling, instead of baptism by immersion as given in the Bible (Acts 8:35-38; Rom 6:3-5). It was a proverb that everything finally came to Rome. And the worldly Christians there were among the first to accept it. From India came the practice of ascetics (monastic hermits) and rosary beads. The burning of candles came from the worship of the Sun God, Mithra. Tertullian (A.D. 196-220), one of the few authenticated Christian writers before 300 A.D. (whose writings we know to be genuine and not later forgeries), who advocated Sundaykeeping by Christians, gives careful instructions how to keep Sunday in place of the Bible Sabbath. And he then adds a brand new heathen practice for the faithful to observe: "the sign of the cross."

"At every forward step and movement, at every going

in and out, when we put on our clothes and shoes, when we bathe, when we sit at table, when we light the lamps, on couch, on seat, in all the ordinary actions of daily life, we trace upon the forehead the sign of the cross."

And what were the faithful Christians doing all this time in Rome? While the bishop of Rome (shortly to call himself the "pope") was gaining in wealth and power through an alliance with heathenism, the men and women who loved God were struggling to keep alive. And their number included some who formerly were civic leaders.

Flavius Clemens (first cousin of the Emperor, Domitian), and his wife Domatilla, were martyred instead of yielding their faith in Christ. Another prominent victim was Acilius Glabrio, a member of one of the foremost families of Rome. During those long centuries Christians fled to the Catacombs. The famous Catacombs of Rome were forgotten for long centuries and only rediscovered by accident in 1578 by Antonia Bosio, when he dug underneath the home of Domatilla.

In the centuries that followed Christ, Rome became the largest inhabited city in the entire world. Christians who were there, in an effort to flee from persecution, dug hiding places for themselves below the city of Rome. These were long tunnels cut out of the porous tufa rock that lay beneath this great metropolis—the capital of the Empire. A labyrinth of passageways went for miles in every direction. Here Christians lived and worshiped, died and were buried in crypts by kind friends. It is estimated that if the passages were placed in a straight line, they would extend more than five hundred miles.

But there were only two ways to escape the terrible persecutions that so frequently came at that time: Either by renouncing one's faith in Christ—or by living so much like the pagans that one's religion hardly seemed different. And this, many chose to do.

To The Glory Of Mithra

7

It happened in the late summer of A.D. 286.

The Roman army was divided into legions, each one numbering nearly seven thousand soldiers, and Roman legions were scattered all over Europe, North Africa and the Near East in order to keep peace throughout the Empire.

But one legion of soldiers, numbering over 6,600 men, was entirely composed of Christians. It was called the Theban Legion, for all of the men had been raised in Thebais. They were stationed in central Gaul (modern France). In July, the Emperor Maximillan ordered a general sacrifice to be made to the Roman gods, and commanded that every soldier throughout the Empire take part. And, in addition, he ordered them to take an oath to assist him in the annihilation of Christianity.

But the men in the Theban Legion refused to sacrifice to the Roman gods, or to promise to kill Christians. Learning of this, Maximillan was so enraged that he ordered every tenth man to be put to the sword. But when it was done, those remaining still refused to submit to the Emperor's requirements. A second time every tenth man was slain.

Now, those still alive wrote an appeal and sent it to the Emperor, declaring their loyalty but maintaining that they must also fear God and could not do this. In a white-hot anger, Maximillan ordered soldiers from nearby stations to go there and slay every one of them.

Out of nearly 7,000 men—not one would deny His faith in Christ. The date: September 22, A.D. 286.

And yet elsewhere at this very same time, Roman soldiers were fast being won over to a new god. While pledging their allegiance to all the old Roman gods, and to the worship of the emperor, they were now rendering their special devotion to Mithra—the Sun god. And, since new emperors frequently came by popular demand from among the best-known army generals, an increasing number of emperors were also worshipers of Mithra.

This growing trend was destined to change Christianity for all time to come.

The only safe religion is Bible religion. Find out what that is and stay by it. There is no alternative that you or I dare follow. How did the Bible Sabbath on the Seventh day of the week turn into Sunday the first day of the week? It is at Rome that we learn this story.

There have been seven days in the week from time immemorial. After God created the world in six days and then rested on the seventh, and hallowed it for worship (Gen 2: 1-3), the seven-day week went all over the world—and down through history to our own time. And we know, from the records of historians and astronomers, that the weekly cycle has never changed: the Seventh day of the week is the same now as it was back in Bible times and before.

We can read the Bible from Genesis to Revelation and we will find only Seventh-day Sabbath worship. There is nothing about first-day worship in the entire book. Where then did it come from?

In order to discover the origin and growth of worship on the first day of the week, we must look outside the Bible—into the pagan world of Christ's time and afterward. In fact, to locate the origin of the word "Sunday," we must look to the same source. For first-day sacredness, and the very name "Sun Day", came from the same place.

In the Bible, the days of the week were simply called the first day, the second day, and so on. The last, or seventh day of the week, was called the Sabbath.

But about the time of Christ, the pagans began giving new names to the days of the week: the *Day of the Sun*, the

Day of the Moon, etc., in honor of their planetary gods. This part of pagnaism is called *"the planetary week."*

Each day was ruled over by a different god, but the most important god ruled the first day-and that was *"the Lord, the Sun."* It was HIS day—the *Lord's Day.*

Of course, this was a clever counterfeit by Satan of the True Lord's Day. The Bible Sabbath is the day unto the Lord (Ex 16:23, 25; 31:15; 35:2), the day of the Lord (Ex 20:10; Lev 23:3; Deut 5:4), and His own day (Isa 58:13). Jesus, the Creator who gave us the Sabbath and everything else (Eph 3:9; Jn 1:3; Col 1:16; Heb 1:2; Gen 2:1-3) was the one who said "I am the Lord of the Sabbath day" (Matt 12:8; Mk 2:28).

Now, although these names for the days of the week were fairly new, the Sun god was not new. The orb of the sun had been worshiped for thousands of years.

"Sun worship was the earliest idolatry."—Fausset, Bible Dictionary, page 666. The Arabians appear to have worshiped the solar disc directly without the use of any statue or other symbol (Job 31:26-27). Abraham was called out of all this when he went to the promised land. Ra was the Sun god of Egypt, and On (Heliopolis—City of the Sun) was the city of Sun worship in that country (see the Hebrew of Jeremiah 43:13).

Entering Canaan under Joshua, the Hebrews again met Sun worship. Baal of the Phoenicians, Molech or Milcom of the Ammonites, and Hadad of the Syrians,—and later the Persian god Mithras (Mithra)—all these were ancient pagan Sun gods. Shemish was an important Sun god in the Middle East. Later, in Egypt, Aton was the god of the Sun disc. The famous temple at Baalbek was dedicated to Sun worship.

All through ancient history, Sun worship was the great counterfeit of the true worship of God, the Creator of heaven and earth.

By associating with Sun worshipers, the Israelites frequently practiced it themselves (Lev 26:30; Isa 17:8). King Manasseh worshiped the Sun (2 Kg 21:3, 5). Josiah destroyed the chariots that were dedicated to the Sun god, and then removed the horses consecrated to Sun-worship processions (2 Kg 23:5, 11-12). Incense was burned on Sun altars on the housetops in worship of the Sun (Zeph 1:5). In vision, the prophet Ezekiel was shown the greatest of abominations: direct Sun worship at the entryway to the temple of the true God. This was done by facing eastward to the rising sun (Ezek 8:16-17). In our own time, this practice of worshiping toward the rising sun is to be found both in Christianity and heathenism. The entrance of every major cathedral of Europe faces west. By this custom, borrowed from ancient paganism, the worshipers inside will face the rising sun as they worship God. (In contrast, the ancient Sanctuary of Israel faced east, so that the worshipers would have their backs to the sun.)

It was only a short time before Christ, that the days of the week were dedicated to pagan planetary gods. The first day was the high day for worship: It was *"dies Solis"*—the day of the Sun. All the other days were subservient to it (*"dies Lunae,"* the day of the moon, etc.).

All of this was in decided contrast with the religion of the Bible—in which we worship the Creator God of the Universe, and His worship day is the Seventh day of the week, as He commanded in the Ten Commandments.

"Remember the Sabbath day, to keep it holy. Six days shalt thou labour, and do all thy work. But the Seventh day is the Sabbath of the Lord thy God. In it thou shalt not do any work: thou, nor thy son, nor thy daughter, thy manservant, nor thy maidservant, nor thy cattle, nor thy stranger that is within thy gates. For in six days the Lord made heaven and earth, the sea, and all that in them is, and rested the seventh day: wherefore the Lord blessed the Sabbath day, and hallowed it."—Exodus 20:8-11. The Fourth Commandment.

The sacred day of the people who believed the Bible was the memorial of Creation—the true Sabbath—the Seventh-day Sabbath: the only weekly rest day given in the Bible. The sacred day of paganism was the memorial of the Sun god. It was the first day of the week. His day was called *"the venerable day of the Sun."*

Sunday sacredness is never found in the Old and New

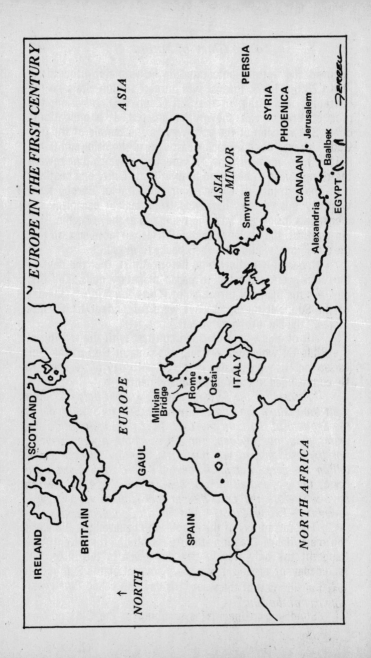

EUROPE IN THE FIRST CENTURY

Testaments, nor was it commanded there. In the time of Christ and the Apostles, the official religion of the Roman government did not have a sacred day, but gradually many of the heathen in Rome began keeping Sunday.

This was due to the influence of the Roman soldiers. Traveling to far lands in order to fight the wars and keep the peace, they brought back with them new cultures and new religions. But the one they especially preferred was Mithraism.

Mithra (also called *Mithras*) was originally an ancient god of Persia (where Iran is now located). He had been worshiped as the god of strength and war for centuries. But in the First Century A.D., he was transformed, oddly enough, into the leading Sun god of the Roman Empire.

Mithra was destined to become the leading pagan god of the western civilized world. The Romans gave him a new name —Sol Invictus, which means "the Invincible Sun." He was the great god of the Roman soldiers, and soon the masses began to worship him also.

By the middle of the Second Century, Mithraic Sun worwas the greatest heathen rival of Christianity.

The worship of Mithra was a clever counterfeit by Satan to draw men and women from the worship of the true God. Mithraism imitated the worship of Christ in several ways: It had a dying, rising Saviour god, whose birth and resurrection was celebrated every year. It had special religious suppers, or communion services, when the believers partook of their god. Its converts had to be baptized (by standing under an iron grating, over which a bull was slaughtered). And it had one day in the week that was sacred to its god—the first day of the week—the *Day of the Sun.*

Mithraism counterfeited the religion of the true God more cleverly than any other religion up to that time in history.

Gradually the new Roman holiday became popular, as large numbers of non-Christians began observing Sunday as a holy day in honor of Mithra. He was especially idolized by the Roman soldiers, for his worship included athletic feats of skill and "warlike manliness."

When Caesar Augustus became emperor, just before the birth of Christ, Mithraism was already spreading westward from Asia into Europe and the Roman Empire.

But of crucial importance was the fact that Roman generals frequently became the new emperor, upon the death of the caesar already in power. This greatly favored the rapid acceptance of Mithraism by the people of Rome. Sun worship was rapidly spreading across the empire.

This was to culminate in the rise of an emperor—Constantine—whose family was especially dedicated to the Sun god,—and who, as we shall see, was to actively work with the Christian Church leaders at Rome in bringing Mithra's holy day into the worship of the God of Heaven.

Mithra was the strongest rival of Christianity back in those days. Both religions strongly attracted the people. And great numbers in the Empire began keeping the Sun day of Mithra or the Sabbath of Christianity.

Even back in the First Century, when Christ walked this earth, many peoples of the Empire began worshiping on the Seventh-day Sabbath of the Bible. This was in great measure due to their respect for the Christians and the Jews.

But then two important events occurred that shattered this. In A.D. 70 (nearly forty years after the death of Christ), and again in A.D. 135, serious Jewish revolts were put down amid much bloodshed. In reaction, Roman hatred of everything Jewish became intense. Soon after this second Jewish rebellion, Emperor Hadrian issued an edict, strictly prohibiting the observance of the Seventh-day Sabbath. But, fortunately, imperial decrees tended to be short-lived, and Christians scattered throughout the Empire generally disregarded it. However, in the city of Rome itself, the capital of the empire, matters were different.

Anicetus, the local bishop (religious leader) of the Christian church in the city of Rome (men would today call him the "pope"), demanded that all of the Christians everywhere keep holy the first day of the week instead of the true Bible Sabbath, which was on the Seventh day of the week. At the risk of his life, the aged Polycarp of Smyrna (a close friend of the Apostle John before his death about 100 A.D.) traveled all the way to Rome to protest this apostasy. This was about the year 155 A.D. Anicetus, the Roman bishop, listened to what he had to say but refused to change his position. Polycarp returned home and was martyred the next year.

By the middle of the Second Century, Mithric Sun worship was becoming very popular among the Romans. The emperor Antoninus Pius (138-161 A.D.) erected a temple to Mithra at Ostai, a seaport town a few miles below Rome. Pius also had his name written at the base of the famous temple of the Sun at Baalbek (Heliopolis) in Syria.

By this time, the teachings of Mithraism were becoming popular among the teachers at the Christian Theological Seminary in Alexandria. (Alexandria, Egypt, was at that time one of the largest cities in the Roman Empire, and next to Rome itself, had the lowest morals.)

Consistently, for the next two centuries, the pattern was this: The worldly instructors at the Christian preacher-training school in Alexandria would adopt pagan and philosophical religious ideas and practices, teach them to their students, and write books on "Christian philosophy." Alexandria was extremely inventive when it came to new ideas. Then, the leaders of the Christian Church in the capital city of Rome would adopt these heathen theories and rituals as "new light" —and begin demanding that all the Christian churches throughout the civilized world practice these errors—just because the Church at Rome had so decreed it!

The purpose of all this was quite simple: The local Christian Church at Rome wanted to gain dominion over all the other local Christian churches throughout Christendom. And they used their demand that new ideas be adopted as a wedge with which to gain this control. And the plan succeeded.

From about 125 A.D. till 325 this concerted effort continued. Finally, with the accession of Constantine to the throne in 312, they gained the help needed for the final takeover. This, in brief, is the story behind the rise of the "Roman Catholic Church" to power.

Gradually, the worship of the *Invincible Sun* became

even more popular and widespread throughout the Roman Empire. Emperor Aurelian (270-275 A.D.), whose mother was a priestess of the Sun, made this solar cult the official religion of the empire. His biographer, Flavius Vopiscus, says that the priests of the Temple of the Sun at Rome were called *"pontiffs"* They were priests of their dying-rising saviour-god Mithra, and *"Vicegerents"* (second in command, next to him) of the Mithraic Church. At a later time, the bishops of the local Christian Church at Rome adopted both of these titles as their own—and became the "vicegerents" of Christ and the "pontiffs," before whom all the faithful in Christendom must bow on pain of death.

So it came to be that by the middle of the Second Century—150 A.D. (only 120 years after the death of Christ),—worldly Christians in Alexandria and Rome began keeping Sunday as a holy day. One of the reasons they gave for this practice was that it made them better accepted by their pagan neighbors—and thus made Christianity more appealing to worldlings. The same method of "converting the world" by becoming more like it is still being used today by a number of Christians.

Because Sunday sacredness was pagan and not Scriptural, many of the worldly Christians observing it excused their practice by calling it "the Lord's Day," even though it was obvious that Revelation 1:10 said nothing about Sunday. "Christian" philosophers at the seminary at Alexandria declared that Sunday was the "Lord's Day" of Revelation 1:10, but the entire Bible reveals that the "Lord's Day" is the Bible Sabbath. (Read Exodus 20:10; 16:23, 25; 31:15: 35:2; Leviticus 23:3; and Deuteronomy 5:4.) God, Himself, calls the Bible Sabbath "My holy day" in Isaiah 58:13.)

Then the ball bounced back the other way. Picking up this idea from the worldly Christians, the followers of Mithra began calling their Sun day, the *"day of the Lord Mithra,"* and *"the Lord's day."* This led to Emperor Pius' official declaration that the great god Mithra was to be called *"Sol Dominus Imperii Romani"*—"The Sun, Lord of the Roman Empire." This new title and the name *"Sol Invicto"* appeared together on his coinage.

Most of the new rituals and theology that came into the Christian Church from paganism in these early centuries (125 A.D. to 350 A.D.) originated in Alexandria, and were then decreed by the local church at Rome upon Christians everywhere. But, for the most part, before Constantine became emperor, many of the other local churches ignored the demands of the Roman bishop as ridiculous. Because of this trend, Egypt and North Africa (heavily influenced by that theological school in Alexandria), and Italy (under the domination of the bishop of Rome), tended to have more errors than the Christian churches in Palestine, Syria, Asia Minor, Central Europe, Britain, Scotland and Ireland, which remained closer to the teachings of the Bible.

Mithraic Sun worship gradually came to dominate the empire as the leading Sun-god religion, until Constantine I defeated Licinius in 323 A.D. After that date, Constantine worked steadily with the Christian bishop of Rome—to make the worldly Christianity of Rome the official religion of the entire Empire.

Within a few short years, Constantine, working closely with the bishop of the Christian church at Rome, demanded a new Roman holiday of Christians everywhere.

And when this happened, Mithraism died—for Satan no longer needed it,—for all Rome was now "Christian."

But the changeover was made at great cost to genuine Christianity.

.. For Rome had become the new City of the Sun.

8

City Of The Sun

Constantine, the man who changed the way of life of hundreds of millions. And that includes millions around you right now.

Who was Constantine?

Roman historians will tell you that he was the forty-eighth Roman emperor. But world historians will tell you that he was one of the most influential men in all history.

For he changed the entire future course of Christianity in less than twenty-five years.

Here is what happened—and why:

By the time of the reign of Emperor Diocletian (A.D. 284-305), Mithraism had reached its greatest power in the west. Diocletian divided the empire into four sections, and then determined to forever blot out Christianity. Some of the most terrible persecutions took place at this time. Fortunately, the worst of it lasted only ten years. Edicts were issued demanding that all Christian churches be torn down, the land sold and the proceeds turned over to the State.

Here is what happened:

It was clear to all that this internal turmoil only deepened the problems within the Empire. What was needed was peace and a strong unity.

On the retirement of Diocletian in 305, it was an uphill fight among several men for the coveted title of Emperor. But out of it, Constantine was to emerge as the sole ruler of the vast Roman empire.

Constantine's family was especially dedicated to the Sun god. And Constantine himself recognized that there were only two strong religions in the empire—Mithraism, the worship of the sun, and Christianity, the worship of Christ. Constantine's objective was to strengthen the empire in order to better resist the growing number of enemies to the north. He saw that in order to weld the empire into a single, powerful force able to meet the demands of the hour, there must be a uniting of the major religions. We are told that the bishop of Rome counseled with Constantine and advised him of the best course to take in order to win everyone into a single imperial church.

The crucial battle took place in October 312 at the Battle of Milvian Bridge. Soon afterward, Constantine enacted the *Edict of Milan*, by which Christianity was given full legal rights, equaling that of every other religion in the empire. More favors to the Church were soon to follow.

Then, on March 7, 321, the long-awaited unifying edict was issued—destined to unite the two leading religions into a single powerful State Church. This was his famous *Sunday Law Decree*, in which he required the observance of the day of the Lord Mithra—*the Sun day*—as a day of worship by all peoples throughout the empire.

Here is the text of this decree:

"Let all judges and townspeople and occupations of all trades rest on the Venerable Day of the Sun [Sunday] ; nevertheless, let those who are situated in the rural districts freely and with full liberty attend to the cultivation of the fields, because it frequently happens that no other day may be so fitting for ploughing grains or trenching vineyards, lest at the time the advantage of the moment granted by the provision of heaven be lost. Given on the Nones [seventh] of March, Crispus and Constantine being consuls, each of them, for the second time."—*Recorded in the Code of Justinian, Book III, title 12, law 3.*

Constantine was not a Christian. At this very same time he was embellishing the Temple of the Sun in Rome. He continued to be a sun-worshiper until his death. The very next day after giving the Sunday law of March 7, 321, quoted above, Constantine enacted another law giving pagan soothsayers

official acceptance in the Empire. In this law he stated that
whenever lightning should strike the imperial palace or any
other public building, the gods should be asked why it had
happened—and that this was to be done through the heathen
priests. They were to look at the entrails of beasts, freshly
slaughtered in sacrifice to the pagan gods, and then tell the
meaning of the lightning bolt.

Five additional Sunday Laws were to be issued by Constantine within a very few years to strengthen this basic one of
A.D. 321.

Sunday was the great day of the Sun-worship cults as
well as of compromising Christians. In his Sunday law, Constantine does not mention Christianity or Jesus or the Bible.
The day is called "the Venerable Day of the Sun" (*verarabili
die solis*). —This was the mystical name for the Day of the
Lord Mithra, god of the Sun. Both the heathen and the Christians well knew this. It is a recognized historical fact that
when Constantine issued this first imperial Sunday edict of
321, enforcing the observance of Sunday, he was still a worshiper of *Sol Invictus*—the "Invincible Sun"—Lord Mithra.
And he was also the *Pontifix Maximus* (supreme pagan pontiff
or priest) of all the Roman gods, which was the state religion.

In another of his six Sunday laws, he gave the order that
all of the army troops be marched out on the drill field each
Sunday in order to recite a prayer composed by the emperor
for this purpose. It was worded in such a way that it could be
addressed to any god adored by mankind, and the soldiers
were required to face the rising sun while uttering this prayer.

A French historian, Victor Duruy, explains the meaning
of these weekly Sunday worship services:

"He [Constantine] sent to the legions, to be recited
upon that day [Sunday], a form of prayer which could have
been employed by a worshiper of Mithra, of Serapis, or of
Apollo, quite as well as by a Christian believer. This was the
official sanction of the old custiom of addressing a prayer to
the rising sun."—*Victor Duruy, History of Rome, Volume 7,
p. 489.*

Constantine always favored the Sun god, but he was wise
enough to know that he must unite it with Christianity in

order to win all of the people to the worship of the Sun god on his day.

Although the True God had never appointed Sunday-keeping in place of the sacred Seventh-day Sabbath, yet Constantine, in counsel with the bishop (the "pope") of the local Christian Church at Rome, recognized that a combining of the principal features of the two dominant religions of the empire could bring peace and prosperity, both to the nation and to the religions within it. Unity based on compromise had the effect of bringing the world into the Christian Church in the Fourth Century, during the reign of Constantine. For before his death, Constantine had made Christianity the State Church of the Empire.

One excellent historical work tells us that Eusebius, bishop of Caesarea (c. 260-340), was "the special friend and flatterer of Constantine" (Great Controversy, p. 574). Eusebius was one of those who convinced the emperor that Sunday legislation would unite the Sun-god worshipers (the Mithraites) with the followers of Jesus. In one of his statements, Eusebius clearly explains that the apostate church was responsible for what Constantine did—and then he tells why: to transfer Christian worship to the "day of light"—the day of the holy Sun.

"The Logos [Christ] has transferred by the New Alliance [new covenant] the celebration of the Sabbath to the rising of the light. He has given us a type of the true rest in the saving day of the Lord, the first day of light . . In this day of light—first day and true day of the sun—when we gather after the interval of six days, we celebrate the holy and spiritual Sabbaths . . All things whatsoever that were prescribed for the [Bible] Sabbath, WE have transferred them to the Lord's day, as being more authoritative and more highly regarded and first in rank, and more honorable than the Jewish Sabbath. In fact, it is on this day of the creation of the world that God said, 'Let there be light and there was light.' It is also on this day that the Sun of Justice has risen for our souls."—*Eusebius, Commentary on the Psalms, Psalm 91, in Patrologie Cursus Completus, Series Latina, ed. J.P. Migne, p. 23, 1169-1172.*

Here are some comments by historians in regard to this momentous event, by which the pagan religions of the western civilized world were united with Christianity:

"This [Sunday law] legislation by Constantine probably bore no relation to Christianity. It appears, on the contrary, that the emperor, in his capacity as Pontifix Maximus, was only adding the day of the sun, the worship of which was then firmly established in the Roman Empire, to the other ferial days of the sacred calendar."—*Hutton Webster, Rest Days, pp. 122-123. [Webster was an American anthropoligist and historian.].*

"The [Catholic] Church made a sacred day of Sunday . . largely because it was the weekly festival of the sun;—for it was a definite Christian policy [at Rome] to take over the pagan festivals endeared to the people by tradition, and to give them a Christian significance."—*Arthur Weigall, The Paganism in Our Christianity, 1928, p. 145. [Dr. A.E. Weigall (1880-1937) was a high-ranking British Egyptologist in the Egyptian Government.]*

"Remains of the struggle [between Christianity and Mithraism] are found in two institutions adopted from its rival by Christianity in the fourth century, the two Mithraic sacred days: December 25th, dies natalis solis [birthday of the sun], as the birthday of Jesus,—and Sunday, 'the venerable day of the Sun,' as Constantine called it in his edict of 321."—*Walter Woodburn Hyde, Paganism to Christianity in the Roman Empire, p. 60. [Hyde (1870- ?) was an American ancient history professor and writer.].*

Certain historians agree that it was the pagan sun-worshipers—and not the Christians—who first gave the name 'Lord's Day' to Sunday. "The first day of each week, Sunday, was consecrated to Mithra [the most widely known sun-god of the early Christian centuries] since times remote, as several authors affirm. Because the Sun was god, the Lord par excellence, Sunday came to be called the 'Lord's day,' as later was done by Christianity."—*Agostinho de Almeida Paiva, O Mitraiomo, p. 3.*

"The festival of Sunday, like all other festivals, was always only a human ordinance, and it was far from the intentions of the apostles to establish a Divine command in this respect,—far from them, and from the early Apostolic Church, to transfer the laws of the Sabbath to Sunday."—*Augustus Neander, The History of the Christian Religion and Church, Rose's translation from the first German edition, p. 186. [Neander is generally considered to be one of the most important of the Protestant church historians of modern times.]*

"Unquestionably the first law, either ecclesiastical or

civil, by which the Sabbatical observance of that day is known to have been ordained, is the edict of Constantine, 321 A.D."
—*Chambers' Encyclopedia, article, "Sabbath."*

"This [Sunday decree of A.D. 321] is the 'parent' Sunday law making it a day of rest and release from labor. For from that time to the present there have been decrees about the observance of Sunday which have profoundly influenced European and American society. When the Church became a part of the State under the Christian emperors, Sunday observance was enforced by civil statutes, and later when the Empire was past, the Church in the hands of the papacy enforced it by ecclesiastical, and also by civil enactments."—*Walter Woodburn Hyde, Paganism to Christianity in the Roman Empire, 1946, p. 261. [Hyde was an ancient history professor in several American universities.]*

"Constantine's decree marked the beginning of a long, though intermittent series of imperial decrees in support of Sunday laws."—*Vincent J. Kelly, Forbidden Sunday and Feast-day Occupations, 1943, p. 29. [Catholic University of America dissertation.]*

"What began, however, as a pagan ordinance, ended as a Christian regulation; and a long series of imperial decrees, during the fourth, fifth, and sixth centuries, enjoined with increasing stringency abstinence from labor on Sunday."—*Hutton Webster, Rest Days, 1916, pp. 122-123, 270. [Dr. Webster was an historian teaching at the University of Nebraska.]*

"Concerning the power of the Mithras cult [on Christianity], we still have evidence in the fact that it is not the Jewish Sabbath that is the sacred weekday (which Christianity, coming out of Judaism, had nearest at hand), but Sunday, dedicated to the Sun-god Mithra."—*H. Lamer, "Mithras," Wurterbuch der Antike, 2nd ed., 1933. [Hans Lamer (1873-?) was an archaeological writer and a student of ancient religions and civilizations.]*

"There is scarcely anything which strikes the mind of the careful student of ancient ecclesiastical history with greater surprise than the comparatively early period at which many of the corruptions of Christianity, which are embodied in the Romish system, took their rise; yet it is not to be supposed that when the first originators of many of these unscriptural notions and practices planted those germs of corruption, they anticipated or even imagined they would ever grow into such a vast and hideous system of superstition and error as is that of popery."—*John Dowling, History of Romanism, 13th edition, p. 65. [Dowling was a Protestant clergyman and his-*

torian of the early nineteenth century.]

"It would be an error to attribute ["the sanctification of Sunday"] to a definite decision of the Apostles. There is no such decision mentioned in the Apostolic documents [the New Testament]."—*Antoine Villien, A History of the Commandments of the Church, 1915, p. 23. [Catholic priest and professor at the Catholic University of Paris.]*

"Rites and ceremonies of which neither Paul nor Peter ever heard, crept silently into use, and then claimed the rank of divine institutions. Officers for whom the primitive disciples could have found no place, and titles which to them would have been altogether unintelligible, began to challenge attention, and to be named apostolic."—*William D. Killen, The Ancient Church, preface, p. xvi. [Killan (1806-1902) was a Protestant church history professor in Belfast, Ireland.]*

"In the year 321 the Emperor Constantine, who was not yet a declared Christian, but was still hovering between paganism and Christianity, issued a decree making Sunday a compulsory day of rest: but the fact that he speaks of Sunday as 'the venerable day of the Sun' [the pagan Sun-worship name for the day] shows that he was thinking of it as a traditional sun-festival at the same time that he thought of it as a Christian holy-day . . Sunday came to be observed throughout Europe as it is still observed by Roman Catholics, namely, as a day on which, like our Christmas, people went to church in the morning and then gave themselves over to rest or to holiday-making and sports."—*Arthur Weigall, The Paganism in Our Christianity, 1928, pp. 236-237. [Dr. A.D. Weigall (1880-1927) was a British historian, Egyptologist and inspector-general of antiquities for the Egyptian Government.]*

"The retention of the old pagan name, 'Dies Solis' [Day of the Sun] or 'Sunday' for the weekly Christian festival, is, in great measure, owing to the union of pagan and Christian sentiment, with which the first day of the week was recommended by Constantine to his subjects, pagan and Christian alike, as the 'venerable day of the sun' . . It was his mode of harmonizing the discordant religions of the empire under one common institution."—*Dean Stanley, Lectures on the Eastern Church, Lecture 6, p. 184. [Stanley was an Episcopalian historian and church leader.]*

"Constantine labored at this time untiringly to unite the worshipers of the old [pagan] and the new [Christian] faith in one religion. All his laws and contrivances are aimed at promoting this amalgamation of religions. He would by all lawful and peaceable means melt together a purified heathenism and a moderated [compromised] Christianity .. Of all his blending and melting together of Christianity and heathenism, none is more easy to see through than his making of his Sunday law. The Christians worshiped their Christ, the heathen their sun-god; according to the opinion of the Emperor, the objects for worship in both religions being the same [the worship of the deities on a single day of the week]*."—H.G. Heggtveit, Illustreret Kirkehistorie, 1895, p. 202. [Hallvard Heggtveit (1850-1924) was a Norwegian church historian and teacher.]*

"The Jewish, the Samaritan, even the Christian, were to be fused and recast into one great system, of which the sun was to be the central object of adoration.*"—Henry Hart Milman, The History of Christianity, Book 2, chap. 8 (Vol. 22, p. 175). [Dr. Milman (1791-1868) was an important historian of England and dean of St. Paul's Cathedral in London.]*

And so it was, that Constantine turned Rome into the City of the Sun, and every passing century witnessed the passage of additional laws and decrees requiring the worship of Christ on the day earlier dedicated to Mithra—on pain of death.

And yet, ironically, Mithra himself was to pass away within fifty years after Constantine's time. For he wasn't needed anymore. Many of his errors had been made a part of official Christianity, and he disappeared from history. The same happened to the worship of Isis and Horus—the Egyptian Queen of Heaven and her infant son. Within half a century after the worship of Mary was required by Rome, the worship of Isis ceased. Its pagan devotees had switched over to Christianity and to the worship of statues of Mary of the sacred heart, holding an infant Son.

When Rome became the City of the Sun, a persecution of Christians—far more bitter than anything they had experienced earlier—began in earnest. And it continued for centuries.

More than fifteen additional Sunday laws were enacted and enforced by the State or the Catholic Church over the next several centuries. These laws restricted what could be done on Sunday, and forbade Sabbathkeeping. Each law became more strict, each penalty more severe. It is obvious that humble Christians were determined not to stop keeping the

Bible Sabbath—the worship of God on the Seventh-day of the week. Sunday sacredness was responsible for the death of large numbers of Christians in the ages that followed.

Pope Gregory the Great (Gregory I - 590-604), in his edict against Sabbathkeepers, declared that they were the preachers of antichrist. Here are his words:

"**Gregory, bishop by the grace of God to his well-beloved sons, the Roman citizens: It has come to me that certain men of perverse spirit have disseminated among you things depraved and opposed to the holy faith, so that they forbid anything to be done on the day of the Sabbath [the seventh day]. What shall I call them except preachers of antichrist, who when he comes, will cause the Sabbath day to be kept free from all work . . He compels the people to Judaize . . [and] wishes the Sabbath to be observed.**

"**On the Lord's day [Sunday], however, there should be a cessation of labor and attention given in every way to prayers, so that if anything is done negligently during the six days, it may be expiated by supplications on the day of the Lord's resurrection.**"—*Gregory 1, Epistles, Book 13, epis. 1, in Labbe and Cossart, Sacrosancta Concilia, Vol. 5, col. 1511.*

Gregory well knew that the Bible Sabbath was given to mankind by the God of Heaven 1500 years before the first Hebrew was born (compare Gen 2:1-3—the Creation of the world, with Gen 12:1—the call of Abraham, the first Jew). It is an insult to the Creator to declare the Seventh-day Sabbath "Jewish." The Bible Sabbath came from God; it was not invented by the Jews.

Here are two other quotations from Catholics who lived in the Dark Ages:

"**They do not hear the masses of Christians [Catholics] . . they flee the image of the Crucifix as the devil, they do not celebrate the feasts [Catholic holy days] of the divine Virgin Mary and of the apostles, . . Some indeed celebrate [keep] the Sabbath that the Jews observe!**"—*Translated by J.J. von Doellinger, Beitraege zur Sektengeschiechte des Mittelalters, Vol. 2, no. 61, p. 662.*

"**Convicted heretics should be put to death just as surely as other criminals.**"—*Thomas Aquinas. [Aquinas (1225-1275) is the most important Roman Catholic theologian in all history. He was made a saint in 1323, and in 1889, Pope Leo XIII decreed that Acquinas' writings be the basis of all Catho-*

lic theology and belief.]

For centuries, Christians were persecuted to the death for worshiping God on the Bible Sabbath. And yet, they refused to compromise their faith. The Seventh-day Sabbath is clearly in the Bible; Sunday-sacredness is clearly not. And so they were willing to die for genuine Bible religion.

Surprisingly enough, the great majority of all Christians still kept the Bible Sabbath as late as the Fifth Century—a hundred years after Constantine's time!

"As we have already noted, excepting for the Roman and Alexandrian Christians, the majority of Christians were observing the seventh-day Sabbath at least as late as the middle of the fifth century. The Roman and Alexandrian Christians were among those converted from heathenism. They began observing Sunday as a merry religious festival in honor of the Lord's resurrection, about the latter half of the second century A.D. However, they did not try to teach that the Lord or His apostles commanded it. In fact, no ecclesiastical writer before Eusebius of Caesarea in the fourth century even suggested that either Christ or His apostles instituted the observance of the first day of the week.

"These Gentile Christians of Rome and Alexandria began calling the first day of the week 'the Lord's day.' This was not difficult for the pagans of the Roman Empire who were steeped in sun worship to accept, because they referred to their sun-god as their 'Lord.' "—*E.M. Chalmers, How Sunday Came into the Christian Church, p. 3.*

Sozomen and Socrates Scholasticus were two historians who lived in the Fifth Century A.D. They clearly state that the majority of Christians everywhere (except at Rome and Alexandria which were more corrupt) steadfastly worshiped God on the Bible Sabbath:

"Although almost all churches throughout the world celebrate the sacred mysteries on the Sabbath every week, yet the Christians of Alexandria and at Rome, on account of some ancient tradition, have ceased to do this."—*Socrates, Ecclesiastical History, Book 5, chap. 22. [This is a very important statement, for it shows that most Christians were still keeping the Bible Sabbath in the Fifth Century—one hundred years after Constantine's Sunday law. Socrates Scholasticus was a Fifth Century historian who wrote shortly after A.D. 439.]*

"The people of Constantinople, and almost everywhere,

assemble together on the Sabbath, as well as on the first day of the week, which custom is never observed at Rome or at Alexandria."—*Sozomen, Ecclesiastical History, vii, 19, in A Select Library of Nicene and Post-Nicene Fathers, 2nd series, Volume II, p. 390. [This valuable statement reveals that Christians were keeping the Bible Sabbath in the Fifth Century, but were also trying to satisfy the requirements of Constantine's Sunday law edict by observing the first day also. Hermias Sozomen was a Greek Christian church historian. He wrote this after A.D. 415.]*

Don't let anyone tell you that Christ and the Apostles kept Sunday holy. They did not. And don't let anyone tell you that most Christians kept Sunday within a century or two after the Bible was finished. They did not. The great majority of Christians were still keeping the Seventh-day Sabbath holy unto God—as late as the Fifth Century (400-499) A.D. It was only by letting the streets flow with blood, that the apostate church of Rome was able to turn the City of the Sun into an Empire of the Sun.

But now, we need to go back in history - to a time before this corrupted Christianity - to a holocaust that Jesus said would take place.

9

The Forgotten Prayer

For better than half a century the prayer was remembered. But in later centuries it would be forgotten.

Christ was nearing the end of His earthly ministry. Only a few days stood between Him and Golgotha. One day He was seated with His disciples on the summit of the Mount of Olives. Spread out before them, across the Valley of Kidron, were the massive battlements and pinnacles of the Temple at Jerusalem. Constructed of massive blocks of white marble, it was surrounded by outer walls, covered colonnades, terraces, stairways and gates.

His disciples, seated around Him, remarked on the immense stones that formed the foundation of the Temple. Josephus, a contemporary Jewish writer of that time, tells us that the temple was made of massive blocks of stone that were forty-two feet in length.

But, at that moment, they were numbed to the silence of utter shock as they heard Him say, "See ye not all these things? Verily I say unto you, There shall not be left here one stone upon another, that shall not be thrown down." Matthew 24:2.

Slowly recovering from their amazement, His disciples pled with Him to tell them when this would happen—and to explain the rest of world history down to the end of time. "Tell us, when shall these things be? and what shall be the sign of Thy coming, and of the end of the world?" Matthew 24:3.

The reply of Jesus fills Chapter 24 of the book of Matthew. It contains warnings—serious warnings. It has information we need as we face into the future. And it also contains help—precious help—for souls trying to stay close to Jesus in these times that try men's souls.

All through history, crises have come to the people of God. In verses 15 through 20, Jesus describes what to do when the crisis comes and we must flee.

And then in verse 20 He gives us the prayer to keep sending up—in all coming ages till He returns to earth for His own:

"But pray ye that your flight be not in the winter, neither on the Sabbath day."—Matthew 24:20.

And then, speaking specifically about the final crisis, just before His return, He gives still further counsel in verses 21 and 22.

During His earthly life, Jesus had continually given an example of obedience to the Moral Law of Ten Commandments. And He told His disciples to obey it also.

And then having taught His followers how to live godly lives, He was crucified. At His death the disciples faithfully observed the Bible Sabbath—the Seventh-day Sabbath, and then came back on the first work-day of the week—the first day—to anoint His body, since they had not had time on Friday to do it. (Read Luke 23:50-24:4; Matthew 27:55-28:2; Mark 15:42-16:9.)

And they continued to keep it later during their missionary work (Acts 13:14-16, 40-46; 16:12-15; 17:1-4). They declared that we ought to obey God rather than men (Acts 5:29), and Paul could sincerely say of himself and his fellow believers: "Do we then make void the law through faith? God forbid: yea, we establish the law." Romans 3:31.

And all through those years the prayer that Jesus gave them was sent up by humble believers in the Word of God. As the crisis neared they prayed for help and strength to obey God and keep His Sabbath in spite of what might happen. And over and over again that prayer was answered.

Then came the first great crisis—the very first great crisis that Jesus warned in Matthew 24 was soon to come—the crisis of the siege and destruction of Jerusalem and its temple.

Thirty-five years after it had been predicted, the storm suddenly broke with a fury unimaginable. In the hills of Samaria and in the byways of Galilee where Jesus had walked and talked with His disciples, men by the thousands perished by the sword and engines of war. One by one the Jewish strongholds were reduced to smoking ruins. Even the lake that Jesus once ordered to be still of storms became, during the battle for Taricheae, bloody from the dead and dying.

But all through this time, men and women of God were praying the prayer that Jesus had given them.

The beginning of the end came to Jerusalem in August of A.D. 66. For the next four years Jerusalem was to know no peace as Jew fought Jew or Roman, within and without its walls. But the Christians continued to pray as Jesus had directed them to do.

Then came the day that a Roman regiment was cornered in Jerusalem and massacred, and Cestius Gallus, Roman legate of Syria, marched southward at the head of 30,000 troops. Burning Joppa and subduing Galilee and the coasts, he headed for Jerusalem. The siege of the capital city began, and the moderates within the walls were on the verge of handing the city over to him,—when a strange thing happened: The Roman general, Cestius, suddenly retreated from the city, for no reason. This unexplainable withdrawal encouraged the Jews to rush out of the city after them, and to attack the retreating Roman forces so severely that history tells us only the coming of nightfall saved the Romans from annihilation. The Jews captured Cestius' siege engines and killed 5,300 Roman foot soldiers and 380 horsemen. "Running and singing," the Jews returned to their metropolis, ignorant of the terrible ordeal that awaited them before the next three years would be concluded.

Jesus had promised His disciples that they would know when to safely flee. And the promise was fulfilled. Praying the prayer given them thirty-six and a half years before, the children of God pled with Him to protect them and help them to escape—and not to do it on the holy Sabbath day.

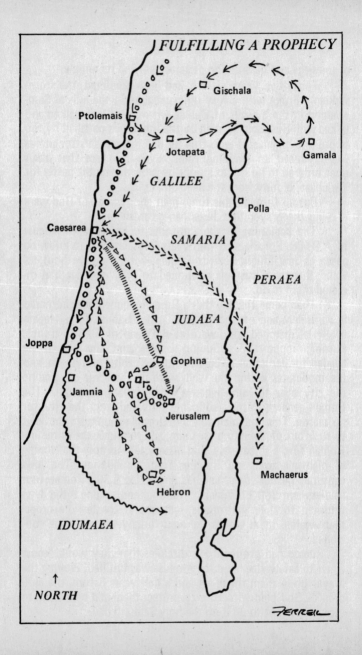

FULFILLING A PROPHECY

Gischala

Ptolemais

Jotapata

Gamala

GALILEE

Pella

Caesarea

SAMARIA

PERAEA

Joppa

JUDAEA

Gophna

Jamnia

Jerusalem

Hebron

Machaerus

IDUMAEA

↑
NORTH

FERREL

THE DESTRUCTION OF JERUSALEM IN A.D. 70
– A KEY TO THE MAP –

 1 – In A.D. 64, Gessius Florus became the Roman procurator, or governor, of Palestine. Riots by the Jews caused Florus to raid the Temple funds and massacre many Jews. Total rebellion in Jerusalem resulted. It was spring of A.D. 66. The Roman garrison fled to Caesarea. Cestius Gallus, Roman legate of Syria was given command and arriving with reinforcements, fought his way to Jerusalem, but then unaccountably retreated before penetrating the walls. At Beth-horon this retreat turned into a rout, for Jerusalem had been emptied of men in order to pursue his army. The Christians immediately fled to Pella. This Jewish victory transformed all Palestine into open rebellion.

2 – The Roman general, Vespasian, arrived in A.D. 67 at Ptolemais, and circling through Galilee, captured the Jewish general, Flavius Josephus, at Jotapata, and then went on to take Gamala and Gischala as well.

3 – Selecting the port city of Caesarea as his base of operations, early in A.D. 68 Vespasian headed south and took Joppa, southwest Judaea and all of Idumaea.

4 – By May 68, Vespasian had conquered Samaria, Peraea and the Transjordan region. Only the fortress of Machaerus held out to the last. After taking it, he returned to Caesarea. It was during this eastern campaign that the Qumran community, where the Dead Sea Scrolls were made, was destroyed.

5 – In June 69, Vespasian swept through the area around Jerusalem and desolated it of opposition. Gophna and Hebron were two major battles in this mop-up operation.

6 – Upon the death of Nero by suicide, Vespasian returned to Rome and within a few months was proclaimed emperor. Most of Palestine was now under Roman control, but Jerusalem had yet to be dealt with. Titus, Vespasian's son, now took command and laid siege to Jerusalem in April 70. A large number of Jews had moved into Jerusalem—and three Jewish factions were warring within the city when the siege began. This in-fighting continued throughout the three-month siege. More than 100,000 Jews died within the city between early May and late July. In August the Temple was burned to the ground, and in September the southern half of the city fell. Over 1 million Jews lost their lives in the siege. Another 97,000 were taken captive to foreign lands.

When Cestius suddenly retreated, and the Jews sallied forth after him,—the Christians knew that the time had come. The entire countryside was empty of warriors; all were engaged in the battle taking place north of Jerusalem. Immediately, every Christian left Judea and fled to Pella, in the land of Perea, east of the Jordan River. In answer to prayer, God had sent help. The flight was not on the Sabbath, and it was made safely. We are told that no Christians perished in the later destruction of Jerusalem. The date: October of A.D. 67. It was the twelfth year of Nero's reign.

And what did the flight save the Christians from? Come, let us see the power of prayer. This is what God spared His people from experiencing:

On May 10, A.D. 70, the shadow of Titus, general of the armies of Rome, fell across the walls of Jerusalem. Son of Vespasian, Emperor of all western civilization, Titus was thirty years old and a seasoned veteran of war. But his legacy was a difficult one: to capture Jerusalem.

When Cestius mysteriously withdrew from it in October of 67, the city was given a little more time. The following year, in July, Vespasian was about to surround it, when Nero committed suicide and Vespasian began a three-month fight to become the next emperor.

But now there was to be no more reprieve. It took Titus' army of 65,000 men 139 days to gain control of the whole city—and during that time every horror took place by Jew and Roman. Every tree within twelve miles of the city was cut down to make crosses to crucify captured Jews upon. But in spite of what was taking place outside the city—a terrible slaughter of Jew by Jew took place within it.

Finally, with the help of battering rams, banks, seventy-five-foot towers, and machines that hurled immense stones, darts, and javelins nearly five hundred yards, the Romans gained possession of the two outer walls.

So many were trying to escape from the harrowing scenes within the doomed capital, that Titus now encircled the city with a five-mile wall, and then went on with the siege.

On August 7, the morning and evening offerings at the

Temple were stopped "for want of men to offer it." Titus pled with the Jews to fight with him elsewhere so that he would not have to defile the Temple. In reply, John of Gischala mounted his artillery on the gates of the sacred building and Titus was forced to continue attacking it.

But then fires were started in the Temple gates, and Titus, determined to save the Temple, sent soldiers to put out the fire. But they were attacked by Jews as they tried to quench the flames. The ensuing fight brought the soldiers alongside the Temple. Josephus, a Jewish historian who lived at that time, tells us what happened next:

"One of the soldiers, without staying for any orders, being hurried on by a certain divine fury and being lifted up by another soldier, set fire to a golden window, through which there was a passage to the rooms that were about the holy house on the north side of it . . The fatal day had come, it was the tenth day of the month of Ab,—[the same day] upon which it was formerly burnt by the King of Babylon."—*Josephus, Wars of the Jews.*

The end had come.

"Titus rushed to the place, followed by his generals and legionaries, and commanded the soldiers to quench the flames. His words were unheeded. In their fury the soldiers hurled blazing brands into the chambers adjoining the temple . . Titus found it impossible to check the rage of the soldiery; he entered with his officers, and surveyed the interior of the sacred edifice. The splendor filled them with wonder; and as the flames had not yet penetrated to the holy place, he made a last effort to save it, and springing forth, again exhorted the soldiers to stay the progress of the conflagration. The centurion Liberalis endeavored to force obedience with his staff of office; but even respect for the emperor gave way . . to the fierce excitement of battle, and to the insatiable hope of plunder.

"The soldiers saw everything around them radiant with gold, which shone dazzlingly in the wild light of the flames; they supposed that incalculable treasures were laid up in the sanctuary. A soldier, unperceived, thrust a lighted torch between the hinges of the door: the whole building was in flames in an instant. The blinding smoke and fire forced the officers to retreat, and the noble edifice was left to its fate."—*The Great Controversy, pp. 33-34.*

All this happened because the chosen people of God

would not obey the Ten Commandments and live godly lives. And so the God of heaven had to separate from them and call those who would hear and come and obey Him. Jerusalem and its Temple were destroyed, just as Christ predicted nearly forty years before, because a nation would not submit their ways to the Word of God.

"It was an appalling spectacle to the Roman—what was it to the Jew? The whole summit of the hill which commanded the city, blazed like a volcano. One after another the buildings fell in, with a tremendous crash, and were swallowed up in the fiery abyss. The roofs of cedar were like sheets of flame; the gilded pinnacles shone like spokes of red light; the gate towers sent up tall columns of flame and smoke. The neighboring hills were lighted up; and dark groups of people were seen watching in horrible anxiety the progress of the destruction: the walls and heights of the upper city were crowded with faces, some pale with the agony of despair, others scowling unavailing vengeance.

"The shouts of the Roman soldiery as they ran to and fro, and the howlings of the insurgents who were perishing in the flames, mingled with the roaring of the conflagration and the thundering sound of falling timbers. The echoes of the mountains replied or brought back the shrieks of the people on the heights; all along the walls resounded screams and wailings; men who were expiring with famine rallied their remaining strength to utter a cry of anguish and desolation."—*The Great Controversy, p. 34.*

Josephus tells us that 1,100,000 Jews were killed in this siege and conquest of Jerusalem. And yet not one Christian died in that siege—because the followers of Jesus were praying the prayer He had given them, and all made their escape when Cestius suddenly retreated.

But that prayer of Jesus has yet to meet its climax. We are still living in a terrible world; every day it becomes more terrible. And today we must pray that prayer—that Jesus will protect us in the days ahead and that we will be enabled to keep His Sabbath—the Bible Sabbath—on the Seventh day of the weekly cycle. We know from historians and astonomers that this weekly cycle has never changed down through the ages. The Seventh day of the week today—is the same day that Jesus kept as the Bible Sabbath when He was here on earth

2,000 years ago.

And that prayer is for us today. For centuries men have forgotten it. The Church of Rome has been quite successful in blotting out the observance of the Seventh-day Sabbath. And yet God has not changed, and His Sabbath has not changed.

In Genesis 2:1-3 God gave the Seventh-day Sabbath to mankind when He first created our world. Indeed, we are to keep it in honor of His creative power. In Exodus 20:8-11, He included it as the fourth of the Ten Commandments. But following that time,—never has God declared in Scripture that He has changed the sanctity of the Seventh-day Sabbath to Sunday, the first day of the week. We can not obey God's Sabbath requirement by keeping a different day than the one He specified in His Word.

Although many have forgotten that prayer that Jesus gave us in Matthew 24:20, it is time for men and women to come back to it. Their own eternal safety depends upon it.

Will you and I—just now—begin praying that prayer again?

"And as He sat upon the mount of Olives, the disciples came unto Him privately saying, Tell us, when shall these things be? and what shall be the sign of Thy coming, and of the end of the world?

"And Jesus answered and said unto them, Take heed that no man deceive you. For many shall come in My name, saying, I am Christ; and shall deceive many. And ye shall hear of wars and rumours of wars . . For nation shall rise against nation, and kingdom against kingdom: and there shall be famines, and pestilences, and earthquakes, in divers [various] places. All these are the beginning of sorrows.

"Then shall they deliver you up to be afflicted, and shall kill you: and ye shall be hated of all nations for My name's sake. And then shall many be offended, and shall betray one another, and shall hate one another. And many false prophets shall rise, and shall deceive many. And because iniquity shall abound, the love of many shall wax cold. But he that shall endure unto the end shall be saved. And this gospel of the kingdom shall be preached in all the world for a witness unto all nations; and then shall the end come . .

"But pray ye that your flight be not in the winter,

neither on the Sabbath day. For then shall be great tribulation, such as was not since the beginning of the world to this time, no, nor ever shall be. And except those days should be shortened, there should be no flesh be saved: but for the elect's sake those days shall be shortened . .

"And then shall appear the sign of the Son of man in heaven: and then shall all the tribes of the earth mourn, and they shall see the Son of man coming in the clouds of heaven with power and great glory. And He shall send His angels with a great sound of a trumpet, and they shall gather together His elect from the four winds."—Matthew 24:3-31.

It is clear that Jesus was predicting the future all the way down to His Second Advent. We were to keep the Sabbath all through those long ages. And we are to keep it today.

Men are embarrassed because of the real reason that the Protestant churches keep the first day of the week holy. The real reason is because Constantine, in counsel with the church leaders at Rome, tried to change the Sabbath to Sunday in A.D. 321. But what Constantine and apostate church leaders attempted in that Sunday law is a little late: It came 290 years after the death of Christ on Calvary, and 226 years after the last book in the Bible was finished.

Sunday sacredness is simply not in the Bible—anywhere. It does no good to say that we know that the Sabbath has been changed to Sunday because the disciples ate a meal that day. And it does no good to say that we should keep Sunday instead of the Bible Sabbath "in honor of the resurrection of Jesus." The truth is that we are to do what God tells us in the Bible to do—not what we imagine we would like to do. Yes, indeed, please God—but don't do it at the cost of giving your approval to a man-made change in the Ten Commandments!

We want the living fire of the Holy Spirit kindled and burning within our hearts—in hearts dedicated to serving and obeying Him in every way.

Otherwise we may find a fire kindled in our gates that will destroy us.

10

Fire In The Gates

It was late fall of 589 B.C., and Nebuchadnezzar left the Golden Metropolis—the greatest city of his time—to settle an account with a rebellious king. And, all unknowingly, to fulfill a prophecy of God.

Down the Processional Way of Marduk, through the Ishtar Gate, and out of Babylon, first north and then west, this ruler of kings marched with his soldiers. Behind them lay the fabled riches of the capital of Neo-Babylonia, with its Hanging Gardens, Temple Tower, palaces, estates and pleasure groves.

Ahead of him lay Jerusalem and a people who had defied him;—a people who had also refused to obey the God of heaven.

But let us go back still earlier—to an amazing prediction given by the King above all kings. We find it recorded in Jeremiah 17:

"Thus said the Lord unto me; Go and stand in the gate of the children of the people, whereby the kings of Judah come in, and by the which they go out, and in all the gates of Jerusalem. And say unto them:

"Hear ye the word of the Lord, ye kings of Judah, and all Judah, and all the inhabitants of Jerusalem, that enter in by these gates:

"Thus saith the Lord; Take heed to yourselves, and bear no burden on the Sabbath day, nor bring it in by the gates of Jerusalem; Neither carry forth a burden out of your houses on the Sabbath day, neither do ye any work, but hallow ye the Sabbath day, as I commanded your fathers.

"But they obeyed not, neither inclined their ear, but made their neck stiff, that they might not hear, nor receive

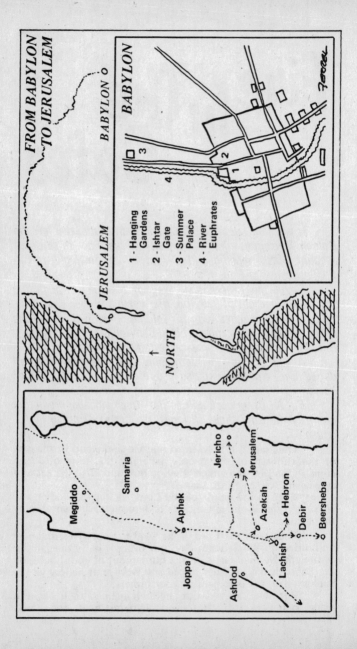

FROM BABYLON TO JERUSALEM

BABYLON

BABYLON

JERUSALEM

NORTH

1 - Hanging Gardens
2 - Ishtar Gate
3 - Summer Palace
4 - River Euphrates

Megiddo

Samaria

Joppa

Ashdod

Aphek

Jericho

Jerusalem

Azekah

Lachish

Debir

Hebron

Beersheba

instruction.

"And it shall come to pass, if ye diligently hearken unto Me, saith the Lord, to bring in no burden through the gates of this city on the Sabbath day, but hallow the Sabbath day, to do no work therein:

"Then shall there enter into the gates of this city kings and princes sitting upon the throne of David, riding in chariots and on horses, they, and their princes, the men of Judah, and the inhabitants of Jerusalem—and this city shall remain forever.

"And they shall come from the cities of Judah, and from the places about Jerusalem, and from the land of Benjamin, and from the plain, and from the mountains, and from the south . .

"But if ye will not hearken unto Me to hallow the Sabbath day, and not to bear a burden, even entering in at the gates of Jerusalem on the Sabbath day,—then I will kindle a fire in the gates thereof, and it shall devour the palaces of Jerusalem, and it shall not be quenched."—Jeremiah 17:19-27.

When Zedekiah, the last king of Judah, made a secret pact with Psamtik II, Pharaoh of Egypt, his doom was sealed. Learning of it, Nebuchadnezzar moved quickly. Devastating the land as he went, he arrived at the walls of Jerusalem in January of 588 B.C. The siege, beginning on the 15th of the month, continued for thirty months. The wall was broken through on July 19, 586 B.C. when the city was taken and looted.

And then a fire was set by the Babylonians in the gates that went like an inferno through the desolated metropolis— and utterly destroyed it.

That which God had predicted in 608 B.C. had finally taken place. When a people knowingly refuse to obey God, they are headed for trouble. Israel had refused to keep the Law of God and observe His holy Sabbath. And so the fire came and swept everything away.

"Now in the fifth month, in the tenth day of the month, which was the nineteenth year of Nebuchadrezzar king of Babylon, came Nebuzaradan, captain of the guard, which served the king of Babylon, into Jerusalem. And burned the house of the Lord, and the king's house; and all the houses of the great men, burned he with fire. And all the army of the Chaldeans, that were with the captain of the guard, brake

down all the walls of Jerusalem round about."—Jeremiah 52:
12-14.

The prophecy was given and the prophecy was fulfilled.
But the Bible tells us more:

"Zedekiah was one and twenty years old when he began
to reign, and reigned eleven years in Jerusalem. And he did
that which was evil in the sight of the Lord his God, and
humbled not himself before Jeremiah the prophet speaking
from the mouth of the Lord.

"And he also rebelled against king Nebuchadnezzar, who
had made him swear by God: but he stiffened his neck, and
hardened his heart from turning unto the Lord God of Israel.
Moreover all the chief of the priests, and the people, trans-
gressed very much after all the abominations of the heathen;
and polluted the house of the Lord which He had hallowed in
Jerusalem.

"And the Lord God of their fathers sent to them by His
messengers, rising up betimes, and sending; because he had
compassion on His people, and on His dwelling place.

"But they mocked the messengers of God, and de-
spised His words, and misused His prophets, until the wrath of
the Lord arose against His people, till there was no remedy.

"Therefore He brought upon them the king of the Chal-
dees, who slew their young men with the sword in the house
of their sanctuary, and had no compassion upon young man or
maiden, old man, or him that stooped for age: He gave them
all into his hand. And all the vessels of the house of God, great
and small, and the treasures of the house of the Lord, and the
treasures of the king, and of his princes; all these he brought to
Babylon.

"And they burned the house of God, and brake down
the wall of Jerusalem, and burnt all the palaces thereof with
fire, and destroyed all the goodly vessels thereof. And them
that had escaped from the sword carried he away to Babylon;
where they were servants to him and his sons until the reign of
the kingdom of Persia;

"To fulfill the word of the Lord by the mouth of Jeremiah, until the land had enjoyed her Sabbaths: for as long as
she lay desolate she kept Sabbath, to fulfill threescore and ten
years."—2 Chronicles 36:11-21.

For hundreds of years the people of God had refused
to keep His Sabbaths. Now the land was to lie desolate for
seventy years because of their refusal.

When God speaks, we can do no better thing than to

obey. God has given you and me—and everyone else in this world—the Seventh-day Sabbath as a day to come apart and rest and worship Him.

He gave us this holy day at the Creation of this world when He had finished making all things.

11

Birth Of A World

All around, for vast distances, can be seen island universes. 100 million of these galactic nebulae are within reach of our present telescope lenses. And each island universe contains perhaps 200 quadrillion immense suns—stars.

Circling each of these stars there are probably planets, and some of them will be inhabited. We know this, for Scripture tells us that God creates with a purpose: He creates that there might be inhabitants (Isaiah 45:18).

Countless millions of people love God and obey Him throughout the vast depths of space. Keep this thought in mind as you trace your path through this present life. If you love God and are trying to obey Him, you are on the side of the majority.

Scriptural records indicate that it was about 6,000 years ago, that a new world was created—ours.

The day came when the inhabitants of all those earths paused to watch God make an entire world and everything in it. And what they saw took place within a single week.

Here are the first words of holy Scripture:

"In the beginning God created the heavens and the earth. And the earth was without form, and void; and darkness was upon the face of the deep. And the Spirit of God moved upon the face of the waters.

"And God said, Let there be light: and there was light. And God saw the light, that it was good: and God divided the light from the darkness. And God called the light Day, and the darkness He called Night. And the evening and the morning were the first day."—Genesis 1:1-5.

And reading further, we find that on each successive day more things were made. We are told repeatedly that each day was composed of the night and the day portion, each was one twenty-four-hour day, as we would call it.

How did God make everything in one week? If you and I wanted to make something, we would form it out of something already in existence. But God made this world and everything in it—out of nothing! Scripture tells us that He simply spake it into existence.

"By the word of the Lord were the heavens made; and all the host of them by the breath of His mouth .. For He spake, and it was done; He commanded, and it stood fast."—Psalm 33:6-9.

God made this world for you and me. He made it to be inhabited.

"For thus saith the Lord that created the heavens; God Himself that formed the earth and made it; He hath established it, He created it not in vain, He formed it to be inhabited."—Isaiah 45:18.

God the Father made this world—and everything else—through God the Son:

"All things were made by Him; and without Him was not anything made that was made."—John 1:3. "For by Him [the Son] were all things created, that are in heaven, and that are in earth, visible and invisible .. all things were created by Him and for Him."—Colossians 1:16. "God .. hath .. spoken unto us by His Son, whom He hath appointed Heir of all things, by whom also He made the worlds."—Hebrews 1:1-2.

And God, who made all things by His word, sustains it by His word.

"Upholding all things by the word of His power."—Hebrews 1:3. "For in Him we live, and move, and have our being."—Acts 17:28.

Never forget that there is power in everything that God says. By the enabling grace of Christ,—listen to those words, think about those words, and obey those words—and you will inherit eternal life.

The Creation of this world reveals the massive immensity of God's power. It also reveals the fathomless depths of

His love.

"As the earth came forth from the hand of its Maker, it was exceedingly beautiful. Its surface was diversified with mountains, hills, and plains, interspersed with noble rivers and lovely lakes; but the hills and mountains were not abrupt and rugged, abounding in terrific steeps and frightful chasms, as they now do; the sharp, ragged edges of earth's rocky framework were buried beneath the fruitful soil, which everywhere produced a luxuriant growth of verdure. There were no loathsome swamps or barren deserts. Graceful shrubs and delicate flowers greeted the eye at every turn. The heights were crowned with trees more majestic than any that now exist. The air, untainted by foul miasma, was clear and healthful. The entire landscape outvied in beauty the decorated grounds of the proudest palace. The angelic host viewed the scene with delight, and rejoiced at the wonderful works of God."—*E. G. White, Patriarchs and Prophets, p. 44.*

God made this beautiful world in six literal days, and at its close gave mankind the Seventh-day Sabbath. Wisely, He knew that if we were to forget Him and His Creatorship, we would turn this world into a hell.

Why is it so important that we remember our Creator? —Because it is our Creator—alone—who is to be worshiped. Only the One who made us is our God; only He is to be bowed down before and given our heart's deepest devotion.

Never underestimate the Bible Sabbath. You need it and everyone else does also. A people that knowingly leaves the Sabbath will always leave the God of the Sabbath. All true worship of God is based on Sabbathkeeping.

On the Sixth Day of Creation Week, God made the land animals and man. Then, on the Seventh Day He rested. And that day He did something else: He blessed that last day in the weekly cycle and hallowed or dedicated it for mankind to sacredly observe thereafter.

"Thus the heavens and the earth were finished, and all the host of them. And on the Seventh day God ended His work which He had made; and He rested on the Seventh day from all His work which He had made.

"And God blessed the Seventh day, and sanctified it: because that in it He had rested from all His work which God created and made."—Genesis 2:1-3.

This is God's own day—the day of the Lord—the Lord's Day—given to mankind to worship Him upon.

We have just learned that Jesus Christ created all things (Col 1:16; Jn 1:3; Heb 1:1-3). He calls Himself the Lord of the Sabbath (Matt 12:8; Mk 2:28). It is His day: the Lord's Day. He calls it "My holy day" in Isaiah 58:13, and He not only wants us to keep it, but to restore it in the hearts and lives of those around us who may have forgotten it:

"And they that shall be of thee shall build the old waste places. Thou shalt raise up the foundations of many generations; and thou shalt be called, The repairer of the breach, The restorer of paths to dwell in.

"If thou turn away thy foot from the Sabbath, from doing thy pleasure on My holy day; and call the Sabbath a delight, the holy of the Lord, honourable; and shalt honour Him, not doing thine own ways, nor finding thine own pleasure, not speaking thine own words;

"Then shalt thou delight thyself in the Lord; and I will cause thee to ride upon the high places of the earth, and feed thee with the heritage of Jacob thy father; for the mouth of the Lord hath spoken it."—Isaiah 58:12-14.

Jesus made the Seventh-day Sabbath for man—all mankind—2000 years before the first Jew, Abraham, was born. Jesus is the Lord of the Sabbath, and if, as sincere followers of Christ, we would keep the Lord's Day, we must rest from our labors on the Seventh-day Sabbath and worship Him on that day.

"And He said unto Them, The Sabbath was made for man, not man for the Sabbath: Therefore the Son of man is Lord also of the Sabbath."—Mark 2:27.

2500 years after this world was created and the Bible Sabbath was first given to mankind—the Moral Law of God was written down for the first time.

Some people think that there was no moral code for people before it was written down on Mount Sinai. But this is not true. If there were no Ten Commandments before that time, then it would have been all right for Cain to kill Abel. But it is clear from Genesis 4 that it was not right for him to do this. Can you imagine a parent bringing a child into the world—and then raising him without teaching him any moral standards? It would not be a very good parent who would do such a thing. And our Father, the God of heaven, is a good parent. We can know that He immediately explained the principles of morality to Adam and Eve.

And then, 2500 years after giving them the Seventh-day Sabbath, He wrote it on the most enduring thing in the world —rock.

12

To Meet The King

It was about the year 1445 B.C. Dusty from traveling over the desert, the two men, who had only been in the country a day or two, entered the palace of the Pharaoh of all Egypt. Passing through a gateway which towered above their heads to a height of twenty-six feet, they approached the royal precinct and felt themselves dwarfed by its size—for it covered approximately thirteen acres of ground. The outer wall alone was twenty-one feet thick.

But no wave of welcome awaited them at the opening of the gates. The guards saw before them only two of the hated Hebrews. "Which slave labor gang did they run away from?" a guard may have remarked as they walked by.

It is a miracle that Moses and Aaron were permitted that day to pass from hall to hall and finally stand before the god-king of this ancient land.

And now they stood in the throne room itself. On either side were massive limestone columns that were elaborately carved, painted and gilded with figures of the Pharaoh standing before the other gods. Beyond them, on either side, the stuccoed walls and floors gleamed with brilliantly-painted scenes. Shafts of sunlight, streaming down from narrow clerestory windows higher up, lighted up the gold, glitter and brightly-painted figures.

Far away, down the length of the throne room could be seen the throne of the Pharaoh above a raised platform. The throne and everything nearby was made of solid gold. As the two men drew closer, they could see carefully-wrought figures on the side of the platform, showing enemies whom the Pharaoh had captured prior to enslaving or killing them.

Amid such majestic grandeur and surrounded by armed guards—and now with the eyes of Pharaoh upon them,—who could have found voice to speak at such a moment?

But Moses was made of sterner stuff. He came with a message from the God of Heaven. The time had come for the eighty-year old shepherd to deliver what would become a death warrant to thousands in Egypt.

Stepping up before the astonished ruler, Amenhoptep II, Moses demanded that he let the people of Israel go.

"Thus saith the Lord God of Israel: Let My people go." —Exodus 5:1.

The story that followed is a familiar one. Stubborn resistance to the will of God brought one plague after another, each more devastating than the one before it, until the land was finally desolated and the people of God departed from the country.

They had left to meet with the King.

Traveling swiftly over the shifting sands of the desert, that vast people, numbering nearly two million, knew that they were not out of danger yet. At any time Pharaoh and his well-trained and equipped army might pursue them to again take them into bondage.

High overhead, an immense cloud shaded them from the heat as they traveled. And it also guided them, for it stretched before them, they followed as it led, for so Moses had instructed them to do.

But now darkness was nearing as they hurriedly moved in a south-easterly direction—and the hearts of many sank: Before them was an impassable mountain on the south, and to the east lay the Red Sea: ocean water stretching for miles—and beyond it the distant shore of the Sinai Peninsula.

This was where the miraculous cloud had brought them.

What were they to do now? There was no way they could proceed further without heading toward Egypt.

And then screams were heard. "They are coming! They are coming!" Pharaoh and his entire army were rapidly approaching from the rear.

And now the cloud seemed to be leaving them also! Slowly it lifted majestically and moved to a point midway between the Israelites and the Egyptians. And as they gazed in astonishment, it drew to a stop—and turned into a boiling pillar of fire before their eyes!

Little realizing that the cloud had become a great wall of impenetrable darkness to the Egyptians, the Hebrews watched in amazement as Moses arose from prayer and walked calmly over to the bank of the sea—and raised his rod over the sea—and it split into two parts!

A powerful wind hurled water into two immense walls, and just as miraculously, immediately dried up the bed of the sea which only a moment before was many feet thick with mud.

Picture it for yourself! Two million men, women and children, with all their cattle and flocks—walking across the channel, now totally dry,—amid mountains of living, seething, foaming masses of water, held back moment-by-moment by a miracle of God!

People spoke in solemn tones as they made their way across, for they well knew that they had been saved from a fate worse than death—only because they were willing to trust God and obey His every command.

And so it will be today—if you and I will trust and obey Him also. The only reliable thing we have is the Word of God. That Bible in your home is the only imperishable thing there. For it contains principles that are eternal. And if those principles are in your heart and life, you will be safe in the care of the God of Moses.

The Creator of the universe was leading out a people to serve Him. They were to be His special people—called to learn His will and declare it to all nations on the face of the earth.

And so it was that He brought them to the valley of

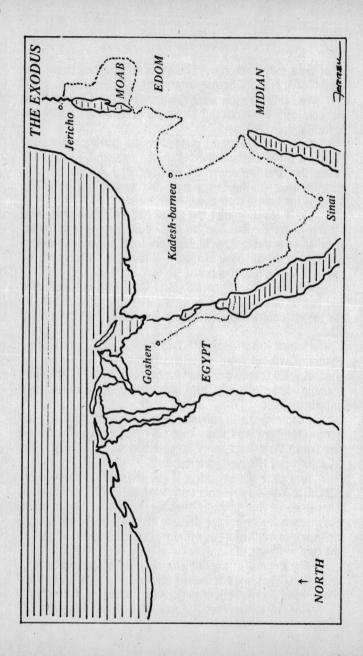

Jebel Musa—the Mountain of Moses—that they might learn the Divine Will and do it, and teach it to all about them in the years ahead—until the whole world could know the truth that amid all the false gods, there IS a True God. And that all the world might know that He has a Moral Law of Ten Commandments—and all men everywhere must, in His strength, obey that Law.

Arriving at the mountain (also called Mount Sinai or Horeb), they spread their tents in the valley beneath its massive granite walls, and quietly awaited the next revealing of the will of God for them.

They had come to meet with the King over all kings.

"On the morning of the third day [after arriving at the Mount], as the eyes of all the people were turned toward the mount, its summit was covered with a thick cloud, which grew more black and dense, sweeping downward until the entire mountain was wrapped in darkness and awful mystery. Then a sound as of a trumpet was heard, summoning the people to meet with God; and Moses led them forth to the base of the mountain.

"From the thick darkness flashed vivid lightnings, while peals of thunder echoed and re-echoed among the surrounding heights. 'And Mount Sinai was altogether on a smoke, because the Lord descended upon it in fire: and the smoke thereof ascended as the smoke of a furnace, and the whole mount quaked greatly.' 'The glory of the Lord was like devouring fire on the top of the mount' in the sight of the assembled multitude. And 'the voice of the trumpet sounded long, and waxed louder and louder' . . And now the thunders ceased; the trumpet was no longer heard; the earth was still. There was a period of solemn silence—and then the voice of God was heard.

"Speaking out of the thick darkness that enshrouded Him, as He stood upon the mount, surrounded by a retinue of angels, the Lord made known His Law."—*E.G. White, Patriarchs and Prophets, p. 304.*

On what other occasion, later in the Old Testament, did the God of heaven give such a massive display of power and glory to a group of people? He never did. On what occasion in the New Testament or afterward, down to our own time, has He done so? At no time.

And why did he do it then? —Because He wanted all

men everywhere to know—either in person or from reading the written record—that the Moral Law of the Ten Commandments should be one of the most important things in their lives. It should lie at the foundation of all their religion. It should guide and direct all their secular duties.

The twin truths that we can and must obey God—and that we can and must do it only through the grace of Jesus Christ—lies at the heart of all holy Scripture. "Trust and obey, for there's no other way, to be happy in Jesus, but to trust and obey" is the basis of Christian experience. And it is your passport to heaven. For God will take no one to heaven, who on earth was determined to live in sin and disobey His Law.

Here is the great Moral Code for mankind. Every part of it is perfect, for it was given to us by our Creator:

AND GOD SPAKE ALL THESE WORDS, SAYING:

"I am the Lord thy God, which have brought thee out of the land of Egypt, out of the house of bondage.

THE FIRST COMMANDMENT
"Thou shalt have no other gods before Me.

THE SECOND COMMANDMENT
"Thou shalt not make unto thee any graven image, or any likeness of any thing that is in heaven above, or that is in the earth beneath, or that is in the water under the earth.

"Thou shalt not bow down thyself to them, nor serve them: For I the Lord thy God am a jealous God, visiting the iniquity of the fathers upon the children unto the third and fourth generation of them that hate Me. And shewing mercy unto thousands of them that love Me, and keep My commandments.

THE THIRD COMMANDMENT
"Thou shalt not take the name of the Lord thy God in vain; for the Lord will not hold him guiltless that taketh His name in vain.

THE FOURTH COMMANDMENT
"Remember the Sabbath day, to keep it holy.

"Six days shalt thou labour, and do all thy work.

"But the Seventh day is the Sabbath of the Lord thy God: in it thou shalt not do any work, thou, nor thy son, nor thy daughter, thy manservant, nor thy maidservant, nor thy cattle, nor thy stranger that is within thy gates.

"For in six days the Lord made heaven and earth, the sea, and all that in them is, and rested the Seventh day: wherefore the Lord blessed the Sabbath day, and hallowed it.

THE FIFTH COMMANDMENT

"Honour thy father and thy mother: that thy days may be long upon the land which the Lord thy God giveth thee.

THE SIXTH COMMANDMENT

"Thou shalt not kill.

THE SEVENTH COMMANDMENT

"Thou shalt not commit adultery.

THE EIGHTH COMMANDMENT

"Thou shalt not steal.

THE NINTH COMMANDMENT

"Thou shalt not bear false witness.

THE TENTH COMMANDMENT

"Thou shalt not covet thy neighbour's house, thou shalt not covet thy neighbour's wife, nor his manservant, nor his maidservant, nor his ox, nor his ass, nor any thing that is thy neighbour's."—*Exodus 20:1-17.*

On Mount Sinai, the God of heaven spoke the Ten Commandments and then wrote them on rock, as His Moral Law for mankind. Rock is the most enduring thing in the world. And God's Law, written on rock, will endure as long as the boulders of the mighty mountains around us. "His commandments . . stand fast forever."—Psalm 111:7-8.

But His Law is not only to be placed on rock. It is also to be written in our hearts.

"I will put My Spirit within you, and cause you to walk in My statutes, and ye shall keep My judgments, and do them."—Ezekiel 36:27. "I will put My law in their inward parts, and write it in their hearts."—Jeremiah 31:33. "For this is the covenant that I will make with the house of Israel after those days, saith the Lord; I will put My laws into their mind, and write them in their hearts: and I will be to them a God, and they shall be to Me a people."—Hebrews 8:10.

The Seventh-day Sabbath is the sign that He is our

Creator and Redeemer:

"Keep the Sabbath, to observe the Sabbath forever . . for a perpetual covenant. It is a sign between Me and the children of Israel for ever: for in six days the Lord made heaven and earth, and on the Seventh day He rested, and was refreshed."—Exodus 31:16-17.

"Verily My Sabbaths ye shall keep: for it is a sign between Me and you throughout your generations; that ye may know that I am the Lord that doth sanctify you."—Exodus 31:13.

"Morever also I gave them My Sabbaths, to be a sign between Me and them, that they might know that I am the Lord that sanctify them."—Ezekiel 20:12.

"And hallow My Sabbaths; and they shall be a sign between Me and you, that ye may know that I am the Lord your God."—Ezekiel 20:20.

Thus we see that the keeping of the Seventh-day Sabbath is a sign that He is our Creator (Ex 31:17), our Redeemer (Ezek 20:12), that we belong to Him (Ezek 20:20), and that He is sanctifying us (Ex 31:13).

We cannot know our duty toward our God unless we find it in the Bible. It is not a matter of what others around us do. It is a matter of what is written in the archives.

The story of the rosebush will help you understand this.

13

Opening The Archives

One of the czars of Russia, while walking in his park, came across a sentry standing guard over a little patch of weeds.

"What are you doing here?" he asked.

The sentry replied, "I don't know. All I know is that the captain of the guard ordered me to stand over this spot."

The czar sent for the captain.

"Captain,—what is this man guarding?"

The captain answered, "All I know is that the regulations call for a sentry to be posted here."

Then the ruler ordered a major investigation, but no one in the government of Russia could discover why that spot needed guarding.

Then they opened the royal archives—containing accurate records of the past—and the mystery was solved.

The chronicles showed that a hundred years before, in the late Eighteenth Century, Catherine the Great, queen of the Russians, had planted a rosebush on that plot of ground. So satisfied was the watching queen when the gardeners had completed their work, that she ordered a sentry to be posted there to keep people from trampling on it.

Eventually the rosebush died, but nobody thought to cancel the order, especially since it had been issued by such an important person.

And for a hundred years men stood guard over a spot where a rosebush once had grown—and didn't know what they were guarding.

Year after year. At first, no one knew how long. Guarding something that wasn't there.

Men today are carefully guarding Sunday. They rest on that day; they attend weekly church services on that day. Many do it because they think that God commanded it.

But it is not until we open the archives of God's Word that we can see the truth of the matter. There is no Sunday sacredness in the Bible. There is no command there to keep it holy. There was no changing of Sabbath to Sunday by Heaven in those hallowed pages.

Then we open the archives of history, and we learn that Sundaykeeping, like a little rosebush, was indeed planted in the Christian Church. But it happened after the Bible was finished and the Bible writers were all dead.

God has a beautiful plan for your life. He is part of that plan, and you are in it too. He asks us to come apart and rest with Him on His holy day, that we may deepen our hold on Him. "Abide in Me, and I in you," He tells us (John 15:4). Our greatest need is to be linked with Christ. And it is the Sabbath rest that can give us the blessings we crave. "He that abideth in Me, and I in him, the same bringeth forth much fruit: for without Me ye can do nothing." (John 15:5).

That first Sabbath must have been a sweet experience. All the earth was brand new, and the first sunset that Adam saw—began a Sabbath. On this first Seventh day the Creator rested, and Adam rested with Him.

The Sabbath is something special that has come down to us—all the way from Paradise. It is worth finding. It is worth keeping . . for the remainder of our lives.

And ever since Eden, God has planned for the Seventh-day Sabbath to be a holy meeting-time between Himself and His people. You see, the Sabbath is a cord of love that binds the created to his Creator by providing a closer fellowship than could be obtained on the six working days.

God intended that the Sabbath would be something that He and His earthly children would keep together through all time to come. And so the Lord declared the Sabbath to be a "perpetual covenant." (Exodus 31:16-17) How thankful we can be for this, for because of God's everlasting purpose, His faithful ones will honor the Sabbath for eternity in the new earth:

"For as the new heavens and the new earth, which I will make, shall remain before Me, saith the Lord, so shall your seed and your name remain. And it shall come to pass, that from one new moon to another, and from one Sabbath to another, shall all flesh come to worship before Me, saith the Lord."—Isaiah 66:22-23.

How long is eternity? It will have to be experienced to be realized. And the Sabbath will be part of that experience. As one begins to see the Sabbath as a token of God's love— both in creation and redemption—that day becomes very precious. Again, let me say it: In a very special sense, the Bible Sabbath is an important link, uniting you with God. Don't run from this beautiful truth, but accept it. For it will draw you nearer to your Creator. The more we pattern our lives after Scripture, the happier we shall become.

We have already seen that God calls the Sabbath a "sign" by which to recognize our connection with Him (Exodus 31: 13,17; Ezekiel 20:12,20). True Sabbathkeeping is a link that will hold men true to their God—if, by faith in Christ, they will always sincerely keep it. Worshiping God on His holy day will draw us nearer to Him all through the week.

Jesus Christ was born into this world just before the beginning of the Christian Era. He grew up and was baptized in A.D. 27, and then began His three-and-a-half year ministry. There had been no prophets or Bible writers for four centuries. Then John the Baptist was sent as a forerunner, to proclaim that the time had come for the Messiah to appear.

While here on earth, Jesus gave us a careful example of obedience to the Sabbath day He had earlier given to mankind.

"And He came to Nazareth, where He had been brought up: and, as His custom was, He went into the synagogue on the Sabbath day, and stood up for to read."—Luke 4:16.

His custom should be ours, for He is our Example. He gave us an example of obedience that we should follow.

"He that saith he abideth in Him ought himself also so to walk, even as He walked."—1 John 2:6. "Leaving us an example, that ye should follow His steps."—1 Peter 2:21. "I have

kept My Father's commandments, and abide in His love."—
John 15:10. "For this is the love of God: that we keep His
commandments."—1 John 5:3.

During His earthly life, Jesus had continually given an
example of obedience to the Moral Law of Ten Commandments. And He told His disciples to obey it also.

"Think not that I am come to destroy the law, or the
prophets: I am not come to destroy but to fulfill. For verily I
say unto you, Till heaven and earth pass, one jot or one tittle
shall in no wise pass from the law, till all be fulfilled. Whosoever therefore shall break one of these least commandments,
and shall teach men so, he shall be called the least in the
kingdom of heaven: but whosoever shall do and teach them,
the same shall be called great in the kingdom of heaven."—
Matthew 5:17-19.

Just as Jesus has not changed, neither has His law
changed. There has been no restructuring by our heavenly
Father of the moral principles that govern mankind since the
Creation of this world. Morality has not changed, as far as God
is concerned, even though some would wish that it had.

Not only did Christ give us a careful example of obedience while here on earth, —but He also rebuked man-made
attempts to change His laws.

"But in vain they do worship Me, teaching for doctrines
the commandments of men."—Matthew 15:9. "Thus have ye
made the commandments of God of none effect by your
tradition."—Matthew 15:6. "Why do ye also transgress the
commandment of God by your tradition?"—Matthew 15:3.

Throughout His life, He did as Scripture predicted He
would do: He magnified the Law and made it honorable.

"The Lord is well pleased for His righteousness' sake; He
will magnify the Law, and make it honourable."—Isaiah 42:21.
"Then said I, Lo, I come: in the volume of the book it is
written of Me: I delight to do Thy will, O My God; yea, Thy
law is within My heart."—Psalm 40:7-8 (compare Hebrews 10:
5,7).

And He did this in the sight of a generation like all the
others in history—crooked and perverse and stubbornly rebellious at the thought of obeying God.

He also taught that others should obey the Law of God,
as He was doing:

"Not every one that saith unto Me, Lord, Lord, shall enter into the kingdom of heaven; but he that doeth the will of My Father which is in heaven."—Matthew 7:21.

"Whosoever therefore shall break one of these least commandments, and shall teach men so, he shall be called the least in the kingdom of heaven: but whosoever shall do and teach them, the same shalll be called great in the kingdom of heaven."—Matthew 5:19.

"Good Master, what good thing shall I do, that I may have eternal life? And He said unto him . . If thou wilt enter into life, keep the commandments."—Matthew 19:16-17.

And yet we fully realize that we are incapable of rendering this obedience to God apart from the enabling grace of Christ.

"I am the vine, ye are the branches: He that abideth in Me, and I in him, the same bringeth forth much fruit: for without Me ye can do nothing."—John 15:5.

In an earlier chapter ("The Forgotten Prayer") we have seen how concerned Jesus was that His followers continue to observe the only Bible Sabbath to be found anywhere in holy Scripture,—and to cling to it decades and centuries after His crucifixion. (Matthew 24:20) And this is very significant. There are so many people today who will tell you solemnly that the Sabbath ended at Calvary, and God did not want anyone to keep it afterward. If you then mention that the Sabbath is the Fourth of the Ten Commandments, they will reply that that is all well—for God got rid of all ten of the commandments at the cross!

Astounded, you then inquire, "Is there then no moral standard to govern the conduct of a Christian today?" And yet some reply: "No moral standard whatever. Jesus fulfilled the law and we no longer need obey it. Love has taken the place of obedience to the Moral Law."

One wonders how such a view can be called "Christian"! According to this theory, people before the crucifixion had to obey the Ten Commandments and not live in sin; but God sent His Son to earth so that men could henceforth live in sin and be saved in sin. Such an error is not to be found in Scripture.

"And she shall bring forth a son, and thou shalt call His

name Jesus: for He shall save His people FROM their sins."—
Matthew 1:21.

Here are some of the things that God said about His
Moral Law and the importance of our obeying it:

"Let us hear the conclusion of the whole matter: Fear
God, and keep His commandments, for this is the whole duty
of man. For God shall bring every work into judgment, with
every secret thing, whether it be good, or whether it be evil."
—Ecclesiastes 12:13-14.

"Whosoever committeth sin transgresseth also the law,
for sin is the transgression of the law."—1 John 3:4.

"For by the law is the knowledge of sin."—Romans
3:20. "For the wages of sin is death."—Romans 6:23. "What
shall we say then? Is the law sin? God forbid. Nay, I had not
known sin, but by the law: for I had not known lust, except
the law had said, Thou shalt not covet."—Romans 7:7. "Do
we then make void the law through faith? God forbid: yea,
we establish the law."—Romans 3:31.

"For whosoever shall keep the whole law, and yet
offend in one point, he is guilty of all. For He that said, Do
not commit adultery, said also, Do not kill. Now if thou commit no adultery, yet if thou kill, thou art become a transgressor of the law."—James 2:10-11.

"For this is the love of God, that we keep His commandments: and His commandments are not grievous."—1 John
5:3.

"The fear of the Lord is the beginning of wisdom: a
good understanding have all they that do His commandments."—Psalm 111:10.

"If ye be willing and obedient, ye shall eat the good of
the land."—Isaiah 1:19.

"Great peace have they which love Thy law: and nothing
shall offend them."—Psalm 119:165. "O that thou hadst
hearkened to My commandments! then had thy peace been as
a river, and thy righteousness as the waves of the sea."—Isaiah
48:18.

"For not the hearers of the law are just before God, but
the doers of the law shall be justified."—Romans 2:13. "But
he that looketh into the perfect law, the law of liberty, and so
continueth, being not a hearer that forgetteth, but a doer that
worketh, this man shall be blessed in his doing."—James 1:25
R.V.

"By this we know that we love the children of God,
when we love God, and keep His commandments."—1 John

5:2.

"Here is the patience of the saints: here are they that keep the commandments of God, and the faith of Jesus."—Revelation 14:12.

It is the Ten Commandment law of God that the saints will keep. When asked "which law?" Jesus replied by naming several of the Ten Commandments (Matthew 19:17-19). And the Apostle James did likewise (James 2:10-12).

Men today claim that there is no law since the death of Christ. But the Bible teaches that where there is no law, there is no sin! Indeed, without the law to identify sin, we cannot know what sin is. Apart from the presence of the law, sin does not exist.

"Where no law is, there is no transgression."—Romans 4:15. "Sin is not imputed when there is no law."—Romans 5:13. "For by the law is the knowledge of sin."—Romans 3:30. "I had not known sin, but by the law."—Romans 7:7.

"Whosoever committeth sin transgresseth also the law: for sin IS the transgression of the law."—1 John 3:4.

The only thing abolished at the cross was the ceremonial law, contained in ordinances. These were the sacrificial laws. After Christ's death, it was no longer necessary to sacrifice lambs at the temple, for Christ our Lamb had died. But after the death of Christ we were still obligated to keep the Moral Law.

Daniel 9:26-27 predicted that at His death, Christ would "cause the sacrifice and the oblation to cease." And the Apostle Paul tells us that this is exactly what happened. When Christ died, the ceremonial ordinances were blotted out. The sacrificial services in the Temple no longer had meaning in the eyes of God.

"Blotting out the handwriting of ordinances that was against us, which was contrary to us, and took it out of the way, nailing it to His cross."—Colossians 2:14. "Having abolished in His flesh the enmity, even the law of commandments contained in ordinances; for to make in Himself of twain one new man, so making peace; and that He might reconcile both unto God in one body by the cross, having slain the enmity thereby."—Ephesians 2:15-16.

A leading Protestant writer, Dr. Albert Barnes, in commenting on Colossians 2:16, said this:

"But the use of the term ["sabbaths"] in the plural number, and the connection, show that he [Paul] had his eye on a great number of days which were observed by the Hebrews as festivals, as a part of their ceremonial and typical law, —and not on the Moral law, or the Ten Commandments. No part of the moral law—no one of the Ten Commandments—could be spoken of as 'a shadow of things to come.' "—*Dr. Albert Barnes, Commentary, on Colossians 2:16.*

The "shadow laws" were the ones that foreshadowed the coming of Christ: the slaying of lambs and goats, the keeping of the yearly Passover, etc. All these ceremonial laws were taken away by the death of Christ.

"For the [sacrificial] law, having a shadow of good things to come, and not the very image of the things, can never with those sacrifices which they offered year by year continually make the comers thereunto perfect. For then would they not have ceased to be offered? . . But in those sacrifices there is a remembrance again made of sins every year. For it is not possible that the blood of bulls and of goats should take away sins."—Hebrews 10:1-4.

And these sacrificial laws included yearly holy days, or yearly "sabbaths." The weekly Sabbath was given to mankind at the foundation of the world and is Fourth of the Ten Commandments. But the yearly sabbaths were gatherings for special sacrificial services, and foreshadowed the death of Christ. At these services there were special "meat offerings" and "drink offerings." A list of these yearly sabbaths will be found in Leviticus 23:4-44. The weekly Seventh-day Sabbath is called "the sabbath" in the Bible, but the yearly sabbaths are easily identified: When mentioned together, an "s" is added: they were the "sabbaths" or "sabbath days." All these yearly gatherings were also abolished at the cross. Paul calls them (and their meat and drink offerings) a "shadow."

"Let no man therefore judge you in meat, or in drink, or in respect of an holyday, or of the new moon, or of the sabbath days; which are a shadow of things to come; but the body is of Christ."—Colossians 2:16-17. "For the law having a shadow of good things to come, and not the very image of the things, can never with those sacrifices which they offered year by year continually make the comers thereunto perfect."

—Hebrews 10:1.

This is because the meaning of the Temple services ended when Christ died. At that moment a hand reached from heaven and tore the veil of the temple in two, thus desecrating it and destroying its significance:

"Jesus, when He had cried again with a loud voice, yielded up the ghost [died]. And, behold, the veil of the temple was rent in twain from the top to the bottom."—Matthew 27:50-51.

"Then said I [Christ], Lo, I come (in the volume of the book it is written of Me,) to do Thy will, O God .. [and] said, Sacrifice and offering and burnt offerings and offering for sin Thou wouldest not, neither hadst pleasure therein: which are offered by the law; then said He, Lo, I come to do Thy will, O God. He taketh away the first, that He may establish the second."—Hebrews 10:7-9.

The first—the shadow laws and ceremonies—were taken away by the death of Christ, that He might solidly establish by His death the principle that man must obey God—and through the merits of Christ can be empowered to do it!

As we come to Jesus just now and accept His life and death for us, we can receive "the righteousness which is of God" (Philippians 3:9), for we are beholding "the Lamb of God, which taketh away the sin of the world." John 1:29. If we will cling to Him, He will enable us to stop sinning and live clean, godly lives. He will take away our sins.

We come to Him in repentance for our sinful past, and we are "justified freely by His grace through the redemption that is in Christ Jesus". (Romans 3:24) And then we are to begin a walk with Christ and a life in Christ. We choose Him in place of our former sinful ways.

"What shall we say then? Shall we continue in sin, that grace may abound? God forbid. How shall we, that are dead to sin, live any longer therein?"—Romans 6:1-2.

"If ye keep My commandments, ye shall abide in My love," Jesus tells us (John 15:10).

The case is clear. We are opening the archives of Scripture and the archives of history—and both reveal the truth about the Bible Sabbath and Sunday.

The Seventh-day Sabbath is the only weekly holy day that the God of heaven ever gave to mankind. And Sunday is not that day.

Here are the facts about the first day of the week—facts from the Bible:

14

It Never Was

Your birthday is the anniversary of when you came into the world. It commemorates the event. That is what your birthday is.

The Bible Sabbath is the birthday of the world. By an express act of God (written down in Genesis 2:1-3), the Seventh day was declared by our Creator to be the weekly anniversary of the creation of this planet, several thousand years ago.

Can a person change his birthday from the day of the year on which he was born to another day? "Impossible," you say. And you would be right.

Suppose he was born on August 7. He might tell people that he was born on August 1, but that would not change his birthday. It would still be August 7.

Well, then,—how could he change his birthday? Even if the federal government enacted a law that his birthday was now August 1, and that he had been born on August 1,—it would not change his real birthday. It would continue to be the 7th of August. He might convince everyone in the world that it was August 1, but this would not alter his actual birthday. August 1 would, in very real fact, remain a fiction—a fake birthday.

In the same manner, the Seventh-day Sabbath—the birthday of our world—cannot be changed to any other day of the week. Christ never changes, and He is the One who created this world out of nothing in the first place.

The Seventh-day Sabbath proves that the Creator is the only personage in all the universe whom we are to worship. The Sabbath is the mark of His creative power and authority.

The Seventh-day Sabbath, given by God to commemorate the Creation of this world, could not be changed—except by going back and changing Creation! The Creation Week, recorded in Genesis 1, would have to be redone. God would have to blot out this world and all its inhabitants and start all over again. Once our world has been created, men may try to deny those facts but they cannot change them: The earth and all in it was created in six days, and then God rested the Seventh and hallowed and sanctified it.

But perhaps you are still wondering: Is there no way to change the Sabbath to another day? Is not the authority of Constantine and the pope sufficient to do it? Is not the fact that Sundaykeeping has been customary for over fifteen hundred years all that is needed? What about the overwhelming number of people who today keep it holy? Isn't that sufficient to authorize the change?

Quite obviously, the answer is no.

And for a very simple reason:

The Bible Sabbath is not just some silly little regulation that mortal man can change whenever he wishes to. It is the great Signpost pointing all mankind to the worship of the only true God—the Creator God. Creation Week would have to be redone in order to change the Sabbath. Here are statements by two prominent Protestants who recognized this fact:

"The reason for which the [Sabbath] command was originally given,—namely, as a memorial of God's having rested from the Creation of the world,—cannot be transferred from the seventh day to the first; nor can any new motive be substituted in its place, whether the resurrection of our Lord or any other,—without the sanction of a divine command [in Scripture] . .

"For if we under the gospel are to regulate the time of our public worship by the prescriptions of the Decalogue,—it will be far safer to observe the seventh day, according to the express commandment of God, than on the authority of mere human conjecture to adopt the first [day of the week]."—*John Milton, A Posthumous Treatise on the Christian Doctrine, Book 2, chap. 7 [John Milton (1608-1674) was the most famous poet of English literature, and the author of "Paradise Lost"].*

"If it [the Ten Commandments] yet exists, let us observe it . . And if it does not exist, let us abandon a mock observance of another day for it. 'But,' say some, 'it was changed from the seventh to the first day.' Where? when? and by whom?—No, it never was changed, nor could be, unless creation was to be gone through again. For the reason assigned [in Genesis 2:1-3] must be changed before the observance or respect to the reason, can be changed.

"It is all old wives' fables to talk of the change of the sabbath from the seventh to the first day. If it be changed, it was that august personage changed it who changes times and laws [Dan 7:25] ex officio.—I think his name is 'Doctor Antichrist.' "—*Alexander Campbell, "The Christian Baptist," February 2, 1824, vol 1, no. 7 [Campbell (1788-1866) was an Irish Protestant who founded in America the denomination known as the Disciples of Christ.]*

People can talk all they want about honoring Christ's resurrection by going to church that morning and then taking the rest of the day off as a holiday. But by working on the Seventh day—the day before Sunday,—they have broken the Fourth Commandment. It is as simple as that. Will we obey God's words, or will we follow our own opinions? We now know that people today keep Sunday only because Christian apostates at Alexandria and Rome wanted the favor of the Sun-worshipers more than the favor of God.

Here then is the question: Are we told anywhere in the New Testament that we should keep Sunday holy? Is there even one text in all of Scripture that officially changes God's holy Sabbath from the Seventh day to the first day?

There is not one text—not one—anywhere in the Bible that commands us to do such a thing.

Sunday is never called sacred or holy anywhere in the Bible. It is never called the Sabbath or the Lord's Day. Sunday is only mentioned eight times in the entire Bible. The first time is Genesis 1:5, where the first day of Creation Week is spoken of. No Sunday sacredness here. It is just one of the six working days of Creation Week.

The next five times refer to Jesus' appearances on Sunday to His disciples after His rest in the tomb on the Bible Sabbath (Matt 28:1; Mk 16:1-2, 9; Lk 24:1; Jn 20:1, 19). Jesus went and found His disciples and told them the good news that He was alive. But there is nothing here about Sunday holiness.

Here are the eight texts in the New Testament that mention the first day of the week:

Matthew 28:1 is the first first-day text in the New Testament: Here we see that the Sabbath ends before the first day of the week begins—and that is all that this passage tells us. Matthew wrote his record several years after the resurrection of Christ.

Mark 16:1-2 is the second first-day text, and Mark 16:9 is the third: We here learn that the Sabbath was past before the first day began. They are two different days. The Seventh-day Sabbath is holy, the other is but one of the six working days. Years after the resurrection, Mark knew of no first-day sacredness.

Luke 24:1 is the fourth one: Nothing new here. Luke does point out in the two preceding verses (Luke 23:55-56) that some of Jesus' most faithful followers "rested on the Sabbath day according to the commandment" (the Fourth Commandment of Exodus 20:8-11). In all His years of instruction, Jesus had said nothing about Sundaykeeping—or we would see His followers faithfully observing it. But this is not to be found, for Sunday-sacredness is foreign to Scripture.

John 20:1 is the fifth first-day text in the New Testament: Again the same simple record of the early morning experience, and nothing more.

John 20:19 is the sixth one: As with the others, John's record gives no account that Jesus ever mentioned the first day of the week. What John does say is that the disciples were gathered together "for fear of the Jews." He specifically points out that this was not a worship gathering. They were simply in hiding, fearful that they too would soon be killed as Jesus was. Some have suggested that the disciples were celebrating Christ's resurrection. This is incorrect, for they did not yet believe Jesus had risen. They were frightened men with a dead Saviour, for all they knew. Twice, Mark shows that by that time they still could not or would not believe it (Mark 16:11

and 16:12-13). Later Christ appeared to them (Luke 24:33-37) but had a difficult time convincing them that it was He.

Acts 20:7-8 is the seventh text: After having spent seven days at Troas, Paul and his missionary company held a farewell gathering with them that night, which lasted till midnight. The first day of the week (Bible time) begins Saturday evening at sunset, and ends Sunday evening at sunset. Inasmuch as this meeting in Acts 20:7-11 was held on the first day of the week and at night, it must therefore have been held on what we today would call "Saturday night." For the first day of the week, according to the Bible, had already begun at sunset on Saturday evening. Had it been held on what we call "Sunday night," the meeting would have been held on the second day of the week.

"It was the evening which succeeded the Jewish Sabbath. On the Sunday morning the vessel was about to sail."—*Conybeare and Howson, Life and Epistles of the Apostle Paul, Vol. 2, p. 206. [This is the most authoritative and complete book on the life of the Apostle Paul.]*

"The Jews reckoned the day from evening to morning, and on that principle the evening of the first day of the week would be our Saturday evening. If Luke reckoned so here, as many commentators suppose, the apostle then waited for the expiration of the Jewish Sabbath, and held his last religious service with the brethren at Troas . . on Saturday evening, and consequently resumed his journey on Sunday morning."—*Dr. Horatio B. Hackett, Commentary on Acts, pp. 221-222. [Dr. Hackett was Professor of New Testament Greek in Rochester Theological Seminary.]*

After the Saturday night meeting at Troas (Acts 20:7-11), Paul's company immediately set to work. They set sail that night. Paul preferred to go alone part of the way, so the next morning, Sunday morning, he walked nineteen miles across a point of land to Assos, where his friends took him on board ship (Acts 20:11-14).

If Sunday was Paul's holy day, why then did he stay with the brethren at Troas seven days, and then leave them on Sunday morning in order to walk eighteen-and-a-half miles that day. The Bible says, "for so had he appointed" to do. That was planning quite a bit of work for Sunday.

They had spent seven days at Troas, and then on Saturday night (after the Sabbath was past) they had a farewell gathering with the believers, "ready to depart on the morrow." What does it mean "to break bread"? This is the common Bible expression for partaking of food. The disciples broke bread daily from house to house (Acts 2:46), and they "did eat their meat with gladness" (2:46). It should here be mentioned that even if they had held an actual communion service that night, this would in no way make it a holy day. The Lord's Supper may be celebrated on any day. (1 Cor 11:26) The Lord's Supper commemorates Christ's death, not His resurrection. "Ye do shew the Lord's death till He come." verse 26.

The book of Acts is as silent on first-day sanctity as are Matthew, Mark, Luke and John.

1 Corinthians 16:1-2 is the eighth and last text: It is the final mention of the first day of the week in the New Testament, and the only mention in Paul's writings. Although Paul wrote many, many letters, this is the only mention of the first day of the week.

Paul wanted the folk to save aside money for the poor folk in Jerusalem. He was an evangelist who didn't like to make calls for money in Sabbath services. "That there be no gatherings when I come," is what he said. He evidently observed that if people did not lay aside at home systematically, on a basis of weekly income,—there would have to be a gathering when he came—not only a gathering of money, but gatherings of people, also.

"Let every one of you lay by him in store." This plan had no connection with a weekly collection at a church service. It was to be laid aside at home. This text also teaches us to total up our money and work up our budgets on the first day of each week, since there is not time in the Friday afternoon (sixth day) preparation to carefully give attention to this, before the Sabbath begins at sunset. Bookkeeping and the keeping of accounts is not to be done on the Sabbath.

So there we have it: eight texts where Sunday is mentioned in the New Testament—and no indication of a new holy day, much less a direct command by the God of heaven to observe it in place of the Seventh-day Sabbath.

Thank God every day of your life for the Bible! It is your pathway to Christ and to eternal life. Never leave the pathway for that which relatives or learned men may tell you. If their ideas do not agree with the Word of God, you had better stay with the plain words of Scripture.

But, interestingly enough, there are some who will tell you that no command to keep Sunday is needed—for Revelation 1:10 proves that we should now keep the first day instead of the Seventh day.

"I was in the Spirit on the Lord's day, and heard behind me a great voice, as of a trumpet."—Revelation 1:10.

But there is no mention of Sunday in this verse, nor in the verses around it.

We can only understand one scriptural passage by comparing it with other scriptural passages. This is the proper way to study the Bible.

John lived with Jesus throughout His earthly ministry, and he well knew the day of the Lord. For three years they had kept it each week, for Jesus habitually kept the Bible Sabbath. "And as His custom was, He went into the synagogue on the Sabbath day, and stood up for to read."—Luke 4:16.

Later, John tells of an experience he had "on the Lord's day" (Revelation 1:10). This beloved disciple had personally heard Jesus publically declare that He was "Lord even of the Sabbath day" (Matthew 12:8; Mark 2:28). And John well knew that God, in the Old Testament, repeatedly said that the Seventh day was the Sabbath of the Lord. With such a background of information as this—it is inconceivable that this loyal disciple should regard another day as the day of His Lord and Master—when no other day was ever commanded in Scripture!

The only day mentioned in the Bible as being the Lord's day is the Seventh day of the week—the Bible Sabbath. The expression found in Isaiah 58:13 is a good example of this: "If thou turn away thy foot from the Sabbath, from doing thy pleasure on MY HOLY DAY . . " God is here describing the

Sabbath.

So then, what day is the "Lord's day" of the Bible? The Bible clearly tells us the day—and it is only one day of the seven. The Bible tells us that the Seventh day is the day of the Lord:

1—The Bible Sabbath is the day unto the Lord (Exodus 16:23, 25; 31:15; 35:2).

2—The Bible Sabbath is the day of the Lord (Exodus 20:10; Leviticus 23:3; Deuteronomy 5:4).

3—The Bible Sabbath is His own day; He calls it "My holy day" (Isaiah 58:13).

4—The Bible Sabbath is the day that Jesus called Himself the Lord of (Matthew 12:8; Mark 2:28).

So it is easy to understand why John would speak of it as "the Lord's day" in Revelation 1:10. He surely was not referring to Tuesday or Monday, Thursday or Sunday! For these days had no holiness in the weekly cycle, and none of them were ever spoken of by Jesus or His Father as being a new day for worship.

Yes, John knew what day was the Lord's Day. It is the Seventh-day Sabbath: This is the day that is the Memorial Day of the Creator (Genesis 2:1-3; Exodus 31:17). This is the Memorial Day of the Redeemer (Ezekiel 20:12, 20).

This is the Lord's Day—God's own day; a day He wants to share with you.

To love God and obey Him by the grace of Christ—is the most important thing in the world. And it is obvious that Satan seeks in every way to break up this relationship of man with his God. There are many evidences that we live down at the end of time. But a very significant one is the fact that most of the religious leaders today teach that it is not necessary to obey the Ten Commandments.

A great falling away from loyalty to God and His Commandments has taken place during the past ages.

And God predicted that it would happen.

15

Fulfilling Prophecy

It was the year 553 B.C., and a prophet of God lay down to sleep. Daniel had been an elder statesman of the empire of Babylon for 51 years.

That night as he rested on his couch God gave him in vision a view of future events.

Powerful winds were blowing from every point of the compass, and tore the sea into froth as they strove together. From where he stood near the shore, it seemed that, with wind upon wind hurling upon it, the very waves of the sea were fighting among themselves.

And then, from amid the terrific strife,—four terrible animals arose out of the sea, one after another, and made their way up onto the shore.

As the vision continued, God told Daniel that these beasts would be four successive world empires that would arise.

"In the first year of Belshazzar king of Babylon Daniel had a dream and visions of his head upon his bed: then he wrote the dream, and told the sum of the matters.

"Daniel spake and said, I saw in my vision by night, and, behold, the four winds of the heaven strove upon the great sea. And four great beasts came up from the sea, diverse one from another."—Daniel 7:1-3.

After a description of each of these ferocious beasts, God explains the dream to Daniel.

But first, let us explain a little of the background of this. Earlier in the Book of Daniel, in the second chapter, we are told of a sweeping prophecy that extends from Daniel's time down to the Second Advent of Christ. Under the symbol of a great metal image (Dan 2:31-35), we are shown nation after nation that would arise. Beginning with Babylon as the head of gold, the ruling empire in the time of Daniel (Dan 2: 38), we are carried on down through the centuries that followed and shown the major empires that would later arise (Medo-Persia, Grecia, Rome, and its ten divisions—Dan 2:39-43). In the time of the feet and toes—our time—Christ will return to this earth and take His faithful ones to heaven (Dan 2:44-45).

But then, about 50 years later, Daniel was given a prophetic vision that closely paralleled that of Daniel 2, while adding more information to it.

Now, instead of parts of a metal image, the symbol is large beasts (Dan 7:2-3). Under the figure of four fierce animals, we are again shown Babylon, Medo-Persia, Grecia, and Rome (Dan 7:4-7).

But the fourth beast, and the "little horn" which grew out of it, especially caught Daniel's attention. There seemed to be something terrible about that little horn power. And we therefore find that most of this chapter is concerned with this little horn.

"I considered the horns, and, behold, there came up among them another little horn, before whom there were three of the first horns plucked up by the roots: and, behold, in this horn were eyes like the eyes of man, and a mouth speaking great things . .

"Then I would know the truth of the fourth beast, which was diverse from all the others, exceeding dreadful, whose teeth were of iron, and his nails of brass; which devoured, brake in pieces, and stamped the residue with his feet; And of the ten horns that were in his head, and of the other which came up, and before whom three fell; even of that horn that had eyes, and a mouth that spake very great things, whose look was more stout than his fellows."—Daniel 7:8, 19-20.

There was a very important reason why Daniel was so concerned about this little horn power which was to arise in the territory of the fourth beast: Daniel was shown that this terrible organization would seek to destroy the people of God and change God's laws.

"I beheld, and the same little horn made war with the saints, and prevailed against them; until the Ancient of days came, and judgment was given to the saints of the most High; and the time came that the saints possessed the kingdom.

"Thus he said, The fourth beast shall be the fourth kingdom upon earth, which shall be diverse from all kingdoms, and shall devour the whole earth, and shall tread it down, and break it in pieces.

"And the ten horns out of this kingdom are ten kings that shall arise: and another shall rise after them; and he shall be diverse from the first, and he shall subdue three kings."—Daniel 7:21-24.

And then Daniel was told the three evil things that this little horn religio-political power would do, and the length of time it would have dominion to do this:

"And he shall speak great words against the most High, and shall wear out the saints of the most High, and think to change times and laws. And they shall be given into his hand until a time and times and the dividing of time."—Daniel 7:25.

Very briefly, let us examine the facts about this vicious little horn power that was to rule and slay the people of God for so long a period of time:

1—This little horn power was to rule the earth for 1260 years.

A "time and times and the dividing of time" (Dan 7:25) is the same as the "forty-two months" of Revelation 11:2, and the "thousand two hundred and threescore days" of Revelation 12:6. The period of rule of the little horn power is referred to in each of these prophecies, although under different names. A "day" in Bible prophecy equals a year (Num 14:34; Ezek 4:6), thus 1260 days is equal to 1260 years. A "time" in Bible prophecy is equal to a year (Dan 11:13, margin, and Revised Version), so the "time and times and the dividing of time" is equal to one year, two years, and half a year, or a total of three and a half years. This is the same as 42 months. And both are equal to 1260 prophetic days or literal years. (A prophetic day is equal to 360 days or 12 months of 30 days each.) This is the symbolic time of Bible prophecy. And so as it was predicted, the little horn power ruled and crushed men's lives for over a thousand years.

2—This little horn power was to arise at a certain time in history. It would come up in the territory of the fourth beast, pagan Rome, at the time that this beast was declining in power. Ten "horns" or divisions were coming up at that same time (seven of these were the Saxons: modern England; the Franks: modern France; the Lombards: modern Italy; the Alemanni: modern Germany; the Bergundians: modern Switzerland; the Suevi: modern Portugal; and the Visigoths: modern Spain). But the little horn was also to uproot three others (the Heruli, Vandals, and Ostrogoths) as it was rising to power.

3—This little horn power would be a definite ruling power. It would be a kingdom as the others had been kingdoms before it (Dan 7:24). It would come up in the territory of the fourth beast (pagan Rome) as the others did (Dan 7:8). It would arise after the other horns had come up and as it was uprooting three of them (Dan 7:24). Although a kingdom like the others preceding it, yet it would be a strangely different kind of kingdom (Dan 7:24). It was "diverse" in that it was to be a combination religious-political power that would rule over nations for long centuries. This little horn power would have a leader at its head, for it would speak through the "mouth of a man." "And behold in this horn were eyes like the eyes of man, and a mouth speaking great things."—Daniel 7:8. A man was to be at the head of this power, a man who would defy God as well as the nations.

4—This mouth would speak great things. Revelation 13 is a parallel prophecy of this strange dominating, destroying power, and we are told: "He opened his mouth in blasphemy against His name, and His tabernacle, and them that dwell in heaven."—Revelation 16:6. And this agrees with the description of him given in Daniel 7: "He shall speak great words against the most High."—Daniel 7:25. This kingdom of a man would indeed be different—for this man would be guilty of blasphemy: He would speak against God and even call himself God!

5—This power would try to destroy the people of God for not submitting to its teachings. "I beheld, and the same horn made war with the saints, and prevailed against them"—Daniel 7:21. And God said that it would try to blot His people from the earth (Dan 7:25).

Only Papal Rome answers to the description given in the Inspired Word of God. Daniel 7 is parallel with Revelation 12 to 17. Unveiled before us is the Great Babylon of Revelation. It would hunt the people of God to the death for over a thousand years. But it would also do something else: It would try to change the Law of God.

6—It was predicted that this little horn power would try to "change times and laws" (Dan 7:25). We have already seen, earlier in this book, the procedure used by the bishop of Rome to do part of this. But here is more:

The Roman Catholic Church tried to blot out the Second Commandment, which forbade image worship. It then divided the Tenth Commandment into two, in order to make up the number ("Thou shalt not covet thy neighbor's house" and "Thou shalt not covet thy neighbor's wife."). And Rome tried to change the Fourth Commandment—so that instead of worshiping God on the day He commanded—the Seventh day of the week,—the people would come to mass on the first day —the Sun day—instead. And those that refused were ruthlessly murdered.

We have seen that God predicted in the Bible that a great desolating power would arise that would seek to change His laws and destroy His people. (Dan 7:8, 20-21, 25; 8:9-12) The prediction that the little horn power would especially seek to change God's "time law" is to be found in Daniel 7:25.

"And he shall speak great words against the most High, and shall wear out the saints of the most High, and think to change times and laws."—*Daniel 7:25.*

Only God can change the Moral Law of Ten Commandments, and for anyone to dare attempt such a change of any of those laws would appear to be unthinkable. It would require a power that would dare to call itself God, for only God can change His law.

And so the Apostle Paul predicted the rise of this man of sin who would call himself God.

"Let no man deceive you by any means: for that day [the Second Advent of Christ—verse 1] shall not come, except there come a falling away first, and that man of sin be re-

vealed, the son of perdition; Who opposeth and exalteth himself above all that is called God, or that is worshiped; so that he as God sitteth in the temple of God, shewing himself that he is God."—*2 Thessalonians 2:3-4.*

With boldness, this power was to arise and sit in the temple of God—and call itself God! And it would boastfully admit what it had done—declaring this very act to be the MARK of its authority over mankind.

And indeed, is it not so? Any power that says it has the authority to change the Law of God—must indeed be God!—for only God has the authority to change His own laws.

Let us not become confused between God and man. We are mortal creatures; He is the God of heaven. The Moral Law is the foundation of His government. All His earthly creatures must yield to this law that He has given them. None dare disobey it.

And, of course,—none should dare to change it.

You see, it is like this: I acknowledge and honor God's authority, when I obey His commands and encourage others to do so. But I declare my independence of God when I set aside His law and refuse to keep it.

Further, I set myself up as a rival god, when having set aside His law, I establish in its place a counterfeit law—and then demand that others keep it in place of the law that God commanded!

Here is the word of Scripture:

"Whom ye obey, his servants ye are."—*Romans 6:16.*

Think about that awhile. If you obey God, you are His servant. If you obey man—and disobey God in doing it—then you are serving man in place of God.

And when you learn that fact—you had better do something about it very quickly.

So we see that God's Word declares that obedience to this human god by keeping his counterfeit laws, while knowing that there is not one word or hint in all the Bible to observe such errors—transfers one's worship from the True God, the Creator God, who made heaven and earth and the Seventh-day Sabbath—transfers it to the worship of the man and his organization who gave us the man-made law.

It is as simple as that. By putting man's changes in place of God's Ten Commandments, we find ourselves worshiping the creature rather than the Creator.

There is nothing quite like that little horn power. It has such brazen insolence that it dares to try to change the laws of God.

And then it dares to boast of the fact . . repeatedly, . . over and over.

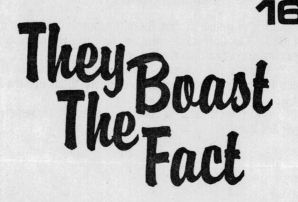

16

They Boast The Fact

Can you use a thousand dollars? Over the years a number of people have offered to give away—free—$1000 to anyone who will show them just one verse of Scripture that tells that the sanctity of the Seventh-day Bible Sabbath has been changed to Sunday, the first day of the week.

They do it, obviously, because they want you to begin reading in the Bible on this important subject—and see for yourself that you should hallow the only weekly Sabbath in that sacred Book.

But the first one to offer $1000 for that missing Bible verse was a Jesuit priest.

He did it to convince Sundaykeepers that if they wanted to stay with Sunday sacredness, they needed to return to Rome.

Thomas Enright, former president of Redemptorist College in Kansas City, Missouri, issued a number of public statements in which he challenged anyone to produce just one text of Scripture stating that the Seventh-day Sabbath had been changed to Sunday. —And he promised to give them $1000 if they would show the Bible passage to him.

The Hartford (Kansas) "Weekly Call," of February 22, 1884, published his challenge:

" 'I will give $1,000 to any man who will prove by the Bible alone that Sunday is the day we are bound to keep . .

The observance of Sunday is solely a law of the Catholic Church . . The church changed the Sabbath to Sunday and all the world bows down and worships upon that day in silent obedience to the mandates of the Catholic Church."—*Hartford "Weekly Call," quoting Priest Thomas Enright, C.S.S.R., February 22, 1884.*

But, try as they might, no one was ever able to claim that $1000 reward. Simply because there is no Bible proof of any kind for Sundaykeeping. Sunday sacredness just isn't in the Holy Scriptures. Enright knew it—and flaunted it—and for a reason.

For, you see, the attempted change of the Sabbath to Sunday marks the basic Roman Catholic "proof" that it is the "true church" that all Protestants should return to and obey. The Roman Catholic leaders declare that Protestants are still part of the Mother Church of Rome—because they keep the papal holy day—Sunday—as their sabbath!

"Sunday is a Catholic institution, and its claims to observance can be defended only on Catholic principles . . From beginning to end of scripture there is not a single passage that warrants the transfer of weekly public worship from the last day of the week to the first."—*Catholic Press, Sydney, Australia, August, 1900.*

"Ques. —Have you any other way of proving that the church has power to institute festivals of precept [command holy-days]?

"Ans. —Had she not such power, she could not have done that in which all modern religionists agree with her.—She could not have substituted the observance of Sunday the first day of the week, for the observance of Saturday the seventh day, a change for which there is no Scriptural authority." —*Stephan Keenan, A Doctrinal Catechism, 1846 edition, p. 176 [Keenan was a Scottish priest, whose catechism has been widely used in Roman Catholic schools and academies].*

"Ques. —Which is the Sabbath day?

"Ans. —Saturday is the Sabbath day.

"Ques. —Why do we observe Sunday instead of Saturday?

"Ans. —We observe Sunday instead of Saturday because the Catholic Church transferred the solemnity from Saturday to Sunday."—*Peter Geiermann, The Convert's Catechism of Catholic Doctrine, 1957 edition, p. 50 [Geiermann, (1870-*

1929) received the "apostolic blessing" of pope Pius X on this book, January 26, 1910].

"It is well to remind the Presbyterians, Baptists, Methodist, and all other Christians, that the Bible does not support them anywhere in their observance of Sunday. Sunday is an institution of the Roman Catholic Church, and those who observe the day observe a commandment of the Catholic Church."—*Priest Brady, in an address at Elizabeth, N.J. on March 17, 1903, reported in the Elizabeth, N.J. News of March 18, 1903.*

"Some theologians have held that God [in the Bible] likewise directly determined the Sunday as the day of worship in the New Law, that He Himself has explicitly substituted the Sunday for the Sabbath. But this theory is now entirely abandoned. It is now commonly held that God simply gave His [Catholic] Church the power to set aside whatever day, or days, she would deem suitable as Holy Days. The Church chose Sunday, the first day of the week, and in the course of time added other days, as holy days."—*Vincent J. Kelly, Forbidden Sunday and Feast-Day Occupations, 1943, p. 2 [Kelly, a Catholic priest, prepared this at Catholic University of America].*

"The pope has authority and has often exercised it, to dispense with the commands of Christ . . The pope's will stands for reason. He can dispense above the law, and of wrong make right, by correcting and changing laws."—*from Pope Nicholas' time.*

"Protestants . . accept Sunday rather than Saturday as the day for public worship after the Catholic Church made the change . . But the Protestant mind does not seem to realize that in accepting the Bible, in observing the Sunday, they are accepting the authority of the spokesman for the church, the Pope."—*Our Sunday Visitor, February 5, 1950 [One of the largest U.S. Roman Catholic magazines].*

"Reason and common sense demand the acceptance of one or the other of these alternatives: either Protestantism and the keeping holy of Saturday, or Catholicity and the keeping holy of Sunday. Compromise is impossible."—*The Catholic Mirror, December 23, 1893 [The Mirror is a Baltimore Roman Catholic weekly newspaper].*

"For ages all Christian nations looked to the Catholic Church, and, as we have seen, the various states enforced by law her ordinances as to worship and cessation of labor on Sunday. Protestantism, in discarding the authority of the Church, has no good reason for its Sunday theory, and ought logically, to keep Saturday as the Sabbath. The State in passing laws for the due Sanctification of Sunday, is unwittingly acknowledging the authority of the Catholic Church, and carrying out more or less faithfully its prescriptions. The Sunday as a day of the week set apart for the obligatory public worship of Almighty God is purely a creation of the Catholic Church."–*John Gilmary Shea, in The American Catholic Quarterly Review, January, 1883, p. 139 [Shea (1824-1893) was an important Catholic historian of his time].*

"It was the Catholic Church which, by the authority of Jesus Christ, has transferred this rest [from the Bible Sabbath] to the Sunday .. Thus the observance of Sunday by the Protestants is an homage they pay, in spite of themselves, to the authority of the [Catholic] Church."–*Monsignor Louis Segur, Plain Talk About the Protestantism of Today, 1868, p. 213 [L.G. Segur (1820-1881) was a French Catholic prelate and apologist, and later a diplomatic and judicial official at Rome.]*

"The Pope is not only the representative of Jesus Christ, but he is Jesus Christ Himself, hidden under veil of flesh."–*The Catholic National, July, 1895.*

"The Catholic Church .. by virtue of her divine mission, changed the day from Saturday to Sunday."–*The Catholic Mirror, September 23, 1893 [The Mirror, a Baltimore-based Catholic weekly, was the official organ for Cardinal Gibbons].*

"Ques. —When Protestants do profane work [regular employment] upon Saturday, or the seventh day of the week, do they follow the Scripture as their only rule of faith—do they find this permission clearly laid down in the Sacred Volume?

"Ans. —On the contrary, they have only the authority of [Catholic] tradition for this practice. In profaning Saturday, they violate one of God's commandments, which He has never abrogated,—'Remember thou keep holy the Sabbath day.'"–*Priest Steven Keenan, A Doctrinal Catechism, pp. 252, 254 [The catechism of this Scottish priest is widely used in Catholic schools to instruct children into their beliefs].*

"If we consulted the Bible only, we should still have to keep holy the Sabbath Day, that is Saturday."–*John Laux, A Course in Religion for Catholic High Schools and Academies, 1936 edition, vol. 1, p. 51 [J.J. Laux (1878-1939) was a Catholic priest, teacher, and author of many Catholic histories as well as biographies of their saints].*

"Some of the truths that have been handed down to us by tradition and are not recorded in the Sacred Scriptures, are the following: That there are just seven sacraments; that there is a purgatory; that, in the new law, Sunday should be kept holy instead of the Sabbath; that infants should be baptized, and that there are precisely seventy-two books in the Bible [66 that are inspired, plus 6 apocryphal]."*—Francis J. Butler, Holy Family Catechism, No. 3, p. 63 [Butler (1859-?) was a Catholic priest of Boston and an author of a series of catechisms.].*

"It is worth while to remember that this observance of Sunday—in which after all, the onlv Protestant worship conists—not only has no foundation in the Bible, but it is in flagant contradiction with its letter, which commands rest on the Sabbath, which is Saturday. It was the Catholic Church which, by the authority of Jesus Christ, has transferred this rest to the Sunday."*—Monsignor Louis Segur, Plain Talk About the Protestantism of Today, p. 213 [L.G. Segur (1820-1881), a French prelate, later was appointed as a diplomatic and judicial official in Rome].*

"All the names which in the Scriptures are applied to Christ, by virtue of which it is established that He is over the church, all the same names are applied to the pope."*—Robert Cardinal Bellarmine, De Conciliorum Auctoriatate (On the Authority of the Councils), Bk 2, chap. 17 [Bellarmine (1542-1621), a professor and rector at the Jesuit Gregorian University in Rome, is generally considered to have been one of the outstanding Jesuit instructors in the history of this organization].*

On April 29, 1922, in the Vatican throne room, a throng of cardinals, bishops, priests, nuns, boys and girls, who had all fallen on their knees in reverence of the one before them, were then addressed from the throne by Pope Pius XI, who said: "you know that I am the Holy Father, the representitive of God on the earth, the Vicar of Christ, which means I am God on the earth."*—Pope Pius XI, quoted in The Bulwark, October, 1922, p. 104 [Pius XI (1857-1939) was pope from 1922-1939, and was the one who signed the Treaty of the Lateran with Mussolini in 1929, whereby Vatican City was established. He consistently backed Mussolini's policies and government until he met with military reverses].*

"The Pope can modify [change] the Divine Law."*—Lucius Ferraris, Ecclesiastical Dictionary [Ferraris (d. before 1763) was an Italian Catholic official of the Franciscan order, highly placed in the Church].*

"We define that the Holy Apostolic See and the Roman Pontiff holds the primacy over the whole world."*—Philippe Labbe and Gabriel Cossart, The Most Holy Councils, vol. 13, col. 1167, on "The Council of Trent."*

"The pope is of so great dignity and so exalted that he is not a mere man, but as it were God, and the vicar of God. He is the divine monarch and supreme emperor, and king of kings. Hence the pope is crowned with a triple crown, as king of heaven and of earth and of the lower regions."—*Lucius Ferraris, Prompta Bibliotheca, vol. 6, art. "Papa II" [Ferraris (d. prior to 1763) was an Italian Catholic canonist and consultor to the Holy Office in Rome].*

"We hold upon this earth the place of God Almighty."— *Pope Leo XIII, in an encyclical letter dated June 20, 1894, The Great Encyclical Letters of Leo XIII, p. 304 [Leo XIII (1810-1903) was pope from 1878 until his death. He was one of the most forceful popes of the nineteenth century].*

"If Protestants would follow the Bible, they should worship God on the Sabbath Day. In keeping the Sunday they are following a law of the Catholic Church."—*Albert Smith, Chancellor of the Archdiocese of Baltimore, replying for the Cardinal in a letter dated February 10, 1920.*

"Protestants often deride the authority of Church tradition, and claim to be directed by the Bible only; yet they, too, have been guided by customs of the ancient Church, which find no warrant in the Bible, but rest on Church tradition only! A striking instance of this is the following:—The first positive command in the Decalogue is to 'Remember the Sabbath Day to keep it holy,' . . But the Sabbath Day, the observance of which God commanded, was our Saturday. Yet who among either Catholics or Protestants, except a sect or two, ever kept that commandment now? None. Why is this? The Bible which Protestants claim to obey exclusively, gives no authorization for the substitution of the first day of the week for the seventh. On what authority, therefore, have they done so? Plainly on the authority of that very Catholic Church which they abandoned, and whose traditions they condemn."—*John L. Stoddard. Rebuilding a Lost Faith, p. 80 [Stoddard (1850-1931) was an agnostic writer most of his life, who later was converted to Catholicism].*

"We Catholics, then, have precisely the same authority for keeping Sunday holy instead of Saturday as we have for every other article of our creed; namely, the authority of 'the church of the living God, the pillar and ground of the truth' (1 Timothy 3:15); whereas you who are Protestants have really no authority for it whatever; for there is no authority for it in the Bible, and you will not allow that there can be authority for it anywhere else. Both you and we do, in fact, follow tradition in this matter; but we follow it, believing it to be a part of God's word, and the [Catholic] Church to be its divinely appointed guardian and interpreter; you follow it [the Catholic Church], denouncing it all the time as a fallible and treacherous guide, which often 'makes the commandments of God of none effect' [quoting Matthew 15:6]."—*The Brotherhood of St. Paul, The Clifton Tracts, Vol. 4, tract 4, p. 15 [Roman Catholic].*

"Now the [Catholic] Church . . instituted, by God's authority, Sunday as the day of worship. This same Church, by the same divine authority, taught the doctrine of Purgatory . . We have, therefore, the same authority for Purgatory as we have for Sunday."—*Martin J. Scott, Things Catholics Are Asked About, 1927, p. 236 [Jesuit theologian and writer].*

"The [Catholic] Church, by the power our Lord gave her, changed the observance of Saturday to Sunday."—*The Catholic Canon, H. Cafferata, The Catechism Simply Explained, 1932 edition, p. 80.*

"The Catholic Church for over one thousand years before the existence of a Protestant, by virtue of her Divine mission, changed the day from Saturday to Sunday . . But the Protestant says: 'How can I receive the teachings of an apostate Church?' How, we ask, have you managed to receive her teaching all your life, in direct opposition to your recognized teacher, the Bible, on the Sabbath question?"—*The Christian Sabbath, 2nd ed., published by the Catholic Mirror of Baltimore, Maryland. [The official paper of Cardinal Gibbons.]*

"If you follow the Bible alone there can be no question that you are obliged to keep Saturday holy, since that is the day especially prescribed by Almighty God to be kept holy to the Lord."—*Priest F.G. Lentz, The Question Box, 1900, p. 98 [Lentz (d. 1917) was a Catholic priest and writer, based in the Illinois area].*

"Prove to me from the Bible alone that I am bound to keep Sunday holy. There is no such law in the Bible. It is a law of the holy Catholic Church alone. The Bible says 'Remember the Sabbath day to keep it holy.' The Catholic Church says, No. By my divine power I abolish the Sabbath day and command you to keep holy the first day of the week. And lo! The entire civilized world bows down in reverent obedience to the command of the Holy Catholic Church."—*Priest Thomas Enright, CSSR, President of Redemptorist College, Kansas City, Mo., in a lecture at Hartford, Kansas, February 18, 1884, and printed in the Hartford Kansas Weekly Call, February 22, 1884, and the American Sentinel, a New York Roman Catholic journal in June 1893, page 173.*

"Of Course the Catholic Church claims that the change was her act . . AND THE ACT IS A MARK of her ecclesiastical power."—*from the office of Cardinal Gibbons, through Chancellor H.F. Thomas, November 11, 1895.*

"Sunday is our MARK of authority! . . The Church is above the Bible, and this transference of sabbath observance is proof of that fact."—*The Catholic Record, London, Ontario, Canada, September 1, 1923.*

We have earlier seen that historians are in agreement on the fact that the attempt to change the Bible Sabbath to Sunday was made after the Bible was finished. And now we have found that the Roman Catholic Church has repeatedly admitted—even boasted—openly of the fact that the change was not made by God or the Bible writers—but by the Vatican.

Surely, in light of all this, there must be learned Protestants who have also admitted that the change is not Biblical but was made in later centuries! And there are—many of them.

Others Agree

Dr. E.R. Hiscox was a leading Baptist scholar and writer of three-quarters of a century ago. He wrote the well-known "Baptist Manual" which went through many printings. He was probably one of the best-known Baptist research and Biblical authorities of his time.

On November 16, 1893, Dr. Hiscox presented the keynote address at a major church gathering, the Baptist Ministers' Convention, which met in New York City.

In his sermon, Dr. Hiscox said this to the assembled ministers of his church:

"There was and is a command to keep holy the Sabbath day, but that Sabbath day was not Sunday. It will however be readily said, and with some show of triumph, that the Sabbath was transferred from the seventh to the first day of the week, with all its duties, privileges and sanctions. Earnestly desiring information on this subject which I have studied for many years, I ask, where can the record of such a transaction be found? Not in the New Testament—absolutely not. There is no Scriptural evidence of the change of the Sabbath institution from the seventh to the first day of the week . .

"I wish to say that this Sabbath question, in this aspect of it, is the gravest and most perplexing question connected with Christian institutions which at present claims attention from Christian people; and the only reason that it is not a more disturbing element in Christian thought and in religious discussion is because the Christian world has settled down content on the conviction that somehow a transference has taken place at the beginning of Christian history.

"To me it seems unaccountable that Jesus, during three years' discussion with His disciples, often conversing with them upon the Sabbath question, discussing it in some of its various aspects, freeing it from its false [Jewish traditional] glosses, never alluded to any transference of the day; also, that during forty days of His resurrection life, no such thing was intimated. Nor, so far as we know, did the Spirit, which was given to bring to their remembrance all things whatsoever that He. had said unto them, deal with this question. Nor yet did churches, counseling and instructing those founded, discuss or approach the subject.

"Of course I quite well know that Sunday did come into use in early Christian history as a religious day, as we learn from the Christian Fathers and other sources. But what a pity that it comes branded with the mark of Paganism, and christened with the name of the sun-god, then adopted and sanctified by the Papal apostasy, and bequeathed as a sacred legacy to Protestantism."—Dr. E.T. Hiscox, author of the Baptist Manual. From a photostatic copy of a notarized statement by Dr. Hiscox.

Leading pastors, writers and administrators of a wide range of the major Protestant denominations have recognized the truth that the Seventh-day Sabbath is the Bible Sabbath— and Sunday sacredness is not to be found anywhere in Scripture.

Here are a few of their statements. Many more could be given if we had the space:

British Congregationalists: "It is quite clear that however rigidly or devotedly we may spend Sunday, we are not keeping the Sabbath . . The Sabbath was founded on a specific, divine command. We can plead no such command for the observance of Sunday . . There is not a single line in the New Testament to suggest that we incur any penalty by violating the supposed sanctity of Sunday."—*Dr. R.W. Dale, The Ten Commandments, Hodder and Stoughton, page 106-107.*

Protestant Episcopal: "Ques. —Is there any command in the New Testament to change the day of weekly rest from Saturday to Sunday?

"Ans. —None."—*Manual of Christian Doctrine, p. 127.*

Disciples of Christ: "Either the [Ten Commandment] Law remains in all its force, to the utmost extent of its literal requirements, or it is passed away with the Jewish ceremonies. If it yet exists, let us observe it according to law. And if it does not exist, let us abandon a mock observance of another day for it."—*Alexander Campbell, "Address to the Readers of the Christian Baptists," part 1, Feb. 2, 1824, pp. 44-45 [Campbell (1788-1866) was the founder of the Disciples of Christ Church].*

American Congregationalists: "The current notion that Christ and His apostles authoritatively substituted the first day for the seventh, is absolutely without any authority in the New Testament."—*Dr. Lyman Abbott, in the Christian Union, June 26, 1890.*

English Independent: "Sabbath in the Hebrew language signifies rest, and is the seventh day of the week, . . and it must be confessed that there is no law in the New Testament concerning the first day."—*Charles Buck, A Theological Dictionary, art. "Sabbath," p. 403 [Buck (1771-1815) was a British Independent minister and author].*

Methodist Episcopal: "The Sabbath instituted in the beginning, and confirmed again and again by Moses and the prophets, has never been abrogated. A part of the moral law, not a jot or tittle of its sanctity has been taken away."—*Bishop's Pastoral, 1874 edition.*

Church of England: "The Lord's day did not succeed in the place of the [Bible] Sabbath, but the . . Lord's day was merely of ecclesiastical institution. It was not introduced by virtue of the fourth commandment, because they for almost three hundred years together kept that day which was in that commandment."—*Jeremy Taylor, The Rule of Conscience, 1851, pp. 456-548 [Dr. Taylor (1613-1667) was chaplain to the King of England, and later appointed a bishop and became president of a college in Wales].*

Christian Church (Christian Connection): "The Roman Church . . reversed the Fourth Commandment by doing away with the Sabbath of God's word, and instituting Sunday as a Holiday."—*Nicholas Summerbell, History of the Christian Church, 3rd ed., 1873, p. 415 [Summerbell (1816-1889) was the president of Union Christian College in Indiana].*

Disciples of Christ: "There is no direct Scriptural authority for designating the first day 'the Lord's Day.' "—*Dr. D.H. Lucas, in the Christian Oracle, January 23, 1890.*

Protestant Episcopal: "The day is now changed from the seventh to the first day; . . but as we meet with no Scriptural direction for the change, we may conclude it was done by the authority of the church."—*The Protestant Episcopal "Explanation of Catechism."*

Baptist: "The Scriptures nowhere call the first day of the week the Sabbath . . There is no Scriptural authority for so doing, nor of course any Scriptural obligation."—*The Watchman.*

Episcopal: "The Sabbath was religiously observed in the Eastern church three hundred years and more after our Saviour's Passion [death]."—*Prof. E. Brerewood of Gresham College, London, in a sermon.*

Baptist: "There was and is a commandment to keep holy the Sabbath day, but that Sabbath was not Sunday. It will, however, be readily said, and with some show of triumph, that the Sabbath was transferred from the seventh to the first day of the week . . Where can the record of such a transaction be found? Not in the New Testament, absolutely not."—*E.R, Hiscox, report of his sermon at the Baptist Ministers' Convention, in New York Examiner, November 16, 1893 [Dr. Hiscox was a well-known Baptist writer and author of their Baptist Manual].*

Presbyterian: "There is no word, no hint in the New Testament about abstaining from work on Sunday. The observance of Ash Wednesday, or Lent, stands exactly on the same footing as the observance of Sunday. Into the rest of Sunday no Divine Law enters."—*Canon Eyton, in The Ten Commandments [Dr. Eyton was the Canon of Westminister in London].*

Anglican: "And where are we told in the Scriptures that we are to keep the first day at all? We are commanded to keep the seventh; but we are nowhere commanded to keep the first day. The reason why we keep the first day of the week holy instead of the seventh is for the same reason we observe many other things, not because the Bible, but because the church, has enjoined [commanded] it."—*Issac Williams, Plain Sermons on the Catechism, Vol. 1, pp. 334, 336.*

Methodist: "It is true that there is no positive command for infant baptism. Nor is there any for keeping holy the first day of the week. Many believe that Christ changed the Sabbath. But, from His own words, we see that He came for no such purpose. Those who believe that Jesus changed the Sabbath base it only on a supposition."—*Amos Binney, Theological Compendium, 1902 edition, pp. 180-181, 171 [Binney (1802-1878), Methodist minister and presiding elder, whose Compendium was published for forty years in many languages, also wrote a Methodist New Testament Commentary].*

Southern Baptist: "There was never any formal or authoritative change from the Jewish Seventh Day Sabbath to the Christian First Day observance . .

"There are in the New Testament no commands, no prescriptions, no rules, no liturgies applying to the observance of the Lord's Day . .

"There is no organic [no actual] connection between the Hebrew Sabbath and the Christian Lord's Day . . It was only a short while until gentiles predominated in the [early church] Christian movement. They brought over the consciousness of various observances in the pagan religions, preeminently the worship of the sun—a sort of Sunday consciousness."—*William Owen Carver, Sabbath Observance, 1940, pp. 49, 52, 54 [Dr. Carver (1868-1954) was professor of comparative religion at the Southern Baptist Theological Seminary, in Louisville, Kentucky].*

Episcopalian: "The observance of the first day instead of the seventh day rests on the testimony of the Catholic church, and the [Catholic] church alone."—*Hobart Church News, July 2, 1894.*

Irish Methodist: "There is no intimation here that the Sabbath was done away, or that its moral use superseded, by the introduction of Christianity. I have shown elsewhere that, 'Remember the Sabbath day, to keep it holy,' is a command of perpetual obligation."—*Adam Clarke, The New Testament of our Lord and Saviour Jesus Christ, Vol. 2, p. 524 [Clarke (1760-1832) was an Irish Wesleyan minister, writer, and three times Methodist conference president].*

Southern Baptist: "As presented to us in the Scriptures the Sabbath was not the invention of any religious founder. It was not at first part of any system of religion, but an entirely independent institution. Very definitely it is presented in Genesis as the very first institution, inaugurated by the Creator Himself."—*W.O. Carver, Sabbath Observance, pp. 40-41 [Dr. Carver (1868-1954) was professor of comparative religion in the Southern Baptist Theological Seminary in Kentucky].*

All this seems amazing to us. How could the heart of the the Bible worship of the God of heaven (the worship of Him on His appointed worship day),—how could any mere mortals dare try to change it—and enforce such a change on everyone around them!

Why did not the Protestant Reformers of the Sixteenth Century bring us back to Sabbathkeeping?

The truth is that they did not have a chance to make all of the needed reforms before Rome threw armies upon them for their destruction.

But, even deeper: Why does not the Vatican confess this terrible change that they had Constantine instigate? Why do they not now lead out in bringing Christendom back to the Bible Sabbath?

At this point the plot thickens. For now we shall learn that, by their own admission, the change of the Sabbath to Sunday is the doctrinal basis upon which the Roman Catholic Church is built. It is the mark of her authority. She dare not change it—for to do so would be to yield that religious authority back to the God of the Sabbath.

Out Of Darkness

The red granite obelisk finally came home.
But here is the story:
Earlier we mentioned that Heliopolis [literally: "city of the sun"] in Egypt was the center of North African sun worship around the time of Christ. And the center of sun worship in Heliopolis was a red granite obelisk that was 83 feet high. What is an "obelisk?" It is a tall pillar, pointed at the top, that anciently was a symbol of the Sun-god. Pagans would place these in front of their churches to identify them.

In A.D. 37-41, Emperor Caligula of Rome, a devoted Sun-worshiper, ordered that this immense obelisk at Heliopolis, Egypt, be carefully packed and brought at great expense to Rome. There it was later erected by Nero in the center of the "Circus" that Caligula had built. Chariot races, often dedicated to Lord Mithra, the Sun-god, were run there.

This Circus was located on one of the seven hills of Rome: Vatican hill. This was fine with everyone, for Vatican hill, back in those days, wasn't used for anything other than the Circus horse races.

But then the years passed, and with them the centuries. And a new ruler over Rome came into power: Pope Sixtus V. His followers all over Europe were busy fighting the Great Reformation that had begun half a century before.

But Pope Sixtus V wanted to add the finishing touch to the sparkling new St. Peter's Cathedral—the largest Catholic

Church in the world. Located in the heart of Vatican hill, it was not far from that old red obelisk.

In the year 1585, a decree from the holy one of Rome went out to all the people: The obelisk that the pagan Emperor Caligula had brought over from Heliopolis—must be brought to the front of St. Peter's and set up in the exact center of the circular court that stood before it. By so doing, the obelisk of the Sun would be placed at the center of the Vatican. And this was understandable.

The decree called for someone to do the moving. But there was no one with enough courage to tackle the operation, even though a large sum of money was offered.

The problem was that the decree included a death penalty to the mover—if he accidently let the obelisk fall to the ground as he was erecting it. This ancient relic of paganism was obviously more important than the lives of Christians.

Finally a man stepped forward and said he would contract to do the job. His name was Domenico Fontana. Using 45 winches, 160 horses, and a crew of 800 men, the moving operation began.

Starting at that ancient pagan carnival site, Caligula's Circus Maximus, Fontana carefully began the job of lowering the immense 83-foot-high sun-image to the ground. Masterful architects like Antonio Da Sangallo and Michelangelo had said the moving operation couldn't be done. (The sun-image weighed over a million Roman pounds.) But Domenico and his brother Giovanni spent a year on the task. Immense machines lowered and transported the pagan worship symbol. Eight hundred men, braced for the task by a sacrament from the pope himself, and working with 160 horses, pulled on 44 ropes, each as thick as a man's arm,—and gradually raised it aloft at the new site. The date: September 10, 1586. The pope himself was present to pray to heaven that the sun-image would not be injured. He also issued an edict while it was being raised that no one in the surrounding crowds could speak aloud, on pain of death, lest the workmen be distracted and the solar idol of Heliopolis be shattered. Only reverent whispers were to be heard as the symbol of the Sun-god was moved to its proper

SUN IMAGE AT THE CENTER

THE POPE SPEAKS
FROM THE BALCONY OF ST. PETER'S

place in front of St. Peter's.

When the job was completed, hundreds of church bells rang out, cannons roared, and the crowds cheered wildly. Coming forth from the cathedral, Pope Sixtus approached the sun pillar and blessed and dedicated it to the "cross." Then, entering St. Peter's at the head of a procession, he performed a solemn mass in its honor, and pronounced a blessing on the workmen and their horses.

Domenico Fontana became the hero of Rome, and Pope Sixtus V sent official announcements to foreign governments. It was clear to all that the Religion of Rome had achieved a new climax in greatness.

The red granite Obelisk of the Vatican can be seen today in the immense circular court in front of St. Peter's. In the exact center of 248 large Doric-style columns (which alone cost nearly a million dollars), stands the sun-red obelisk. Weighing 320 tons, it stands 83 feet high, on top of a 49-foot foundation—132 feet in all.

The great Obelisk of the ancient "City of the Sun" is back home again—standing once more at the entrance to the largest church in town . . to identify it.

It is back at the center of worship—in the City of the Sun.

On October 31, 1517, Martin Luther nailed a sheet of paper containing 95 protests to the door of the University Church in Wittenberg, Germany. That day marks the beginning of the Great Reformation.

But that Reformation was never completed, for Luther and his associates had so recently come out of the darkness of Catholic error, that they only partially perceived those errors. We are deeply thankful for what they did, but the work they began is yet to be finished.

When the Reformation burst upon Europe in the Six-teenth Century, Rome determined to crush out the interest of the people in returning to Bible religion. The three primary methods used to extinguish Protestantism were warfare, Jesuit espionage, and the Council of Trent.

The Council of Trent was convened by the pope and

continued from December 13, 1545 to December 4, 1563. Its assigned purpose was to clarify Roman Catholic doctrine in order to strengthen the Church in its fight against Protestantism. It is generally considered to have been one of the most important councils in the history of Romanism.

Every basic modern doctrine of Catholicism finds its foundation in the decisions affirmed at the Council of Trent.

"From a doctrinal and disciplinary point of view, it was the most important council in the history of the Roman church, fixing her distinctive faith and practise in relation to the Protestant Evangelical churches." — *Schaff-Herzog Encyclopedia, article entitled "Council of Trent."*

The Protestants had launched a campaign that all doctrine must be brought to the test of the Inspired Word. And if not found there it must be rejected. This deep truth lies at the heart of Protestantism.

But Rome was determined to overthrow that truth and again bring the people into bondage to its errors. How they were to do this was the question, for there was a division in the Church over the primacy of Tradition.

The Roman Catholic Church had always been founded on the words of men ("Tradition"), with a sprinkling of the Word of God ("Scripture"). They had always declared Tradition to be superior to Scripture in every dispute over worship, doctrine or practice.

And what is "Tradition?" It is the sayings of men. It is the decisions of Roman Catholic councils, the decrees of its popes, and the words of its canonized saints.

"Like two sacred rivers flowing from Paradise, the Bible and divine Tradition contain the Word of God, the precious gems of revealed truths.

"Though these two divine streams are in themselves, on account of their divine origin, of equal sacredness, and are both full of revealed truths, still, of the two, TRADITION is to us more clear and safe." [Full caps theirs] — *Joseph F. Di Bruno, Catholic Belief, 1884 ed., p. 45. [Di Bruno was an Italian Catholic priest and writer.]*

"Some of the truths that have been handed down to us by Tradition and are not recorded in the Sacred Scriptures, are the following: That there are just seven sacraments; that there

is a purgatory; that, in the new law [Roman Catholic "Canon Law"], Sunday should be kept holy instead of the Sabbath; that infants should be baptized, and that there are precisely seventy-two books in the Bible [66 in our Bible that are inspired, plus 6 apocryphal books]."—*Francis J. Butler, Holy Family Catechism, No. 3, p. 63 [Butler (1859-?) was a Catholic priest of Boston and an author of a series of catechisms].*

But when the Council of Trent convened, there was a battle over this matter. Should Tradition rule over the Bible, or should they carry equal authority? Should the Bible be considered more authoritative, or should Tradition be set aside entirely?

There was much bickering over this matter at Trent. Protestantism was making a powerful attack on Romish beliefs, which were based on Tradition. Since Roman Catholic tradition was nothing more than a hodge-podge collection of confused sayings, many of the archbishops and cardinals attending this very important Catholic council naturally hesitated to officially announce that Tradition was the basis of the Roman Catholic Church.

But then came the deciding point—and it came as a surprise.

What is not generally known is that the entire argument was settled in one day.

When Gaspar del Fosso, the Archbishop of Reggio, stood up and spoke on January 18, 1562, he decided once and for all the entire future course of Catholicism.

Rising to his feet, and calling for attention, he wholeheartedly praised Tradition and then made bitter jibes at those who wanted to downgrade its supremacy in the Church.

Since others had already spoken in defense of Tradition, what is it that made del Fosso's speech so decisive? It was this:

He reasoned that the Church of Rome was founded on Tradition and it and its beliefs would soon perish without it. Then he gave his punch line: He told the assembled delegates that the great proof that the doctrine of "Tradition-above-Scripture" must be right—was the fact that the Church of

Rome had centuries earlier changed the Seventh-day Sabbath, which God Himself had commanded, to Sunday, the first day of the week.

Del Fosso declared that THIS proved that Tradition was more important than the Bible—for Church Tradition had presumed to change the very laws of God Himself—and had apparently succeeded! And what is more, del Fosso climaxed,—the Protestants were obeying Rome and keeping Sunday also. That morning, Del Fosso made it clear that Sunday sacredness was the pivotal proof of the entire doctrinal structure of Catholicism.

His logical speech settled the matter. The tone of the gathering changed. Never again in the councils of Rome was a question to be raised in regard to the supreme authority of Roman Catholic Tradition. For Sundaykeeping had settled it. The fact that Rome had changed the Sabbath to Sunday and the fact that Protestants carefully obeyed the papacy by keeping it, was the "proof" needed to forever establish Rome's authority.

"Finally, at the last opening [session] on the eighteenth of January, 1562, their last scruple was set aside; the Archbishop of Reggio made a speech in which he openly declared that tradition stood above Scripture. The authority of the church could therefore not be bound to the authority of the Scriptures, because the church had changed the Sabbath into Sunday, not by the command of Christ but by its own authority. With this, to be sure, the last illusion was destroyed, and it was declared that tradition does not signify antiquity, but continual inspiration."—*J.H. Holtzman, Canon and Tradition, p. 263.*

Oddly enough, the Protestant leaders who presented the Augsburg Confession, a little over thirty years earlier, had recognized this very fact that Rome's authority was keyed to her attempted change of the Bible Sabbath:

"They [the Catholic bishops] allege the changing of the Sabbath into the Lord's day, contrary, as it seemeth, to the Decalogue; and they have no example more in their mouths than the change of the Sabbath. They will needs have the church's power to be very great, because it hath done away with a precept of the Decalogue."

"But of this question ours do thus teach: that the

Bishops have no power to ordain any thing contrary to the Gospel, as was showed before."—*from the Augsburg Confession, quoted in Library of Original Sources, Volume 5, pp. 173-174.*

Soon after this confession of Protestant faith was made at Augsburg, Germany, in 1530, the Reformers and their followers found themselves deluged in war and intrigue. Fighting for the faith they already had—indeed, for their very lives,—they had little time to carry the Reformation further—and rediscover many of the Biblical truths buried under centuries of error and speculation.

But the Catholic leaders knew—and they tell us in their writings:

"Sunday is a Catholic institution, and its claims to observance can be defended only on Catholic principles . . From beginning to end of scripture there is not a single passage that warrants the transfer of weekly public worship from the last day of the week to the first."—*Catholic Press, Sydney, Australia, August, 1900.*

"It is well to remind the Presbyterians, Baptists, Methodist, and all other Christians, that the Bible does not support them anywhere in their observance of Sunday. Sunday is an institution of the Roman Catholic Church, and those who observe the day observe a commandment of the Catholic Church."—*Priest Brady, in an address at Elizabeth, N.J. on March 17, 1903, reported in the Elizabeth, N.J. News of March 18, 1903.*

The Sunday as a day of the week set apart for the obligatory public worship of Almighty God is purely a creation of the Catholic Church."—*John Gilmary Shea, in The American Catholic Quarterly Review, January, 1883, p. 139 [Shea, (1824-1892) was an important Catholic historian of his time].*

"Protestants . . accept Sunday rather than Saturday as the day for public worship after the Catholic Church made the change . . But the Protestant mind does not seem to realize that in accepting the Bible, in observing the Sunday, they are accepting the authority of the spokesman for the church, the Pope."—*Our Sunday Visitor, February 5, 1950 [One of the largest U.S. Roman Catholic magazines].*

"If Protestants would follow the Bible, they should worship God on the Sabbath Day. In keeping the Sunday they are following a law of the Catholic Church."—*Albert Smith, Chancellor of the Archdiocese of Baltimore, replying for the Cardinal in a letter dated February 10, 1920.*

"Protestants often deride the authority of Church tradition, and claim to be directed by the Bible only; yet they, too, have been guided by customs of the ancient Church, which find no warrant in the Bible, but rest on Church tradition only! A striking instance of this is the following:—The first positive command in the Decalogue is to 'Remember the Sabbath Day to keep it holy,' . . But the Sabbath Day, the observance of which God commanded, was our Saturday. Yet who among either Catholics or Protestants, except a sect or two, ever kept that commandment now? None. Why is this? The Bible which Protestants claim to obey exclusively, gives no authorization for the substitution of the first day of the week for the seventh. On what authority, therefore, have they done so? Plainly on the authority of that very Catholic Church which they abandoned, and whose traditions they condemn."—*John L. Stoddard. Rebuilding a Lost Faith, p. 80 [Stoddard (1850-1931) was an agnostic writer most of his life, who later was converted to Catholicism].*

"Now the [Catholic] Church . . instituted, by God's authority, Sunday as the day of worship. This same Church, by the same divine authority, taught the doctrine of Purgatory . . We have, therefore, the same authority for Purgatory as we have for Sunday."—*Martin J. Scott, Things Catholics Are Asked About, 1927, p. 236 [Jesuit theologian and writer].*

"The Catholic Church for over one thousand years before the existence of a Protestant, by virtue of her Divine mission, changed the day from Saturday to Sunday . . But the Protestant says: 'How can I receive the teachings of an apostate Church?' How, we ask, have you managed to receive her teaching all your life, in direct opposition to your recognized teacher, the Bible, on the Sabbath question?"—*The Christian Sabbath, 2nd ed., published by the Catholic Mirror. [This Baltimore periodical was the official paper of Cardinal Gibbons.]*

"If you follow the Bible alone there can be no question that you are obliged to keep Saturday holy, since that is the day especially prescribed by Almighty God to be kept holy to the Lord."—*Priest F.G. Lentz, The Question Box, 1900, p. 98 [Lentz (d. 1917) was a Catholic priest and writer, based in the Illinois area].*

Yes, now we understand. The Sun day and the worship of God on that day instead of on the Bible Sabbath—IS THE MARK of Rome's authority in religious matters.

Oh, that more people understood this! Oh, that everyone would leave the mark of Rome—and return to the symbol of obedience to the true God—the Sign of creation, sanctification and salvation.

"Keep the Sabbath . . It is a sign between Me and the children of Israel for ever: for in six days the Lord made heaven and earth, and on the Seventh day He rested, and was refreshed."—Exodus 31:16-17.

"Verily My Sabbaths ye shall keep: for it is a sign between Me and you throughout your generations; that ye may know that I am the Lord that doth sanctify you."—Exodus 31:13.

"Moreover also I gave them My Sabbaths, to be a sign between Me and them, that they might know that I am the Lord that sanctify them."—Ezekiel 20:12.

"And hallow My Sabbaths; and they shall be a sign between Me and you, that ye may know that I am the Lord your God."—Ezekiel 20:20.

Yes, it is time to return to God's Sign of Creation, Sanctification and Salvation. It is time to flee the Mark of Roman Babylon.

"Prove to me from the Bible alone that I am bound to keep Sunday holy. There is no such law in the Bible. It is a law of the holy Catholic Church alone.

"The Bible says 'Remember the Sabbath day to keep it holy.' The Catholic Church says, No. By my divine power I abolish the Sabbath day and command you to keep holy the first day of the week.

"And lo! The entire civilized world bows down in reverent obedience to the command of the Holy Catholic Church." —*Priest Thomas Enright, CSSR, President of Redemptorist College, Kansas City, Mo., in a lecture at Hartford, Kansas, February 18, 1884, and printed in the Hartford Kansas Weekly Call, February 22, 1884, and in the American Sentinel, a New York Roman Catholic journal in June 1893, p. 173.*

Cardinal Gibbons was the leading Roman Catholic spokesman for the Vatican in America at the turn of the century. He wrote the well-known "Faith of our Fathers" which went through many printings.

A letter addressed to his office brought the following reply:

"Of course the Catholic Church claims that the change was her act . . AND THE ACT IS A MARK of her ecclesiastical power."—*from the office of Cardinal Gibbons, through*

Chancellor H.F. Thomas, November 11, 1895.

For us, who live down in earth's final hour, these are facts too serious to be ignored. Knowing the truth about the Bible Sabbath and the Sun day, we must individually make our decision.

For the end is just ahead.

End Of Time

The Bible Sabbath hit the headlines in New York City not too long ago. The following article appeared in the "New York Times" on March 14, 1966. The title in bold type said this: "AN APPEAL TO THE POPE OF ROME TO LEAD CHRISTIANS BACK TO THE BIBLE."

"Dr. Ernest R. Palen, pastor of New York's Marble Collegiate Church for more than thirty years, created a stir that hit the headlines, when on March 13, 1966, he delivered a sermon in which he called for Protestants and Roman Catholics to join in returning to the Bible Sabbath that Jesus kept—on Saturday. This Reformed Church in America theologian and pastor startled hearers by quoting from Exodus 20:8, and then saying, 'It should not be too great a break for us . . to observe the same Sabbath day that Jesus Himself observed.' In this sermon, he pled for all the churches to return to the keeping of the Seventh-day Sabbath, and noting that mankind can only truly keep holy that day which the God of heaven has commanded to be kept holy, he said that this 'one day of the week really kept holy by Catholics, Protestants, and Jews would give an uplift to the moral tone of our day that nothing else could do.' Dr. Palen, recognizing the well-known leadership of the pope in Sunday sanctification, asked that Pope Paul VI take the initiative in this matter. Dr. Palen predicted that if the pontiff would designate 'the Seventh day—the historical and Biblical Sabbath—as the day to keep holy,' that most of

*the major Protestant bodies of our time would 'go along.' "—
Article by George Dugan, "Christians Urged to Join Jews in
Observing Saturday Sabbath," New York Times, March 14,
1966.*

And Palen is right. The Ten Commandments given by
God to Moses is to be the great pattern for our lives. Through
the grace of Jesus Christ we can be empowered to keep that
law holy unto God. The purpose of Christianity is to bring
people back to God and enable them to obey Him.

"Till heaven and earth pass, one jot or one tittle shall in
no wise pass from the law." Matthew 5:18. The law of God is
a revelation of His will, and so it is a transcript of His character. Both God and His Moral Law will endure forever. Never
has one command been annulled; not a jot or a tittle has been
changed. The Bible says: "Forever, O Lord, Thy word is
settled in heaven." Psalm 119:89. "All His commandments are
sure. They stand fast forever and ever." Psalm 111:7-8.

And in the very heart of the Ten Commandments is the
fourth, as it was first proclaimed by God on Mount Sinai:

**"Remember the Sabbath day, to keep it holy. Six days
shalt thou labor, and do all thy work: but the Seventh day is
the Sabbath of the Lord thy God: in it thou shalt not do any
work, thou, nor thy son, nor thy daughter, thy man-servant,
nor thy maid-servant, nor thy cattle, nor thy stranger that is
within thy gates: for in six days the Lord made heaven and
earth, the sea, and all that in them is, and rested the Seventh
day: wherefore the Lord blessed the Sabbath day, and hallowed it."—Exodus 20:8-11.**

You and I may in the past have ignorantly broken this
commandment. But now He wants us to return to it. We want
to do what God says. We want this with all our heart. And
now as we learn that the God of heaven who loves us so much
that He let His Son go to Calvary so that sin could be taken
out of our lives;—well, we can do nothing better than to show
Him our loyalty from henceforth. Whatever He says in His
Word, we want to do.

Throughout this book we have been looking at the past.
Now we shall view the present—and the future.

In the Sixth Century B.C., the prophet Daniel was

shown in vision that a terrible organization was later to arise that would seek to destroy God's people and God's law.

"And he shall speak great words against the most High, and shall wear out the saints of the most High, and think to change times and laws."—Daniel 7:25.

But a parallel warning is to be found in Revelation 14. In this chapter we find a threefold warning to be given to all the world in the last days (Revelation 14:6-12). And it comes just before the Second Coming of Christ (Revelation 14:14). Indeed, that message will prepare men and women to meet their Creator in peace when He returns.

Under the figure of three angels flying in midheaven, this important message is revealed. By the first angel of Revelation 14:6-7, men are called upon to "fear God and give glory to Him," and to worship Him as the Creator of the heavens and the earth. In order to do this, they must obey His law. This is a Bible truth that needs to be understood by everyone today. "Fear God and keep His commandments, for this is the whole duty of man." Ecclesiastes 12:13. Without obedience to His commandments, no worship can be pleasing to God. "This is the love of God, that we keep His commandments." 1 John 5:3. "He that turneth away his ear from hearing the law, even his prayer shall be abomination." Proverbs 28:9.

The duty to worship God is based upon the fact that He is the Creator. We owe our existence to Him. Therefore He deserves our worship and our obedience. It is right to worship our Creator; to worship anything else is to make it an idol. "All the gods of the nations are idols; but the Lord made the heavens." Psalm 96:5. "Know ye that Jehovah, He is God: it is He that hath made us, and not we ourselves." Isaiah 40:25-26. "O come, let us worship and bow down: let us kneel before the Lord our Maker." Isaiah 45:18. "Thou art worthy, O Lord, to receive glory and honor and power: for Thou hast created all things." Revelation 4:11. There is no fact more obvious than that we worship God because He is our Creator. And because He is our Creator, we must obey Him.

In Revelation 14, men are called upon to worship the Creator, and this prophecy reveals that those who genuinely do, will be those who keep His commandments.

"And the third angel followed them, saying with a loud voice, If any man worship the beast and his image, and receive his mark in his forehead or in his hand, the same shall drink of the wrath of God, which is poured out without mixture . .

"Here is the patience of the saints: here are they that keep the commandments of God, and the faith of Jesus."—Revelation 14:9-10,12.

In contrast to those who will receive the mark, are those who choose to obey God's commandments. One of these commandments—the fourth or Sabbath commandment—points directly to God as the Creator (Exodus 20:8-11). For the Bible Sabbath is a sign between us and our God. It is "a sign . . that ye may know that I am the Lord your God." Ezekiel 20:20. "It is a sign . . for in six days the Lord made heaven and earth, and on the Seventh day He rested and was refreshed."—Exodus 31:17.

"The importance of the Sabbath as a memorial of creation is that it keeps ever present the true reason why worship is due to God . . The Sabbath, therefore, lies at the very foundation of divine worship; for it teaches this great truth in the most impressive manner, and no other institution does this. The true ground of divine worship, not of that on the Seventh day merely, but of all worship, is found in the distinction between the Creator and His creatures. This great fact must never become obsolete, and must never be forgotten."—*John N. Andrews, History of the Sabbath, chapter 27.*

It was to keep this truth ever before the minds of men, that God instituted the Sabbath in Eden; and so long as the fact that He is our Creator continues to be a reason why we should worship Him, so long the Sabbath will continue as its sign and memorial. The keeping of the Sabbath will ever be a sign of loyalty to the true God.

So the message of the first angel of Revelation 14, is a call to return to the worship of the Creator. And without a full obedience, we cannot genuinely worship Him as He desires. (Rev 14:6-7)

But in contrast with those who keep the commandments of God and have the faith of Jesus, shown in Revelation 14:12, the third angel points to another class, against whose errors a solemn and fearful warning is uttered:

"If any man worship the beast and his image, and receive his mark in his forehead, or in his hand, the same shall drink of the wine of the wrath of God."—Revelation 14:9-10.

What do these symbols mean? What is the "beast," the "image," and the "mark"?

The line of prophecy in which these symbols are found begins with Revelation 12, with the dragon that sought to destroy Christ at His birth. The dragon is said to be Satan (Rev 12:9), for he it was that urged men to put the Saviour to death. But the chief agent of Satan in making war upon Christ and His people during the first centuries of the Christian era was the Roman empire, in which paganism was the prevailing religion. Thus while the dragon primarily represents Satan, it is, in a secondary sense, a symbol of pagan Rome.

In Revelation 13:1-10 is described another beast, "like unto a leopard," to which the dragon gave "his power, and his seat, and great authority" (Rev 13:11). Down through history, most Protestants have recognized this power to be the papacy; an organization which succeeded to the power and seat and authority once held by the ancient Roman empire. Of this leopard-like beast it is declared:

"There was given unto him a mouth speaking great things and blasphemies . . And he opened his mouth in blasphemy against God, to blaspheme His name, and His tabernacle, and them that dwell in heaven. And it was given unto him to make war with the saints, and to overcome them: and power was given him over all kindreds, and tongues, and nations."—Revelation 13:5-7.

This prophecy, which is nearly identical with the description of the little horn of Daniel 7, unquestionably points to the papacy.

"Power was given unto him to continue forty and two months" (Rev 13:5). And, says the prophet, "I saw one of his heads as it were wounded to death" (Rev 13:3). And again, "He that leadeth into captivity shall go into captivity: he that killeth with the sword must be killed with the sword" (Rev 13:10). The forty and two months are the same as the "time and times and the dividing of time," three years and a half, or

1260 days, of Daniel 7:25 and Revelation 12:6. This was the time during which the papal power would so greatly oppress the people of God. This time-span began with the supremacy of the papacy in A.D. 538, and terminated in 1798. At that time, the pope was made captive by the French army, the papal power received its deadly wound, and the prediction was fulfilled, "He that leadeth into captivity shall go into captivity."

At this point in the chapter, another symbol is introduced. Says the prophet, "I beheld another beast coming up out of the earth; and he had two horns like a lamb" (Rev 13:11). Both the appearance of this beast and the manner of its rise indicate that the nation which it represents is unlike those presented under the preceding symbols. The great kingdoms that have ruled the world were presented to the prophet Daniel as beasts of prey, rising when the "four winds of the heaven strove upon the great sea" (Dan 7:2). In Revelation 17:15, an angel explained that waters represent "peoples, and multitudes, and nations, and tongues." Winds are a symbol of strife. The four winds of heaven striving upon the great sea, represent the terrible scenes of conquest and revolution by which the kingdoms have attained to power.

But the beast with lamb-like horns was seen "coming up out of the earth" (Rev 13:11). Instead of overthrowing other powers to establish itself, the nation thus represented must arise in territory previously unoccupied, and grow up gradually and peacefully. It could not arise among the crowded and struggling nationalities of the Old World. It had to come up in the west.

What nation of the New World was in 1798 rising into power, giving promise of strength and greatness, and attracting the attention of the world? One nation, and only one, meets the specifications of this prophecy: the United States of America.

But the beast with lamb-like horns "spake as a dragon. And he exerciseth all the power of the first beast before him, and causeth the earth and them which dwell therein to worship the first beast, whose deadly wound was healed; and . .

saying to them that dwell on the earth, that they should make an image to the beast, which had the wound by a sword and did live" (Rev 13:11-14).

The lamb-like horns and the later dragon voice are in strong contrast. This plainly foretells a development of the spirit of intolerance and persecution that was manifested by the nations represented by the dragon and the leopard-like beast. And the statement that the beast with two horns "causeth the earth and them which dwell therein to worship the first beast," indicates that the authority of this nation is to be exercised in enforcing some observance which shall be an act of homage to the papacy.

Yet such action would be directly contrary to the principles of this government, to the genius of its free institutions, to the direct and solemn avowals of the Declaration of Independence, and to the Constitution. The founders of the nation wisely sought to guard against the employment of secular power on the part of the church, with its inevitable result—intolerance and persecution. The Constitution provides that "Congress shall make no law respecting an establishment of religion, or prohibiting the free exercise thereof," and that "no religious test shall ever be required as a qualification to any office of public trust under the United States." Only in flagrant violation of these safeguards to the nation's liberty, can any religious observance be enforced by civil power.

And an image of the first beast is to be made by this power: "Saying to them that dwell on the earth, that they should make an image to the beast" (Rev 13:14). "They." The legislative power rests with the people in this lamb-like beast. But what is the "image to the beast"? and how is it to be formed? This image, made by the two-horned beast, is an image to the first beast. It is also called an image of that beast.

To understand what the image is like, we must study the characteristics of the first beast—the papacy.

When the early church became corrupted by departing from the simplicity of the gospel and accepting heathen rites and customs, she lost the Spirit and power of God. And then, in order to control the consciences of the people, she sought the support of secular governments. The result was the papacy.

The papacy: a church that for over a thousand years controlled the power of the state, and employed it to further her own ends, especially for the punishment of "heresy,"—and brought darkness and misery to people everywhere.

In order for the image to be formed, the religious power must so control the civil government that the authority of the state will also be used by the church to enforce specific religious observances.

In centuries past, whenever the church has obtained secular power, she has employed it to punish dissent from her doctrines. Rome did it for hundreds of years. Protestant churches in Europe and England did it for long periods of time also. For example, during the sixteenth and seventeenth centuries, thousands of non-conformist ministers were forced to leave their churches, and many, both of pastors and people, were subjected to fine, imprisonment, torture, and martyrdom.

It was apostasy that led the early church to seek the aid of the civil government, and this prepared the way for the development of the papacy. Paul predicted it in 2 Thessalonians 2:3. And 2 Timothy 3:1-5 foretells that this union of church and state will occur again in the last days.

The wide diversity of belief in the Protestant churches is regarded by many as decisive proof that no effort to secure a forced uniformity can ever be made. But for years, there has been a growing sentiment to unite on common points of belief. Yet when this shall be done, the next step will be a movement to require compliance to the new faith by everyone. And this will lead to the use of force to gain it.

Thus, according to Bible prophecy, when the leading churches of the United States, uniting upon such points of doctrine as are held by them in common, shall influence the state to enforce their decrees and to sustain their institutions, then Protestant America will have formed an image of the Roman hierarchy, and the infliction of civil penalties upon dissenters will inevitably result.

The two-horned beast will cause men to receive the

Mark.

"And he causeth [commandeth] all, both small and great, rich and poor, free and bond, to receive a mark in their right hand, or in their foreheads. And that no man might buy or sell, save he that had the mark, or the name of the beast, or the number of his name."—Revelation 13:16-17.

In the next chapter, the third angel has a warning that goes together with the warning you have just read.

"If any man worship the beast and his image, and receive his mark in his forehead, or in his hand, the same shall drink of the wine of the wrath of God."—Revelation 14:9-10.

The "beast" mentioned in this message, whose worship is enforced by the two-horned beast, is the first, or leopard-like beast of Revelation 13,—the papacy. The "image to the beast" is the religion that shall be developed when the churches shall seek the aid of the civil power for the enforcement of their doctrines.

But what is "the mark of the beast"?

After the warning against the worship of the beast and his image, and his mark, the prophecy declares: "Here are they that keep the commandments of God, and the faith of Jesus" (Rev 14:12). Those who keep God's commandments are thus placed in contrast with those that worship the beast and his image and receive his mark. So the point of distinction between the two classes will be the keeping of God's law, on one hand, and a required refusal to keep it, on the other.

The special characteristic of the beast, and therefore of his image, is the breaking of God's commandments. Says Daniel, of the little horn, the papacy: "He shall think to change times and the law" (Dan 7:25, R.V.). Paul called this same apostate power the "man of sin" who was to try and exalt himself above God. These prophecies go together, for only by changing God's law could the papacy exalt itself above God. And whoever should understandingly keep the law as thus changed would be giving supreme honor to that power by which the change was made. Such an act of obedience to papal laws would be a mark of allegiance to the pope in the place of God.

In the coming crisis, the worshipers of God will be especially distinguished by their regard for the fourth commandment, for this is the sign of His creative power, and the witness to His claim upon man's reverence and homage.

But at the same time, the worshipers of the beast will be distinguished by their efforts to tear down the Creator's memorial, to exalt the institution of Rome. It was in behalf of the Sunday that popery first asserted its arrogant claims, and its first resort to the power of the state was to compel the observance of Sunday.

The claim so often put forth, that Christ changed the Sabbath, is disproved by His own words (Matthew 5:17-19). Indeed, it is a fact generally admitted by Protestants, that the Scriptures give no authority for the change of the Sabbath. We have already seen this. And we have observed that Roman Catholics acknowledge that the change of the Sabbath was made by their church, and declare that Protestants, by observing the Sunday, are recognizing her power.

As the sign of the authority of the Catholic Church, papist writers cite "the very act of changing the Sabbath into Sunday, which Protestants allow of; . . because by keeping Sunday, they acknowledge the church's power to ordain feasts, and to command them under sin."—Henry Tuberville, "An Abridgement of the Christian Doctrine," p. 58.

What then is the change of the Sabbath but the sign, or mark, of the authority of the Roman Church—"the mark of the beast"?

The Roman Church has not relinquished her claim to supremacy; and when the world and the Protestant churches accept a sabbath of her creating, while they reject the Bible Sabbath, they virtually admit this assumption. Romanists declare that "the observance of Sunday by the Protestants is an homage they pay, in spite of themselves, to the authority of the [Catholic] Church."—"Plain Talk about Protestantism," p. 213. The enforcement of Sunday-keeping on the part of Protestant churches is an enforcement of the worship of the papacy—of the beast. Those who, understanding the claims of the fourth commandment, choose to observe the false instead of the true Sabbath, are thereby paying homage to that power by which alone it is commanded.

But in the very act of enforcing a religious duty by secular power, the churches would themselves form an image to the beast; hence a national enforcement of Sunday-keeping in the United States would be an enforcement of the worship of the beast and his image.

But Christians of past generations observed the Sunday, supposing that in so doing they were keeping the Bible Sabbath; and there are now true Christians in every church, not excepting the Roman Catholic communion, who honestly believe that Sunday is the Sabbath given by God. Heaven accepts their sincerity of purpose. But when Sunday observance shall be enforced by law, and the world shall be enlightened concerning the obligation of the true Sabbath, then whoever shall transgress the command of God, to obey a precept which has no higher authority than that of Rome,—will thereby honor popery above God. He is paying homage to Rome, and to the power which enforces the institution ordained by Rome. He is worshiping the beast and his image.

As men then reject the institution which God has declared to be the sign of His authority, and honor in its stead that which Rome has chosen as the token of her supremacy, they will thereby accept the sign of allegiance to Rome—"the mark of the beast." Thus it is not until the issue is thus plainly set before the people, and they are brought to choose between the commandments of God and the commandments of men, that those who continue in transgression will receive "the mark of the beast."

The most fearful threat ever addressed to mortals is contained in the third angel's message of Revelation 14: 9-12. That must be a terrible sin which calls down the wrath of God unmingled with mercy. Men are not to be left in darkness concerning this important matter. The warning against this sin is to be given to the world before the final visitation of God's judgments. Prophecy declares that the first angel will make his announcement to "every nation, and kindred, and tongue, and people" (Rev 14:6). The warning of the third angel, which forms a part of the same threefold message, is to be no less wide-spread. It is represented in the prophecy as being proclaimed with a loud voice, by an angel flying in the midst of heaven; and it will command the attention of the world.

In the issue of the contest, all Christendom will be divided into two great classes,—those who keep the commandments of God and the faith of Jesus, and those who worship the beast and his image and receive his mark. Although church and state will unite their power to compel "all, both small and great, rich and poor, free and bond," to receive "the mark of the beast" (Rev 13:16), yet the people of God will not receive it. The prophet John in vision beheld "them that had gotten the victory over the beast, and over his image, and over his mark, and over the number of his name, stand on the sea of glass, having the harps of God," and singing the song of Moses and the Lamb" (Rev 15:2-3).

[Note: pages 140:2-150:1 of this book were condensed from "The Great Controversy," pages 434-450.]

But we are not yet on the sea of glass. Before us in the battle; later the crown. We have seen that the issues are clear in the Bible. And they are clear in history as well. The Seventh day is the Sabbath—for God never changed it.

A number of years ago, a farmer sent a letter to the pope, inquiring about the Bible Sabbath. The letter was sent on to Chicago for reply. Here are both letters:

Thomaston, Georgia
May 22, 1934

Pope Pius XI
Rome, Italy
Dear Sir:

Is the accusation true, that Protestants accuse you of? They say you changed the Seventh Day Sabbath to the, so-called, Christian Sunday: identical with the First-Day of the Week. If so when did you make the change, and by what authority.

Yours very truly,
(Signed)
J.L. Day

Extension Magazine
Published by
The Catholic Church Extension Society
of the United States of America
180 North Wabash Avenue
Chicago

Dear Sir:

Regarding the change from the observance of the Jewish Sabbath to the Christian Sunday, I wish to draw your attention to the facts:

(1) That Protestants, who accept the Bible as the only rule of faith and religion, should by all means go back to the observance of the Sabbath. The fact that they do not, but on the contrary observe the Sunday, stultifies them in the eyes of every thinking man.

(2) We Catholics do not accept the Bible as the only authority of the Church, as a rule to guide us. We say, this Church instituted by Christ, to teach and guide man through life, has the right to change the Ceremonial laws of the Old Testament and hence, we accept the change of the Sabbath to the Sunday. We frankly say, "Yes, the Church made this change, made this law, as she made many other laws, for instance, the Friday Abstinence, the unmarried priesthood, the laws concerning mixed marriages, the regulation of Catholic marriages, and a thousand other laws."

(3) We also say that of all Protestants, the Seventh-day Adventists are the only group that reason correctly and are consistent with their teachings. It is always somewhat laughable to see the Protestant Churches, in pulpit and legislature, demand the observance of Sunday, of which there is nothing in the Bible.

With best wishes,
Peter R. Tramer, Editor

By Rome's own statement, very few people are keeping the right day holy—for only a few are keeping God's Bible Sabbath. What we are told about this is important:

"The Church changed the observance of the Sabbath to Sunday by right of the divine, infallible authority given to her by her founder, Jesus Christ. The Protestant claiming the Bible to be the only guide of faith, has no warrant for observing Sunday. In this matter the Seventh-day Adventist is the only consistent Protestant."—*The Catholic Universe Bulletin, August 14, 1942, p. 4 [This is the official weekly newspaper of the Cleveland Catholic Diocese]*.

"Ques. —(a) The Bible says, 'The seventh day is the Sabbath of the Lord,' and we read in your literature that it is the only Bible Sabbath there is. Will you please explain how the Sunday observance originated? (b) Do you think the Seventh-day Adventists keep the right day?

Ans. —"If you follow the Bible alone there can be no question that you are obliged to keep Saturday holy, since that is the day especially prescribed by Almighty God to be kept holy to the Lord. In keeping Sunday, non-Catholics are simply following the practise of the Catholic Church for 1800 years, a tradition, and not a Bible ordinance. What we would like to know is: Since they deny the authority of the Church, on what grounds can they base their faith of keeping Sunday. Those who keep Saturday, like the Seventh-day Adventists, unquestionably have them by the hip in this practise. And they cannot give them any sufficient answer which would satisfy an unprejudiced mind. With the Catholic there is no difficulty about the matter. For, since we deny that the Bible is the sole rule of faith, we can fall back upon the constant practise and tradition of the Church."—*Francis George Lentz, The Question Box, 1900, p. 98-99 [Lentz, who died in 1917, was an Illinois Catholic priest]*.

"Ques. —What Bible authority is there for changing the Sabbath from the seventh to the first day of the week? Who gave the Pope the authority to change a command of God?

"Ans. —If the Bible is the only guide for the Christian, then the Seventh-day Adventist is right, in observing the Saturday with the Jew . . Is it not strange that those who make the Bible their only teacher, should inconsistently follow in this matter the tradition of the Catholic Church?"—*Bertrand Conway, The Question Box, 1903 ed., pp. 254-255; 1915 ed., p. 179 [Conway (1872-1959) was a Paulist father in the Catholic Church]*.

"The Adventists are the only body of Christians with the Bible as their teacher, who can find no warrant in its pages for the change of day from the seventh to the first . . Reason and common sense demand the acceptance of one or the other of these alternatives: either Protestantism and the keeping holy of Saturday, or Catholicity and the keeping holy of Sunday. Compromise is impossible."—*Catholic Mirror, September 2, and 23, 1893. [The Catholic Mirror, a Baltimore journal that was then the official organ of Cardinal Gibbons.]*

So now we can see it clearly: The attempt of the Roman Catholic Church to change the Sabbath of the Creator—to another day—is the MARK of her authority. It is the MARK of the beast. For it decides whom you will worship:

"Sunday is our MARK of authority! .. The Church is above the Bible, and this transference of sabbath observance is proof of that fact."—*The Catholic Record, London, Ontario, Canada, September 1, 1923.*

"Prove to me from the Bible alone that I am bound to keep Sunday holy. There is no such law in the Bible. It is a law of the holy Catholic Church alone. The Bible says 'Remember the Sabbath day to keep it holy.' The Catholic Church says, No. By my divine power I abolish the Sabbath day and command you to keep holy the first day of the week. And lo! The entire civilized world bows down in reverent obedience to the command of the Holy Catholic Church."—*Priest Thomas Enright, CSSR, President of Redemptorist College, Kansas City, Mo., in a lecture at Hartford, Kansas, February 18, 1884, and printed in the Hartford Kansas Weekly Call, February 22, 1884, and the American Sentinel, a New York Roman Catholic journal in June 1893, page 173.*

Of course the Catholic Church claims that the change was her act .. AND THE ACT IS A MARK of her ecclesiastical power."—*from the office of Cardinal Gibbons, through Chancellor H.F. Thomas, November 11, 1895.*

Today the Bible Sabbath is the great test of loyalty. But soon Jesus will return for His own, and the trials of life will be a thing of the past.

And so we have now come full circle. We started at Pitcairn Island and learned of a people who found that the Bible was the only solution to their lives. And then, gradually over the years, they studied into it more and more deeply, until they came to the Sabbath truth.

The people of Pitcairn were only humble farmers in the middle of the ocean, but they held the Bible above all else. And it gave them a happy way of life as they studied it and made its truths their own. The traditions of Europe were far distant from their home and they were ready to accept the Bible just as it was written. And the high level of peace and morality that it brought them is a marvel to the world.

The Pitcairners carefully studied the Sabbath truth from their Bibles. But in this book we have traveled over large sections of the world in order to verify what they there learned. We have gone back and back, farther and farther into history, and into the most distant past.

And that which we have found has verified to us that the humble folk of Pitcairn were indeed on the right track. All that they had were their Bibles to prove the truth of the Sabbath. We have had that and more—history and astronomy, ancient and modern records, the testimony of church leaders and scientists.

And now we have solved the mystery of Pitcairn. For we know for ourselves that their discovery was correct.

Shortly after Thursday October Christian II (Thursday's son), the leader of the island at the time, and Simon Young, the beloved leader of the church, accepted this truth in October of 1886, the entire island accepted it also.

And so it was that within a few days the church bell was no longer tolling on Sunday, but on Saturday—the Bible Sabbath—calling the people to worship.

Would you like to live with the Pitcairn Islanders? You may not be able to live with them on their little island, but you can worship with them from week to week. Come and worship your Creator on His day—the day He gave us at the Creation of this world, the day He confirmed repeatedly throughout the Bible. Come and worship with your friends, the people with the faith of the Pitcairners—the Seventh-day Adventists. For back in 1886, all on the island of Pitcairn united with the Seventh-day Adventist Church. They wanted to be one with other believers in the true Sabbath all over the world. And now you too may unite in the faith of the Pitcairners. The simple Bible religion of the Word of God is what you have been looking for. How thankful we can be that it is spread out before us in the Holy Scriptures, as we turn from page to page.

Today the Bible Sabbath is the great test of loyalty. We have seen that from our study of Daniel and Revelation. But soon Jesus will return for His own, and the trials of life will be a thing of the past. Oh, how we long for that day!

And how can we identify the remnant people of God in these last days? Bible prophecy explains it. Revelation 12 tells us about the persecutions of the true church from Christ's time on down to the end. And the final verse in this chapter describes our own time, just before Jesus returns:

"**And the dragon was wroth with the woman, and went to make war with the remnant of her seed, which keep the commandments of God, and have the testimony of Jesus Christ.**"—Revelation 12:17.

The remnant—the last end—of the true church before time ends, will be keeping the commandments of God by the grace of Christ! Thank God for Scripture! It tells us the way to go as we seek to pattern our lives in harmony with God's will. But we are told more. In Revelation 14, at the conclusion of the three angels' messages, we are again told what the faithful people of God will be like in the last days, just before the return of Christ in the clouds of heaven for His own:

"**Here is the patience of the saints: here are they that keep the commandments of God, and the faith of Jesus.**"—Revelation 14:12.

It is by faith in Christ that we are enabled to obey His written Word. It is through His strengthening grace that we can obey all ten of His Commandments. Revelation 14:12 describes God's little ones down at the end of time. Two verses later, we are shown the Second Advent of Christ Himself:

"**And I looked, and behold a white cloud, and upon the cloud one sat like unto the Son of man, having on His head a golden crown, and in His hand a sharp sickle.**"—Revelation 14:14.

And then Jesus will call His faithful ones to meet with Him in the clouds.

"**For the Lord Himself shall descend from heaven with a shout, with the voice of the archangel, and with the trump of God: and the dead in Christ shall rise first.**

"**Then we which are alive and remain shall be caught up together with them in the clouds, to meet the Lord in the air: and so shall we ever be with the Lord.**"—1 Thessalonians 4:16-17.

Then Jesus will take His little ones to heaven and as they stand on the sea of glass, He will open to them the gates of the city. His children who on earth have obeyed His Word will enter into the glorious City of God.

"**Blessed are they that do His commandments, that they**

may have right to the tree of life, and may enter in through the gates into the city."—Revelation 22:14.

Thus through all eternity to come, the meek and lowly, who so carefully followed the example of their Master on earth, will witness to the glory of His salvation to millions of worlds throughout the universe.

But amid the splendor and the happiness, from Sabbath to Sabbath they will gather to worship their Creator on His memorial day:

"For as the new heavens and the new earth, which I will make, shall remain before Me, saith the Lord, so shall your seed and your name remain.

"And it shall come to pass, that from one new moon to another, and from one Sabbath to another, shall all flesh come to worship before Me, saith the Lord."—Isaiah 66:22-23.

The sealed ones will bow before their Maker and worship and praise Him. The trials of earth are past, and now they sing to their God.

"And I saw as it were a sea of glass mingled with fire: and them that had gotten the victory over the beast, and over his image, and over his mark, and over the number of his name, stand on the sea of glass, having the harps of God.

"And they sing the song of Moses the servant of God, and the song of the Lamb, saying, Great and marvellous are Thy works, Lord God Almighty; just and true are Thy ways, Thou King of saints."—Revelation 15:2-3.

Come, let us prepare for this great event now. Having gone back—beyond Pitcairn—into the past, we now have time to prepare to go—beyond Pitcairn—into the future.

And the future will be bright for God's faithful ones who on earth learned to walk with Him by faith, and obey Him at the cost of all things. Here they suffered, obedient to His Word. But there they shall inherit all the promises.

God bless you. I want to meet you there.

—Vance Ferrell

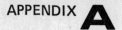

No Time Lost

The little town of Nazareth is located on the most southerly of the mountain ranges of southern Galilee. Quietly it lies nestled on the side of a shallow ridge that runs in a semicircle, somewhat like a horseshoe. Here among the dwellings and groves of this small town, Jesus grew to manhood.

But, just now, come back with me in imagination to that village, where so many years ago the Master walked among men. Another day is quietly dawning, as the early rising sun chases away the bright mists that hang over the slope of Nazareth. From the home of the carpenter, Jesus steps forth and walks to the little church in the center of town. It is Sabbath morning in Nazareth.

Oh, how much you and I would like to go to church with Jesus! And, perhaps more important—how much we would like to go to church on the same weekly Sabbath that He kept. What peace of heart this would bring to us! —to be able to keep the Sabbath of Jesus.

And, my friend, you and I can. For we know enough from Biblical, historical and other records, that we today can know of a certainty the Sabbath of Jesus.

For, you see, in order to trace back to the Sabbath of Jesus, we must know the truth about the weekly cycle itself. And here are the facts:

The seven-day week, as well as the Bible Sabbath that terminates it, had a common origin in history. Both originated at the Creation of our world. We learn this from Genesis 2:1-3. There is no other way of accounting for the existence of the week. It is a towering monument to the fact that the true God made the earth and all things therein in six days, and rested on the Seventh day, just as He tells us in Genesis 2:1-3. It is because of the seven-day Creation Week, and the Seventh-day Sabbath that concluded it, that mankind all over the world today keeps this weekly cycle of seven days.

The Weekly Cycle as we know it has been maintained from Creation without confusion or loss of days. God gave the Seventh-day Sabbath to mankind when He made all things in the beginning. "The Sabbath was made for man," Jesus said (Mark 2:27), and so it shall stand as true—for Jesus said it, and He is our Creator (John 1:1-3,10, Eph 3:9, Col 1:13-17, Heb 1:1-3), the One who made the Sabbath.

From time to time you will hear someone say, "The Weekly Cycle has been lost and so we cannot know the true Sabbath." But when pressed for the facts about this, his words are vague and confused.

The truth is that from the Bible and from the lives of men and races, scientists have an excellent understanding of the preservation of the Weekly Cycle throughout history. Even the records of the astronomers tell us that time has never been lost,—and if somehow that were to happen, now or earlier in history,—they could account exactly for any errors or losses of time in human history: they could restore the missing links in the Weekly Cycle. These are convincing facts, and they are true.

The unbroken continuation of the Weekly Cycle down through history can be established from Scripture, from history, and from science. First, let us consider the Biblical evidence:

If the Weekly Cycle had been lost between Adam's time (when the Sabbath was made) and Moses' day (when God put the Ten Commandments into written form), this situation would at that time have been corrected by the Divine Lawgiver.

A striking illustration of the importance that our God

attaches to Sabbathkeeping, is to be found in the miracle of the manna. For forty years, or 2,080 weeks, the Lord worked a number of miracles every week, thereby identifying the true Sabbath 2,080 times. We are told about this in Exodus 16.

God sent manna for the first five days of each week. That was a miracle. Then on the sixth day, He sent twice as much. Another miracle. And only that which fell on the sixth day could be kept over through the next day. Still another miracle. And then on the Seventh day, He sent none. It is very obvious that God wanted His people who knew about Him to keep the Bible Sabbath. And He worked miracles to help safeguard it. When, after all this evidence, some of them went ahead and broke the Sabbath, He clearly showed His will in the matter. Carefully read Exodus 16.

The great Moral Law of Ten Commandments had governed mankind since the days of Adam. But after the experience of the manna in Exodus 16, God wrote the Ten Commandments on solid rock—the most enduring thing there is. It was written on the most lasting substance in the world—something that would not pass away, in order to show us the enduring nature of that Law. And it is Heaven's plan that it also be written on our hearts,—that every day we may obey these ten precious promises of happiness.

If the Sabbath had been lost between Moses' time and Jesus' time (which it was not), we would have the example of the Saviour Himself to guide us as to the correctness of the weekly cycle—and the Seventh day.

Scripture tells us: "He that saith he abideth in Him ought himself also so to walk, even as He walked." 1 John 2:6. Throughout His earthly life, Jesus gave "us an example, that ye should follow His steps." 1 Peter 2:21.

We want to follow the steps of Jesus. We want to do as He did, with all our hearts! More than anything else in the whole wide world, this is what we want. I want it. And I know you want it also.

Jesus, "as His custom was," kept the Seventh-day Sabbath according to the commandment. (Luke 4:16,31; compare

John 15:10.) If time or the Sabbath had been lost, Jesus would have found it for His followers.

Jesus was crucified on the sixth day of the week which was the day before the Sabbath (Luke 23:54-56). On this same sixth day, which was also called the "preparation day" (Mark 15:42; Luke 23:54), His followers prepared "spices and ointments" to anoint His body for burial, and then "rested on the Sabbath day according to the commandment." Luke 23:56.

And then came the Seventh-day Sabbath, and Jesus rested in the tomb (Matt 28:1-7). The next day He arose. It was the first working day of the week, and Jesus had a lot of work to do. That morning, after speaking with Mary, He traveled all the way to heaven, and then that evening appeared to many of His disciples (John 20:17,19; Luke 24:13-36).

So it was that throughout the life and death of Jesus, He faithfully set us an example of obedience to the Sabbath commandment. And He taught His followers to do the same (Matt 24:20), for after His death, they kept the Sabbath also (Luke 23:56), and later in their missionary work (Ac 13:14-16, 40-46; 16:12-15; 17:1-4). They declared that we ought to obey God rather than men (Ac 5:29), and Paul could sincerely say of himself and his fellow believers: "Do we then make void the law through faith? God forbid: yea, we establish the law."—Romans 3:31. The Word of God was being fulfilled, that Gentiles would one day faithfully keep the Sabbath which the Jews were desecrating (Isa 56:3-7).

There is such a wealth of historical and other information available regarding the unchanged nature of the weekly cycle, that we may know without a doubt that there has been no alteration in it down through the ages.

We can know it from the writings of historians. It is given us in the records of chronographers, who trace it in their study of the calendars of yesteryear. It is revealed in the existence of ancient races and their witness today. It is proven by the languages of earth. It is testified to by the stars of heaven, and verified by the leading astronomers of our own time. It is written in the encyclopedias and other standard reference works that deal with the subject.

Has the Sabbath been lost since Jesus' day? Here are some of the ways that we can know for a certainty that the Seventh day of the week—right now—is the same Seventh day of the week as when Jesus was on earth and kept it holy as an example for us:

1—THE CALENDAR

The Julian calendar was in use when Jesus Christ was upon the earth. Its originator, Julius Caesar, died 44 years before Christ was born. This calendar which continued in use for fifteen centuries was not accurate in the length of its year, for it was 11 minutes, 14 seconds too long. What was needed was our method of "leap years." By 1582 the vernal equinox of March 21 had receded to March 11, making it ten days off schedule.

A change was recommended by astronomers and made at the time that Gregory XIII was the pope, and so the corrected calendar with its "leap year" was called the Gregorian calendar. It began to function on Friday, the 5th of October, 1582. Friday the 5th was changed to Friday the 15th. So that particular month was ten days shorter—but the length of its weeks was not affected. This is due to the simple fact that the number of days in the month or in the year has nothing to do with the number of days in the week. Thus the weekly cycle was not affected in any way.

On a diagram on the next page we will give the calendar change that took place in October, 1582.

The inhabitants of Spain who retired to sleep on Thursday, October 4, awoke the next morning on Friday, the 15th. Some nations began the use of the new calendar at once. This included Spain, Portugal and Italy. Part of Germany made the changeover in 1583 and the rest of the nation waited until 1700. About that time the Netherlands, Sweden and Denmark also accepted it. And then, finally, in 1752, England and the American colonies made the changeover. But all during those years with mixed-up calendars—everyone was on the

THE LATIN CHANGE-OVER	THE ENGLISH CHANGE-OVER
1582	1752

		SEPTEMBER								AUGUST			
						1							1
2	3	4	5	6	7	8	2	3	4	5	6	7	8
9	10	11	12	13	14	15	9	10	11	12	13	14	15
16	17	18	19	20	21	22	16	17	18	19	20	21	22
23	24	25	26	27	28	29	23	24	25	26	27	28	29
30							30	31					

		OCTOBER							SEPTEMBER				
	1	2	3	4	15	16			1	2	14	15	16
17	18	19	20	21	22	23	17	18	19	20	21	22	23
24	25	26	27	28	29	30	24	25	26	27	28	29	30
31													

		NOVEMBER							OCTOBER				
	1	2	3	4	5	6	1	2	3	4	5	6	7
7	8	9	10	11	12	13	8	9	10	11	12	13	14
14	15	16	17	18	19	20	15	16	17	18	19	20	21
21	22	23	24	25	26	27	22	23	24	25	26	27	28
28	29	30					29	30	31				

In October 1582, Portugal, Spain and Italy began the use of this new calendar which included leap years.

This meant that for these three nations of Europe, the year 1582 was ten days shorter than the calendar of the other nations of Europe.

But all during this year, and in the years before and afterward, the weekly cycle never changed as nation after nation gradually changed over to the new calendar.

In September 1752, England finally made the change-over to the new leap year calendar.

This meant that for this important nation of Europe, the year 1752 was eleven days shorter than the calendar of the other nations.

But all during this year, and in the years before and afterward, the weekly cycle never changed as nation after nation gradually changed over to the new calendar.

Between 1582 and 1752—and down to 1919,—all the nations of Europe gradually changed to the new calendar. But all during these 337 years—everyone had the very same days of the week.

same weekly cycle. For, as you will see from the calendars we have included, the weekly cycle was not changed.

By the time England made the changover to the new calendar, eleven days had to be changed instead of ten. Wednesday, September 2 was followed by Thursday, September 14. Russia and Greece continued to use the old-style calendar—the Julian Calendar—for over a hundred and fifty more years! Finally, in 1917 (Turkey), 1918 (Russia), 1919 (Serbia), and 1923 (Greece)—the last modern nations had adopted it! 341 years had elapsed since the changeover began.

For 337 years the calendars of Europe were all mixed up, and the dates of the months varied from country to country. But all during that time the days of the week were alike, for they had not changed. When it was Monday in Russia it was Monday in Germany, England and Italy—although they were all living under different calendars. When the 20th Century began, Sabbath in Russia was the same as Sabbath in England—although the dates were fourteen days apart.

The Encyclopedia Britannica calls it the "unalterable uniformity of the week," for the Weekly Cycle has never been affected by calendar changes.

And because of this, the seven-day week, given by God to mankind at the Creation of the world, has never been touched by the calendar changes down through the centuries.

How many ways may we know that the Weekly Cycle— and with it, the Sabbath cycle—has never been changed? Let us count some more ways:

2—THE JEWISH RACE

Our heavenly Father has given us more than written proof of the permanence of the Weekly Cycle and the Seventh-day Sabbath,—He has given us living proof: The Jewish race.

Every other Near-eastern ethnic group has disappeared: the Hittites, the Sumarians, the Babylonians, the Assyrians, the Moabites, the Philistines—all are gone. But the Jews remain—and with them the Seventh-day Sabbath.

It has been 3400 years since the time that God gave them manna in the wilderness and told them to carefully keep each Seventh-day Sabbath when no manna fell. But all during those long centuries since then, they have observed God's Sabbath, week after week, month after month, year after year, century after century.

Ask any Jewish acquaintance what day is the Sabbath. He will tell you that it is Saturday—the Seventh day.

Orthodox Jews scattered throughout the world have kept strict record of time. They have carefully observed the Seventh-day Sabbath throughout the ages. The existence and testimony of the Jewish race is alone enough to settle the matter. The present writer considers it the most amazing and conclusive means of knowing the ancient Sabbath of Jesus and earlier times. There is no doubt that the God of heaven has carefully guarded the day that He sanctified and blessed at Creation. We have no excuse for not keeping it holy as He commanded.

But, since the time when Christ walked on earth and kept the correct Bible Sabbath, there have been others who have provided living proof also.

3—PROTESTANTS AND CATHOLICS

Several years ago a young man was puzzled. What he read in his Bible did not agree with what the churches were doing. After the worship service one Sunday, he asked if he could speak with his pastor for a moment.

Going aside, he said, Dr. ___, the Bible says to worship God on the seventh day of the week; why do we not do this?"

Quickly the answer came back, "Oh, it doesn't matter, for time has been lost and we cannot know which day was the seventh day of the week in the time of Christ."

"But why, then," said the young man, "do we keep the first day of the week holy today?"

"Oh, you see, we keep the first day of the week holy because Jesus rose on that day, and we know what day of the week He rose on."

The young man walked away and began keeping the Bible Sabbath commanded by God. It was obvious to him that the pastor was only giving excuses for disobedience.

The learned minister had told him that we cannot keep the Seventh-day Sabbath because we do not know what day of the week is the seventh day on which Christ kept the Sabbath 2,000 years ago. And then he added that we must keep the first day of the week holy today—because we know what day was the first day in the time of Christ!

From Christ's time down to our own, there have been faithful Sabbathkeepers who have kept the Seventh-day Sabbath. And there were also worldly Christians who at an early time adopted the holy day of Mithra, the Sun-god, to worship Christ.

The fact is that not only have Jews and Christians kept the Seventh-day Sabbath for the past two thousand years, but Sundaykeepers have also preserved the knowledge of which day is which—all during that same time.

Two facts are indisputable: 1—We KNOW that Jesus Christ kept the right day of the week as the holy Bible Sabbath, and He is our example in all things. 2—We KNOW that the Seventh day of the week now is the same day that Christ observed while here on earth.

4—HISTORICAL AND SCIENTIFIC RECORDS

The Roman Catholic Church has kept an accurate record of time, as down through the centuries they kept the rest day their leaders invented—Sunday.

The majority of Protestants also keep Sunday, not having understood at the time of the Great Reformation that this was but a Catholic institution.

Historians have amassed an immense record of human events going back thousands of years. Those records tell us of people keeping the seventh day holy far back in recorded history.

Astronomers have kept an accurate record of time. And theirs is one of the most accurate that you will find anywhere.

They tell us that if all records of time should suddenly be lost, the astronomers could rediscover time from the mathematics of the stars in their motions. God put the stars in the heavens "for signs, and for seasons, and for days and years." Genesis 1:14.

And then we have the calendars themselves. All calendars agree. There is no evidence whatsoever to support the false claim that "time has been lost."

And lastly, the standard reference works all tell us the same thing: No time has been lost in the weekly cycle. An example of this conclusive agreement is to be found in all of the major encyclopedias.

5—THE LANGUAGES OF MAN

A young Yugoslav immigrant had recently entered the United States. One evening he found himself in front of a church. Quietly sitting down he listened attentively, and afterward went up to the minister and in broken English said:

"Sir, please to answer my question. This a question I have already to asked my bishop in Yugoslavia. But he laugh. And I need for you to answer.

"In my country, Saturday is called 'Subota.' In Exodus 20th in Yugoslav Bible, the commandment says, 'The seventh day is Subota.' Then at calendar I look. It says Subota is the last day of week—your Saturday.

"Now, Sir, why my bishop tell me attend church on the first day of the week instead of on Subota?"

Fortunately, this young man was speaking to an unusual pastor, one that had earlier discovered this wonderful Biblical truth for himself. In reply, the pastor told him:

"This is an important question, but I will not laugh. I will answer your question with what God says about this. Listen carefully, for it is always dark if you close your eyes. Light is good from the lamp, but God's Word is the brightest lamp in all the world. Let us see what the Bible says."

All through this book you have been reading the kind of things that young man learned that evening.

Few of us realize that not only in the Yugoslav language —but in more than 160 of the languages of mankind—the name for the seventh day of the week (the day we call Saturday)—is "Sabbath."

In Polish it is "Sobota," in Arabic it is "As'sabt," in Russian "Subbata," in Spanish "Sabbado," in Persian "Shambin," in Bulgarian "Shubbuta," in Greek "Sabbaton," in Portuguese "Sabbado," in Hindustani "Shamba," in French "Sabbat," in Hebrew "Shabbath," in Italian "Sabbato," in Latin

"Sabbatum." And on and on it goes—through more than one hundred and sixty of the major languages of the earth.

This is because in ancient times, men knew that the true Sabbath fell on the Seventh day of the week. As an example of this, look in a Spanish dictionary and you will find that the word "Sabbado" comes through the Latin word "Sabbatum" from the ancient Hebrew word for "Sabbath."

All over the world men can know what day is the true Sabbath of ancient times. For the day has never changed, just as God has not changed.

Dr. William Mead Jones was a noted London research scholar. He was also something of a linguist. One of his many unusual accomplishments was his "Chart of the Week." From the information given on this chart, it is obvious that the Seventh-day Sabbath was known from the most ancient times.

On this chart are listed the names of the days of the week in 160 ancient and modern languages—and in 108 of these 160 languages the Seventh day is called "the Sabbath."

In every case, the Sabbath is the word used in each of those languages for the seventh day of the week. And the root meaning of the word in each language is "the Sabbath," or "rest day." In a paragraph just before this, we quoted from more than ten of these languages, showing how in each instance the Seventh day is "the Sabbath."

All over the Arab world of the Near East, it is the same, also:

"The only time reckoning on which Christians, Moslems, and Jews agree in the Orient is that of the days of the week. These are numbered and called by their numbers, save [except for] Friday and Saturday, which are known [in Arabic] as 'the day of assembling,' and the 'day of the Sabbath.' "—*Samuel M. Zwemer, D.D., "An Egyptian Government Almanac," quoted in The United Presbyterian, September 26, 1929. [Dr. Zwemer, long known as an authority on Mohammedanism, was for some years a professor at Princeton University.]*

Whether it be called "Sab" in Maba (a central African dialect), or "Subota" in Russian (an eastern European sub-language),—the Sabbath is the day of rest in a large number of the languages of mankind all over the globe.

What an overwhelming array of evidence has been provided for us in these last days that there may be no question that the Seventh-day Sabbath IS the Sabbath, for God never changed it.

6—SCIENTISTS AND HISTORIANS SPEAK

"Seven has been the ancient and honored number among the nations of the earth. They have measured their time by weeks from the beginning. The origin of this was the Sabbath of God, as Moses has given the reasons for it in his writings."— *Dr. Lyman Coleman, Statement.*

"One of the most striking collateral confirmations of the Mosaic history of the creation is the general adoption of the division of time into weeks, which extends from the Christian states of Europe to the remote shores of Hindustan, and has equally prevailed among the Hebrews, Egyptians, Chinese, Greeks, Romans, and northern Barbarians,—nations some of whom had little or no communication with others, and were not even known by name to the Hebrews."—*Horne's Introduction, Volume 1, page 69.*

In the official League of Nations "Report on the Reform of the Calendar," published at Geneva, August 17, 1926, are the following representative statements by noted astronomers:

"The week has been followed for thousands of years and therefore has been hallowed by immemorial use."—*Anders Donner, "The Report," p. 51. [Donner had been a Professor of Astronomy at the University of Helsingfors.]*

"I have always hesitated to suggest breaking the continuity of the week, which without a doubt is the most ancient scientific institution bequeathed to us by antiquity."—*Edouard Baillaud, "The Report, p. 52. [Baillaud was Director of the Paris Observatory.]*

Here are a number of other statements by eminent scientists and historians:

"The week is a period of seven days . . It has been employed from time immemorial in almost all Eastern countries."—*The Encyclopedia Britannica, 11th edition, Volume 4, p. 988, article, "Calendar."*

"As to Question (1)—I can only state that in connection with the proposed simplification of the calendar, we have had occasion to investigate the results of the works of specialists in chronology and we have never found one of them that has ever had the slightest doubt about the continuity of the weekly cycle since long before the Christian era.

"As to Question (2)—There has been no change in our calendar in past centuries that has affected in any way the cycle of the week."—*James Robertson, personal letter, dated March 12, 1932. [Dr. Robertson was Director of the American Ephemeris, Navy Department, U.S. Naval Observatory, Washington, D.C.]*

"As far as I know, in the various changes of the Calendar there has been no change in the seven day rota of the week, which has come down from very early times."—*F.W. Dyson, Personal letter, dated March 4, 1932. [Dr. Dyson was Astronomer Royal, Royal Observatory, Greenwich, London.]*

"Some of these (the Jews and also many Christians) accept the week as of divine institution, with which it is unlawful to tamper; others, without these scruples, still feel that it is useful to maintain a time-unit that, unlike all others, has proceeded in an absolutely invariable manner since what may be called the dawn of history."—*"Our Astronomical Column," Nature, London, number 127, June 6, 1931, p. 869.*

"The week of seven days has been in use ever since the days of the Mosaic dispensation, and we have no reason for supposing that any irregularities have existed in the succession of weeks and their days from that time to the present."—*Dr. W.W. Campbell, Statement. [Dr. Campbell was Director of Lick Observatory, Mt. Hamilton, California.]*

"For more than 3,000 years science has gone backward, and with profound research, reveals the fact that in that vast period the length of the day has not changed by the hundredth part of a single second of time."—*General O.M. Mitchell, Astronomy of the Bible, p. 235.*

"By calculating the eclipses, it can be proven that no time has been lost and that the creation days were seven, divided into twenty-four hours each."—*Dr. Hinckley, The Watchman, July, 1926. [Dr. Hinckley was a well-known astronomer of half a century ago.]*

"In spite of all of our dickerings with the calendar, it is patent that the human race never lost the septenary [seven-day] sequence of week days and that the Sabbath of these latter times comes down to us from Adam, through the ages, without a single lapse."—*Dr. Totten, Statement. [Dr. Totten of New Haven, Connecticut, was Professor of Astronomy at Yale University when this statement was made.]*

"The continuity of the week has crossed the centuries and all known calendars,—still intact."—*Professor D. Eginitis, Statement. [Dr. Eginitis was Director of the Observatory of Athens, Greece.]*

"It is a strange fact that even today there is a great deal of confusion concerning the question of so-called 'lost time.' Alterations that have been made to the calendar in the past have left the impression that time has actually been lost. In point of fact, of course, these adjustments were made to bring the calendar into closer agreement with the natural [solar] year. Now, unfortunately, this supposed 'lost time' is still being used to throw doubt upon the unbroken cycle of the Seventh-day Sabbath that God inaugurated at the Creation. I am glad I can add the witness of my scientific training to the irrevocable nature of the weekly cycle.

"Having been time computer at Greenwich [England observatory] for many years, I can testify .. that all our days are in God's absolute control—relentlessly measured by the daily rotation of the earth on its axis. This daily period of rotation does not vary one-thousandth part of a second in thousands of years. Also .. the year is a very definite number of days. Consequently, it can be said that not a day has been lost since Creation, and all the calendar changes notwithstanding, there has been no break in the weekly cycle."—*Frank Jeffries, Statement. [Dr. Jeffries was Fellow of the Royal Astronomical Society, and Research Director of the Royal Observatory, Greenwich, England.]*

We will conclude this chapter with an interesting historical analysis published by the Presbyterian Church:

"The division of time into weeks .. [is a] singular measure of time by periods of seven days [that] may be traced not only through the sacred history before the era of Moses, but in all ancient civilizations of every era, many of which could not possibly have derived their notion from Moses .. Among the learned of Egypt, the Brahmans of India, by Arabs, by Assyrians, as may be gathered from their astronomers and priests, this division was recognized. Hesiod (900 B.C.) declares the seventh day is holy. And so also Homer and Callimachus. Even in the Saxon mythology, the division by weeks is prominent. Nay, even among the tribes of primitive worshipers in Africa, we are told that a peculiar feature of their religion is a weekly sacred day, the violation of which by labor will incur the wrath of their god. Traces of a similar division of time have been noticed among the Indians of the American continent.

"Now, on what other theory are these facts explicable than upon the supposition of a divinely ordained Sabbath at the origin of the race?"—*"The Christian Sabbath," tract number 271, released by the Presbyterian Board of Publication.*

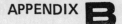

It Is Written

Facts, facts, and more facts. The Bible is full of facts about the true Sabbath,—and here they are:

1   Here are 60 FACTS about Sunday and the Bible Sabbath.
2   Here are 157 BIBLE PASSAGES—every important verse in the Bible.

Here is the information you have always wanted. Here are the Scriptural facts about the Bible Sabbath and Sunday.

1—The first rest in the Bible was on the Seventh day of the week—the Bible Sabbath (Gen. 2:1-3). / The first work done in the Bible was done by our Creator on the first day of the week (Gen. 1:3-5).

2—The first birthday in the Bible was that of the world, and in commemoration of it, God gave us the Sabbath (Gen. 2:1-3). In order to change this to some other day, it would be necessary to recreate the world. / Nowhere in Scripture did God ever tell us that the first day was in honor of anything.

3—The Seventh-day Sabbath is the only rest day God ever gave to man. / The Bible never tells us that the first day is to be regarded as a rest day or that it was ever set apart for this purpose.

4—The Creator blessed the Seventh day (Gen. 2:3). / There is not one occurrence where He ever pronounced a blessing on the first day of the week.

5—The Seventh-day Sabbath was made for 'man'—that

is, for mankind (Mark 2:27). It was not made for one race,— the Hebrews. / Sunday, the first day, was never set aside in Scripture as a special day for any race, nor for mankind as a whole.

6—The Bible Sabbath was given to Adam, as the head of the human race. Through him it was to be passed on to all nations that dwell on the face of the earth. The Sabbath is not "Jewish"—it is of universal obligation in our world. / Sunday, the first day was never given by our Creator to Adam our fore-father to be kept sacred—nor to any one else later on.

7—The Seventh-day Sabbath was given as a sacred legacy to mankind 2,300 years before the first Jew existed. It is not a Jewish institution. / The first day of the week was never given as a sacred legacy to the world—at any time in history.

8—The Bible never calls the Scriptural Sabbath "Jewish," but always "the Sabbath of the Lord thy God." Those who ridicule the Sabbath had better be careful how they treat the holy things of God. / The Bible always calls the first day of the week just that—the "first day"—and nothing else.

9—After God blessed the Bible Sabbath, He sanctified it and set it apart for a holy use (Gen. 2:1-3). The Seventh-day Sabbath is dedicated time that God gave to mankind to wor-ship Him upon. / Nowhere in Scripture did our Creator ever tell us that He had sanctified or dedicated the first day of the week to any purpose other than common work.

10—God specifically commanded us to keep the Seventh day holy unto Him in the Fourth of the Ten Commandments (Ex. 20:8-11). / God specifically commanded us to work upon the first day of the week (Ex. 20:8-11). Is it wrong to obey God?

11—At the express command of God (Ex. 20:10), His followers have kept the Seventh-day Sabbath for thousands of years, until men as predicted in Scripture tried to erase it from their minds. / And at the express command of God (Ex. 20:9), His followers have worked on the first day of the week for thousands of years—until men attempted to change it in their thinking by enforcing by law the sacred observance of the first day, and labor on the Seventh.

12—God Himself calls the Seventh-day "holy" (Ex. 20:8). / God Himself calls the first day a "working" day (Eze. 46:1). When God says something, should we obey Him, or should we obey the opinions that men received centuries ago from paganism?

13—Evident reference is made to the Sabbath and to the seven-day week all through the patriarchial age (Gen. 2:1-3; 8:10, 12; 29:27-28, etc.). / None of the patriarchs ever kept the first day of the week, nor did they even mention it.

14—The Bible Sabbath—the Seventh-day Sabbath—was part of God's Law before it was written down at Mount Sinai (Ex. 16:4, 27-29). / The first day of the week—Sunday—has never been part of God's Law—at any time in history.

15—When God gave manna to His people—and for forty years thereafter—several miracles occurred each week in order to point out the holiness of His Seventh-day Sabbath: (1) A regular portion of manna was given Sunday through Thursday. (2) Twice as much was given on Friday. (3) No manna was given on Sabbath. (Read Exodus 16). / God worked no miracle at that time to prove Sunday holiness—nor at any other time in Scripture.

16—When God wrote His Moral Ten Commandment Law for mankind, He placed the Sabbath Commandment in the center of it (Ex. 20:3-17). / When God wrote down this Law to guide the conduct of all men, He did not place first-day sacredness in the center of the Law, nor on the edge of the Law, nor anywhere else.

17—Obedience to the Seventh-day Sabbath is one of the unchangeable Ten Commandments. Obedience to a first-day rest is not in any of the commandments. The Seventh-day Sabbath Commandment is equal to each of the other nine. Why would God place it there if it were not of equal importance with all the rest? To say that it is of lesser importance is but the talk of men. In the great Day of Judgment I would rather stand on the words of God than on the words of men.

18—Seventh-day sacredness is the Fourth Commandment. / First-day or first-day sanctity has never gone forth from His lips.

20—The requirement that we must keep the Seventh-day Sabbath was written on rock with His own finger (Ex. 31:18). It must be very important if God wrote it with His own finger. How many things in the Bible did God write with His finger? And He wrote it on rock (Deut. 5:22). No other natural, unprocessed substance that could be written upon is as enduring as rock. How dare men stand in the pulpit and say it has been done away with—when God Himself never said so? / God never wrote first-day sacredness on rock—nor did His prophets ever write it on paper.

21—The Ark was beneath the Shekinah Presence of God, within the Most Holy Place of the Sanctuary (Ex. 40, etc.). And within that Ark were the Ten Commandments, which included the Sabbath Commandment (Deut. 10:1-5). The Sanctuary was located in the center of the dwellings of the people of God, and in its heart was the Most Holy Place. In the center of this room was the Ark of the Covenant, and within it, in the heart of the Moral Law, was the Sabbath Commandment. / First-day sacredness was not to be found in the Ark of the Covenant, nor even in the tents of God's people. None were to be found keeping Sunday holy.

22—The Ark is called "the Ark of the Covenant" because it was a chest that contained and safeguarded the Covenant—the Ten Commandments. God called this moral Law His "Covenant" with His people (Deut. 5:2-21). A covenant is an agreement. God agrees to save us if we will let Him give us enabling grace to keep His Law. Both sides agree to do something—that is what a covenant is. / God never made any covenant with us in regard to the first day of the week.

23—The "old covenant" experience is the attempt of God's people to keep His requirements in their own strength. In the old covenant, the fault was with the people (Heb. 8:8). The "New Covenant" is based on better promises than this. It is based on God's promise to enable us to do as He asks (Heb. 8). His enduring Law, written with His own finger on rock, He offers to write upon our hearts, by the enabling power of His Spirit (Heb. 8:10). If we are willing to submit to His rules, we shall in His strength be empowered to obey everything He asks of us. We shall no longer break His Law, but keep it. It will be heart-work (Jer. 31:31-34). / God has never promised to write Sunday-keeping upon our hearts, and He has never agreed to help us sacredly observe it.

24—After God finished giving the Ten Commandments to the people, "He added no more" (Deut. 5:22). We are only to keep one day holy unto God, and it must be the day that He selected for us. It can not be some other day. / God never added the first day as a second holy day, and He never made it the original one.

25—God forbade work upon the Sabbath, even in the most hurrying times (Ex. 34:21). / But He has never forbidden work on the first day, even when we have the least to do.

26—The Bible Sabbath—the Seventh-day Sabbath—is the sign of the true God, by which we are to know Him from all false gods (Eze. 20:20). It is the Creator who made the world. And only our Creator is to be our God. We are to have no other gods. We are to worship no other gods. And we are to worship Him only in the way He tells us to. Are you and I greater than our God, that we can set aside His worship rules and make our own? To do this is to worship our own ideas. The Seventh day was given us at the Creation of the world that we might ever know which was the true God. / Because our Creator did not give us Sunday as the day to worship Him, those who observe it, while knowing that it is unscriptural, are not doing as He asked. The first day is the sign of allegiance to ancient pagan Sun-worship. Many Catholic and Protestant church leaders tell us so, and history proves it. It takes a daring man to knowingly reject the Laws of God for the commandments of men (Matt. 15:9, Mark 7:7).

27—The Seventh-day Sabbath is a memorial of Creation (Ex. 20:11; 31:17). Every time we rest upon the Seventh day, we commemorate that amazing event, and honor Him by whose hand we were made—our Creator. / Sunday, the first day of the week, was never given us as a memorial of anything. Christians will say they keep it "in honor" of the resurrection of Christ,—when the truth is that Chirst never told them to do so—and they only do it simply because everyone else does. It is a known fact that the crucifixion is more important in the salvation of man than is the resurrection, and yet if you discovered that I were regularly keeping Friday holy, you would consider me odd—for you would recognize I am just following my own ideas. God SPOKE the Seventh day into your and my Sabbath. Let's follow what He said rather than what men speculate. God has, indeed, given us in Scripture a Biblical Memorial of Christ's death and resurrection,—it is the Lord's Supper, distinctly commanded three times by Jesus in John 13:3-17. Baptism is the second Memorial of His death and resurrection given us,—as well as a reminder of our covenant to obey Him by faith in Christ's enabling grace (Read Romans 6:1-13). / But we were never told in the Bible that we were to honor Sunday as a memorial of anything.

28—God promised that Jerusalem would stand forever if the Jews would keep the Sabbath (Jer. 17:24-25). He sent them into captivity to ancient Babylon for breaking it (Neh. 13:18; Jer. 52). And for the same reason, He destroyed Jerusalem (Jer. 17:27). / Those who, in our day, knowingly reject His Sabbath for a man-made one, are actually submitting to the authority of a power predicted in Scripture (Dan. 7:25) that would seek to change it. They obey man instead of God.

29—God has pronounced a special blessing on all the Gentiles who will keep the Bible Sabbath (Isaiah 56:6-7). / He has never pronounced any blessing on anyone who decides to keep the first day of the week as a holy day.

30—God not only blesses the Sabbath day,—He blesses those who will faithfully observe it (Isaiah 56:2). / God has promised the opposite of a blessing on those who choose the sayings of men in place of the commandments of God (Jer. 17:5 and the entire chapter, Matt. 15:9, etc.).

31—God requires that we keep His Sabbath and that we call it honorable (Isa. 58:12-13). Let those beware who would dare to ridicule that holy day. It is not "the old Jewish Sabbath," and it is not a "yoke of bondage." / On the other hand, there is no commandment to give honor to Sunday in any way.

32—Isaiah prophesied that after the holy Sabbath had been trodden down for "many generations," it would be restored again (Isaiah\58:12-13). Daniel prophesied that men would seek to change it (Dan. 7:8, 21-22, 25). This is a very important prophecy and links closely with the parallel prophecies of Paul and John. The Little Horn power of Daniel 7:25; 1 John 2:22; 4:3, and 2 John 7; and Mystery, Babylon the Great of Revelation 13 through 17 is an important Biblical study. Men and women today must return to the plain words of Scripture and refuse to bow to this pagan error of Sun-day sacredness. We must return to the keeping of the Ten Commandments just as God gave them (Ex. 20:1-17). Jesus died on Calvary to enable us by grace to obey the Bible.

33—Down to the end of the Old Testament, prophets and men of God faithfully kept the holy Sabbath of God. / But never in one instance, did they observe the first day as sacred.

34—When the Son of God came, He faithfully kept the Seventh-day Sabbath all His life (Luke 4:16; John 15:10), as an example to us—for Scripture says that His earthly life is an Example for us that we are to copy (1 Pet. 2:21; 1 Jn. 2:6). Jesus Christ has not changed (Heb. 13:8), neither has His Father (Mal. 3:6), and neither has His Law (Ps. 111:7-8, Matt. 5:17; Rom. 3:31, etc.). God made the world in six days and then rested on the Seventh-day Sabbath. Jesus faithfully kept that Sabbath while on earth. Shall we not be safe in following the example of both the Father and the Son? / Neither of them ever gave us even one instance in which they kept the first day as a rest day.

35—As with every other week that preceded it, Jesus worked through the final work-week of His life before His Crucifixion. After His death on Friday, "the preparation day" (the day God's people prepared for the Sabbath—Luke 23:54, Matt. 28:1-2), Jesus rested in the tomb during the hours of the Sabbath, and on the first day of the week He began another work-week again—by rising from the tomb (Matt. 28:1; Mark 16:9; Luke 24:1; John 20:1) and traveling all the way to heaven and back again on that day. Repeatedly, Jesus had said, "Mine hour is not come." Every act of His life was guided by the Father. We can clearly see this in His Last Week—working up to Friday afternoon, resting on the Sabbath, and then resuming His work again on Sunday. / But no such example or pattern of Sunday-sacredness was ever given us by our Lord.

36—The Seventh day is the Lord's Day, according to the Bible. We are told about the "Lord's day" in Revelation 1:10, but we are not there told what day it is. Instead, very frequently throughout Scripture, the Seventh-day Sabbath is called the day of the Lord (Ex. 20:10; Lev. 23:3; Deut. 5:4; etc.), the day unto the Lord (Ex. 16:23, 25; 31:15; 35:2; etc.) and His own day (Isa. 58:13). And while on earth, Jesus told us the day He was Lord of—the Bible Sabbath (Mk. 2:28). / Nowhere in Scripture is the first day ever called the "Lord's day" or any similar designation. At no time in the sacred Word did God by word of mouth ever honor the first day of the week. Be honest with yourself: Do you feel safer going by what God says to do or by what the people around you tell you to do?

37—Jesus called Himself the "Lord of the Sabbath" (Matt. 12:8) because it was His work to love and protect it, as the husband is the lord of the wife, to love and cherish her (1 Pet. 3:6). Should you not love and cherish it also? / But never did He call Himself the lord of the first day.

38—Repeatedly, Jesus vindicated the Sabbath as a merciful institution designed for man's good (Mk. 2:23-28). / But He never had anything to say about the first day of the week.

39—Far from abolishing the Sabbath, Jesus carefully taught men how to observe it (Matt. 12:1-13). / But we were never taught in Scripture how we might keep Sunday holy.

40—Just before His death, He instructed His disciples that the Sabbath should be carefully observed after His death at the time of the predicted destruction of Jerusalem—thirty-nine years later, and also at the end of the world (Matt. 24:2-3 and 20). / But He was totally silent in regard to any sanctity of Sunday after His death.

41—Christ's followers carefully kept the Sabbath because of the Bible commandment after He died (Luke 23: 53-56). They loved Him and this was the day He had always taught them to keep. / But we are never once told that they kept the first day as sacred—because of a Bible commandment or for

A SABBATH TIME LINE FROM EDEN TO EDEN

In Twelve Links
A Chain of Truth

Linking God to His People
In the Holy Sabbath

At the Creation —
The Sabbath given to mankind.
Genesis 2:1-3
Exodus 31:16-17

Before Sinai —
The Sabbath for 2500 years.
Exodus 16:4,26,28,30

At Sinai —
The Sabbath written down
Exodus 20:8-11

After Sinai —
The Sabbath in the Old Testament.
Numbers 15:32-35
Jeremiah 17:21-27
(Fulfilled: Jer 52:7-15; 2 Chr 36:19-21)

Jesus Our Example —
The Sabbath of Christ
Luke 4:16, 1 Peter 2:21
Mark 2:28, Isaiah 42:21
Mark 1:21, 1 John 2:6

The Disciples —
The Sabbath of His people
Luke 23:56-24:1

Paul —
The Sabbath of the Apostles
Acts 17:2, 13:14,42,44, 16:13

After the Time of Christ —
(At the destruction of Jerusalem and the end of the world)
Matthew 24:1-3,20

The Dark Ages and the Last Days —
The Sabbath in the Christian Era
Revelation 12:17

Last Day Restoration Predicted —
The Sabbath of our time
Isaiah 58:12-14
Revelation 12:17, 14:12

Heaven and the New Earth —
The Sabbath for eternity
Revelation 22:14
Isaiah 66:22-23

Your Special Day with God —
The Sabbath founded upon Scripture
Exodus 31:13,17
Isaiah 56:2,4,6
Ezekiel 20:12,20

All through the Bible, we find much information about the precious Bible Sabbath. And this is as we would expect, for the Sabbath is the connecting link between man and his God.

Can we do any better than to do the best? And the best is given us in the pages of Holy Scriptures. There we find God's plan for our lives. And it is a wonderful plan.

Just now, become a link in God's Sabbath time line. For it reaches to eternity.

A SUNDAY TIME LINE FROM EDEN TO EDEN

In Twelve Links
A Chain of Fact

Disproving a man-made error
The Sunday-sacredness error

At the Creation —
  Sunday sacredness not
  known
  Bible texts vindicating
  Sunday: None

Before Sinai —
  Sunday sacredness never
  found
  Bible texts vindicating
  Sunday: None

At Sinai —
  Sunday sacredness totally
  missing
  Bible texts vindicating
  Sunday: None

After Sinai —
  Sunday sacredness
  completely absent
  Bible texts vindicating
  Sunday: None

Jesus Our Example —
  Sunday sacredness
  totally ignored
  Bible texts vindicating
  Sunday: None

The Disciples —
  Sunday sacredness not
  mentioned
  Bible texts vindicating
  Sunday: None

Paul —
  Sunday sacredness never
  spoken of
  Bible texts vindicating
  Sunday: None

After the time of Christ
(At the destruction of
  Jerusalem and the end of
  the world)
  Sunday sacredness
  entirely missing
  Bible texts vindicating
  Sunday: None

The Dark Ages —
  Sunday sacredness—such
  an error predicted!
  Daniel 7:25, 8:10-12
  Revelation 13:6-7
  Revelation 17:5-6

Last Days —
  Sunday sacredness—No,
  but return to Bible
  Sabbath predicted
  Isaiah 58:12-14
  Revelation 12:17, 14:12

Heaven and the New Earth —
  Sunday sacredness totally
  missing
  Bible texts vindicating
  Sunday: None

Your Special Day with
God —
  Sunday sacredness—
  nowhere found in
  Scripture
  Bible texts vindicating
  Sunday: None

All through the Bible we find absolutely nothing said about Sunday sacredness.
    There is no text anywhere in Scripture that tells us that Sunday is holy unto the Lord, or that it has become the new sabbath.

any other reason.

42—Thirty years after Christ's resurrection, the Holy Spirit specifically calls it "the Sabbath day" (Acts 13:14). / But at no time did men under the moving of the Spirit of God tell us that Sunday was to be regarded as anything other than a common day.

43—Paul was the apostle to the Gentiles, and he called it the "Sabbath day" in A.D. 45 (Acts 13:27). Is Paul to be regarded as less intelligent than our modern theologians who tell us that the Sabbath ceased at the Resurrection of Christ? / Paul never recommended Sunday to the Gentile believers.

44—The Gentile converts called it the Sabbath (Acts 13:42). / But we have no record in Scripture that they ever observed the first day as sacred unto God.

45—In the great Christian council of c. 49 A.D., in the presence of the apostles and thousands of disciples, James calls it the "Sabbath day" (Acts 15:21). / At this important council, Sunday should have been mentioned if it had been decided upon as the new day for worship. But this did not happen.

46—It was customary to hold prayer meetings on the Sabbath (Acts 16:13). / But neither God nor His prophets ever said one word in favor of Sunday as a holy day.

47—Paul read the Scriptures in public meetings on the Sabbath (Acts 17:2-3). / But if you will read those same Scriptures you will find only nine times in all the Bible that the first day is even mentioned (Gen. 1:5; Matt. 28:1; Mk. 16:2,9; Lk. 24:1; Jn. 20:1, 19; Acts 20:7; 1 Cor. 16:2).

48— It was Paul's custom to preach upon the Sabbath day (Acts 17:2-3). Acts mentions stop-over meetings, that Paul held on several different days of the week as He was traveling through an area. But within the book of Acts alone is given the record of his having held eighty-four meetings upon the Sabbath (Acts 13:14, 44; 16:13; 17:2; 18:4,11). / In all the Bible we have a record of only one religious meeting held on Sunday, and that was a night meeting (Acts 20:5-12). There is no intimation that another such Sunday meeting was ever held before or after it. Nothing was said about Sunday sacredness at that meeting. A meeting does not make a day sacred—Paul held a lengthy gathering a few days later (Acts 20:17-38). And "breaking bread" does not make a day sacred. This was their term for a meal. Jesus did it on Thursday night (Lk. 22) and His disciples later did it every day of the week (Acts 2:42-46). [The gathering of the disciples in the upper room on the Sunday of Christ's resurrection was not for a religious meeting— but "for fear of the Jews" (Jn. 20:19). They were not gathered in honor of the resurrection of Christ, for they did not yet believe in it (Mk 16:11 and 12-13).]

49—There never was any dispute or question between the Christians and the Jews, who opposed them, over the Sabbath day. This is additional proof that the Christians still observed the same day that the Jews did. / And in Scripture, there never was any argument between them over Sunday-sacredness—for neither of them believed in it. At the time of Christ, in the First Century of our era, only the pagans were keeping Sunday sacred. They had been doing this for at least a hundred years. In later centuries, Christians were to adopt this pagan custom and begin keeping the first day as though it were holy.

50—In all their accusations against him, the Jews never charged Paul with disregarding the Sabbath. Why did they not, if he did not keep it? / On the other hand, Paul taught the Christians that they should do their secular business at home on the first day (1 Cor. 16:2). Why would he do this if it were to be sacredly observed? This is the only time in all his writings that Paul ever mentions the first day of the week.

51—It was Paul himself, who expressly declared that he had kept the law: "Neither against the law of the Jews, neither against the temple, nor yet against Caesar, have I offended anything at all." (Acts 25:8). How could this be true if he had not kept the Sabbath? / But never once did he tell us that he kept Sunday holy.

52—The Sabbath is mentioned in the New Testament fifty-nine times,—and always with respect, bearing the same title it had in the Old Testament: "the Sabbath day." / Sunday is mentioned in the New Testament only eight times, and not in one instance does it bear the title of sanctity, or is it spoken of as a sacred day.

53—God has never given any man permission to work upon the Bible Sabbath. Reader, by what authority do you use the Seventh day for common labor? / God has never given any man permission to regard Sunday, the first day, as anything other than a common day.

54—In not one instance did New Testament Christians—either before or after the resurrection—ever do ordinary work on the Seventh day. Why should modern Christians do differently than Bible Christians? This is a very important question. / The apostles never rested on the first day and they never said that it was sacred.

55—There is no record that God has ever removed His blessing or sanctification from the Seventh day. / There is no record that He spoke it about Sunday.

56—The Seventh-day Sabbath was written by His own finger upon stone at Sinai (Ex. 20, etc.). When Jesus began His work, He expressly declared that He had not come to destroy the law. "Think not that I am come to destroy the law, or the prophets" (Matt. 5:17). / Never at any time did He speak about establishing the sanctity of the first day of the week.

57—Jesus, the One who redeemed us is the One who created us (Isa. 43:1; Jn. 1:1-3, 14; Col. 1:16-18; Eph. 2:10; Heb. 1:2). He is the One who gave us the Sabbath in the beginning (Gen. 2:1-3). / He was the first One to use the first day as a common working day (Gen. 1:3-5).

58—Jesus existed before Abraham (Jn. 8:58), even from old and from everlasting (Micah 5:2). He who was with the children of Israel all through their wilderness experience (1 Cor. 10:1-12) was the One who as our Creator, spoke the Law on Mount Sinai (Ex. 20), and who wrote it and the Sabbath on rock that we might ever observe it (Ex. 31:18 and Deut 5:22). On earth, Jesus severely condemned the Pharisees as hypocrites for pretending to love God, while at the same time they made void—set aside—one of the Ten Commandments by their traditions (Matt 23, etc.). / It was Jesus who commanded that we work on the first day of the week (Ex. 20:8-11), and it is Jesus who would today tell men that they should keep His

Commandments instead of setting them aside by their traditions (the sayings of men).

59—Not one word is said anywhere in the Old or New Testament about the Sabbath being abolished, done away, or changed. / And there is not a text anywhere in Scripture that tells us that the sacredness God gave to the Seventh day of the week has been transferred to Sunday, the first day of the week. I have repeatedly in print and over the radio offered large sums of money to the one who would discover and present to me such a text—but to this day no such text has ever been sent to me. The reason for this is simple: There is no such text. It does not exist. The first day was made into a counterfeit sabbath many centuries ago, by men who at that time wanted to control men's religious worship. And men today are ignorantly keeping that day in honor of these ancient pagan practices.

60—Not only was the great apostasy and the effort to change the Law of God—and the Bible Sabbath—predicted in Scripture (Dan. 7:25), and its eventual restoration in the last days, as well (Isa. 58:12-14),—but the comforting promise has been given us that it will be kept in the New Earth through all eternity by the people of God (Isa. 66: 22-23). We hardly need mention that no such promise concerning Sunday was ever made. Thank God for the clear teachings of His Word—and for the precious Bible Sabbath—the Seventh-day Sabbath—the only Sabbath God ever gave to mankind.

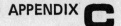

The Twelve Pillars

What happens when a leading churchman and Biblical scholar tells the truth about Sunday sacredness and the Bible Sabbath?

Well, it happened not long ago. And the reaction was a strong one. But more: it was revealing, for it provided the "reasons" advanced by learned clergymen for keeping the first day of the week holy.

Here, in two newspaper items, is the story:

"TORONTO, Oct. 27 (BUP).—Rev. Philip Carrington, Anglican Archbishop of Quebec, sent local clergymen into a huddle today by saying outright that there was nothing to support Sunday being kept holy.

"Carrington told a church meeting in this city of straight-laced protestantism that tradition, not the Bible, had made Sunday the day of worship.

"He quoted the biblical commandment which said the seventh day should be one of rest, and then stated: 'That day is Saturday.'

"He quoted the biblical commandment [Exodus 20: 8-11] which said the seventh day should be one of rest, and then stated: 'That day is Saturday.'

" 'Nowhere in the Bible is it laid down that worship should be done on Sunday,' the Archbishop told a hushed, still audience.

"Local parsons read his comments today with set, determined looks. They refused comment."—*News item, "The Albertan [Calgary], Canada, Oct. 28, 1949.*

The above news item appeared a thousand miles to the

west of Toronto. But in Toronto itself, the "Daily Star" was able to obtain those comments. The first sentence of the following news clip quite nicely summarize why Sunday is kept holy in our day:

"Oct 27.—Sunday is kept holy by Christians, not because there are any Scriptural injunctions [reasons], but because there are religious traditions associated with that day among Christians, Protestant and Catholic spokesmen said today. They were commenting on a statement of Most Rev. Philip Carrington, Anglican Archbishop of Quebec, that there is no commandment which states Sunday must be kept holy.

"Rabbi's Recollections

"A rabbi recalled that the first Christians were Jews and celebrated the Sabbath on the last day of the week and it was not until the reign of the Emperor Constantine [321 A.D.] that the day was changed by Christians.

"At a service commemorating the 400th anniversary of the Church of England prayer book, Archbishop Carrington declared that 'the Bible commandment says on the seventh day thou shalt rest. That is Saturday. Nowhere in the Bible is it laid down that worship should be done on Sunday.' Tradition [man-made ideas], he said, had made it a day of worship.

"A spokesman for St. Augustine's, the Roman Catholic seminary for the diocese of Toronto, said: 'Strictly speaking, that archbishop is right. There is no Scriptural evidence for the observance of Sunday. But he doesn't go far enough.

"Evidence in the Bible

" 'In the Bible, there is evidence that Christ established a church, to carry on his work. He gave that Church [the Catholic Church] authority to carry out God's rule on earth. Because the resurrection occurred on Sunday, and because of the general acceptance today of Sunday as a day of rest, it's fitting that now Sunday should be observed instead of Saturday, as under the old rule [the Bible rule].

" 'The [Catholic] Church has a specific church commandment stating Sunday should be observed.

" 'Protestants observe Sunday because for many centuries they had been part of the Roman Catholic Church, and had observed the Church commandment,' he said.

" 'There is no specific command in the New Testament about which day shall be kept holy' [An error. The truth is that the true Sabbath is found throughout the Bible, but Sunday sacredness is found nowhere within its pages], said Rev. G.H. Dowker of Grace Church-on-the-Hill. 'The simple fact is, we keep holy the first day of the week because it was the day of the resurrection of Christ.'

"Rev. Northcote Burke of Christ church, Deer Park, said he thought the archbishop [Philip Carrington] used the statement merely to illustrate church tradition. 'Certainly the tradition of the sabbath has always been to keep the Lord's day on the first day of the week. The early Christians used it because it was the day Christ arose again.' [The great majority of early Christians did not keep it until they were forced to, in the fifth century and afterward.]

"Jesuit Gives His View

" 'Our Lord rose from the dead on the first day of the week,' said Father Hourigan of the Jesuit Seminary. 'That is why the [Catholic] Church changed the day of obligation from the seventh day to the first day of the week. The Anglicans and other Protestant denominations retained that tradition when the Reformation came along.'

"Rabbi David Monson, of Beth Sholam synagogue, said the change was made because of Emperor Constantine [Roman emperor from A.D. 306 to 337]. 'He changed the Christian Sabbath to Sunday,' he said. 'The original Christians celebrated the Sabbath on Saturday . .

"Rev. Herbert Delaney, speaking for the chancery of the Roman Catholic diocese of Toronto, agreed that under the old rule of the Scriptures [the present rule for Christians], the Sabbath was the holy day. But he said Sunday was observed under a specific commandment of the [Catholic] Church, after the coming of Christ, in an 'interpretation' of the original commandment.

"Father Delaney said the reason for the change from Saturday to Sunday under the new rules [of decrees and councils] was that Christ had risen on Sunday.

"Not Only Tradition

"Dr. E. Crossley Hunter of Trinity United church said the explanation lies not only in tradition, but also in records of the New Testament.

" 'Again and again in the New Testament we find references to the Lord's day as the first day of the week, whereas in the Old Testament it refers to the seventh day,' he said. [Untrue. There is not one instance anywhere in the Bible in which the first day of the week is called "the Lord's day."] 'However, the archbishop is quite right in the literal meaning of the commandment" [given in Exodus 20:8-11, as applying only to the seventh day of the week].

"One minister remarked: 'We've become so accustomed to keeping Sunday as our holy day that it isn't likely this belated discovery is going to change our attitude overnight. Certainly not in Toronto.' "—*News Item, Toronto [Canada] "Daily Star," Oct. 27, 1949.*

Philip Carrington was born in 1892 in England, and earned many degrees (M.A., D.D., Litt.D.) and later, because of his scholarship, received two honorary ones (S.T.D., D.C.L.). He rapidly rose to important positions in the Church of England and became the Anglican Archbishop of Quebec. Author of many books and articles, he was a leader in his church, as well as an acknowledged authority in religious affairs. And he had a personal integrity that would tell the truth, even when it was not popular to do so.

He recognized that the commandments of God rank higher than the commandments of men.

"And when they had brought them, they set them before the council .. Then Peter and the other apostles answered and said, We ought to obey God rather than men."—*Acts 5:27, 29.*

Here is what the Bible says about this:

"But in vain they do worship Me, teaching for doctrines the commandments of men."—*Matthew 5:9.*

"For the time will come when they will not endure sound doctrine; but after their own lusts shall they heap to themselves teachers, having itching ears; and shall be turned unto fables."—*2 Timothy 4:3-4.*

"But the Pharisees and lawyers rejected the counsel of God against themselves."—*Luke 7:30.*

"And He said unto them, Full well ye reject the commandment of God, that ye may keep your own tradition."—*Mark 7:9 (Acts 4:19-20).*

"Prove all things; hold fast to that which is good."—*1 Thessalonians 5:21.*

"To the law and to the testimony: if they speak not according to this word, it is because there is no light in them."—*Isaiah 8:20.*

"All Scripture is given by inspiration of God, and is profitable for doctrine, for reproof, for correction, for instruction in righteousness: that the man of God may be throughly furnished unto all good works."—*2 Timothy 3:16-17.*

"Holding fast the faithful word as he hath been taught, that he may be able by sound doctrine both to exhort and to convince the gainsayers."—*Titus 1:9.*

How thankful we can be that we have the Bible—the precious Word of God! What would we do without it! We dare not leave it for the words of men—when those words teach disobedience to the Inspired Word of God. Cling to Jesus and to your Bible all your life, and obey all that it tells you—and you will be safe.

"Who will have all men to be saved, and to come unto a knowledge of the truth."—*1 Timothy 2:4.* "They received not the love of the truth, that they might be saved."—*2 Thessalonians 2:10.*

"God hath from the beginning chosen you to salvation through sanctification of the Spirit and belief of the truth."—*2 Thessalonians 2:13 (1 Peter 1:2).*

"Ye have purified your souls in obeying the truth through the Spirit."—*1 Peter 1:22.*

"If ye continue in My Word, then are ye My disciples indeed; and ye shall know the truth, and the truth shall make you free."—*John 8:31-32.*

"Sanctify them through Thy truth; Thy Word is truth." —*John 17:17.*

"Open ye the gates, that the righteous nation which keepeth the truth may enter in."—*Isaiah 26:2.*

"And I saw a new heavens and a new earth . .Blessed are they that do His commandments, that they might have right to the tree of life, and may enter in through the gates into the city."—*Revelation 21:1; 22:14.*

We are told in Proverbs 9:1 that wisdom hath builded her house out of many pillars. Here are the twelve Biblical pillars that undergird the Sabbath Truth. Here are the foundation stones that prove the Bible Sabbath to be the only weekly rest day you should keep today:

PILLAR NUMBER ONE — The Sabbath was given to mankind at the Creation of this world.

"Thus the heavens and the earth were finished, and all the host of them. And on the Seventh day God ended His work which He had made; and He rested on the Seventh day from all His work which He had made.

"And God blessed the Seventh day, and sanctified it: because that in it He had rested from all His work which God created and made."—*Genesis 2:1-3.*

In Pillar Number 1 we have three unanswerables:

(1) God did three wonderful things to the Seventh day: First, He Himself rested upon it. What an honor that is to any day! Second, He blessed it. How many things—all through the Bible—did God bless? Not very many. But He blessed the Seventh day. And He made it a rest day. Do we dare do our common labor on a day that He blessed and set aside for rest? Third, He sanctified, or hallowed it. How many things did God hallow in the Bible? Very, very few things. How many things did He bless *and* hallow? Hardly any. Let no man tell you that the Seventh-day Bible Sabbath is unimportant. It is important to your Creator; it ought to be important to you also.

(2) The Bible Sabbath was the first divine institution for mankind in the history of the world, and along with marriage, is one of the only institutions to come down, past Eden, into human history. The Sabbath is as sacred as is marriage and is to be as sacredly guarded.

(3) God dedicated and set aside the Sabbath as a rest day —2,000 years before the first Jew. Abraham is considered by all to have been the first Jew. He lived about 2000 B.C. Biblical records indicate that the Creation of this world took place about 4000 B.C. —The Bible Sabbath is not Jewish! It is for mankind; it is for all the world.

"The Sabbath was made for man."—*Mark 2:27.*

PILLAR NUMBER TWO — The Sabbath is a memorial as well as a symbol.

First, it is a memorial of Creation.

"It is a sign between Me and the children of Israel forever: for in six days the Lord made heaven and earth, and on the Seventh day He rested, and was refreshed."—*Exodus 31: 17.*

As a memorial of the Creation of this world, it cannot pass away without first having this world pass away. Our planet could not have a new or different Sabbath day without having it first hurled into oblivion—and then a new planet created from nothing, in the place of Planet Earth which no longer has existence. But no such event has occurred.

Second, it is a symbol of our salvation. When we keep it, we tell all the world that we belong to God and that we serve Him and obey Him. The Seventh-day Sabbath is a sign of our conversion, sanctification and salvation:

"Verily My Sabbaths ye shall keep: for it is a sign between Me and you throughout your generations; that ye may know that I am the Lord that doth sanctify you."—*Exodus 31:13.*

"Moreover also I gave them My Sabbaths to be a sign between Me and them, that they might know that I am the Lord that sanctify them."—*Ezekiel 20:12.*

"And hallow My Sabbaths; and they shall be a sign between Me and you, that ye may know that I am the Lord your God."—*Ezekiel 20:20.*

Nowhere in Scripture were we told to keep any day in honor of Christ's resurrection. To do so is unscriptural. —But to set aside the Creation and sanctification Sabbath of the Bible—for another day of the week—and excuse it by saying that we do so "in honor of Christ's resurrection,"—is indeed to do a very daring thing. Who dare presume to set aside the Memorial of Creation and salvation for any reason! To knowingly do so, flies in the face of direct commands by the God of heaven, and thus denies our creation and salvation by Him.

And then having done it, we can, in the Judgment, only plead that we did so because others did so. For there is no other reason for keeping the first day of the week holy instead of the Seventh day.

PILLAR NUMBER THREE — The people of God kept the Bible Sabbath before the Ten Commandments were given at Mount Sinai.

And this is understandable. The Sabbath Truth was first given to our race in Eden before the fall of man. It was given before sin and apart from it. It was given to mankind to link him to his God. And if Adam needed the Sabbath, we need it all the more today.

It is of interest that when Moses initially returned to Egypt, he told his enslaved people that they must begin keeping the Sabbath again. God was about to do great things for them, and they must identify themselves as His worshipers.

"And the king of Egypt said unto them, Wherefore do ye, Moses and Aaron, let [keep] the people from their works? Get you unto your burdens. And Pharaoh said, Behold, the people of the land now are many, and ye make them rest from their burdens."—*Exodus 5:4-5.*

Moses had not told them to stop working. But he had told them to keep the weekly Sabbath rest. Pharaoh was angry about this.

And then, four chapters before the Ten Commandments were given on Mount Sinai, the God of heaven spoke in such a way that it is obvious that the Seventh-day Sabbath was already well-known—but not always well-kept:

"Then said the Lord unto Moses, Behold, I will rain bread from heaven for you; and the people shall go out and gather a certain rate every day, that I may prove them, whether they will walk in My law, or no. And it shall come to pass, that on the sixth day they shall prepare that which they bring in; and it shall be twice as much as they gather daily . .

"And it came to pass, that on the sixth day they gathered twice as much bread . . And he [Moses] said unto them, This is that which the Lord had said, Tomorrow is the rest of the holy Sabbath unto the Lord . . Six days ye shall gather it; but on the Seventh day, which is the Sabbath, in it there shall be none. And it came to pass, that there went out some of the people on the Seventh day for to gather, and they found none. And the Lord said unto Moses, How long refuse ye to keep My commandments and My laws? . . So the people rested on the Seventh day."—*Exodus 16:4-5, 22-23, 26-28, 30.*

There are those who say that the Seventh-day Sabbath was not commanded by God nor kept by man before Exodus 20 and its proclamation on Mount Sinai. But Genesis 2:1-3 and Exodus 16 prove otherwise.

PILLAR NUMBER FOUR — The Seventh-day Sabbath Commandment lies in the very heart of the Moral Law of Ten Commandments.

"Remember The Sabbath day, to keep it holy.

"Six days shalt thou labour, and do all thy work. But the Seventh day is the Sabbath of the Lord thy God: in it thou shalt not do any work, thou, nor thy son, nor thy daughter, thy manservant, nor thy maidservant, nor thy cattle, nor thy stranger that is within thy gates.

"For in six days the Lord made heaven and earth, the

sea, and all that in them is, and rested the Seventh day: wherefore the Lord blessed the Sabbath day, and hallowed it." —*Exodus 20:8-11.*

And here we find still more unanswerables:

(1) The Sabbath Commandment is part of the Moral Law of Ten Commandments. The Apostle James tells us that if we break any part of this law, we have broken it all (James 2:10-12). We cannot tear out the Fourth Commandment without setting aside all the others as well. They all stand together, because the God of Heaven put them all together.

(2) This "sabbath commandment" is not a one-day-a-week-holy commandment, but the Seventh-day-holy commandment. We do not obey this commandment by keeping holy the third day of the week or the first. We only obey the commandment by keeping the Seventh day—the Bible Sabbath. Adam and Eve could not select at random any tree in the garden and call it the "tree of life." They had to go to the one that God had appointed as the Tree of Life. And the same for the "tree of knowledge of good and evil." God made the decision as to which tree was which. And this He did with the weekly Sabbath;—*He* choose the Seventh day, and not any other day with it or in place of it. We do not decide which day of the week is to be kept holy unto God; He alone is to do this. It is for Him to command; it is for us to obey.

(3) Some say that Genesis 2:1-3 is not a command for man to keep the Sabbath, and therefore we need not do so. But Exodus 16 and 20 clearly show that man *is* commanded to keep it holy. And who dare say that the Ten Commandments were only for the Jewish race? Are the rest of us permitted to lie, steal, cheat, and commit adultery. Are only the Hebrews to observe these ten moral principles?

(4) The reason for the commandment is the Creation of this world: "For in six days the Lord made heaven and earth." This is not something local, merely for a Semitic race;—it is a commandment for all in the entire world who shall bow down and worship their Creator in humble thankfulness for His plan to save them through the life and death of Jesus Christ.

(5) The commandment says to "remember." The people

of God were not being told of some new concept. They were to keep in mind that which they already knew.

(6) God wrote these ten commandments with His own finger (Ex 31:18; Deut 9:10). He wrote them on the most enduring thing in the world—rock (Ex 31:18). And He wishes to write them also on our hearts.

"This is the covenant that I will make with them after those days, saith the Lord: I will put My laws into their hearts, and in their minds will I write them."—*Hebrews 10:16 (Heb 8:10; Jer 31:33)*.

And through the New Covenant He will write His holy law upon our hearts, if we will let Him. To have the Ten Commandments written on our hearts means two things: First, to be willing to obey them, and, second, to let God enable us to do so by the grace of Jesus, His Son.

PILLAR NUMBER FIVE — The weekly Sabbath—the Seventh-day Sabbath—is part of the Moral Law contained in Ten Commandments. It will stand forever. The yearly sabbaths were part of the ceremonial laws that prefigured or foreshadowed the death and ministry of Christ.

These "shadow laws," such as Passover and the Wave Sheaf, which were a part of the ceremonial or sacrificial law, would not endure past the death of Christ.

"For the [ceremonial] having a shadow of good things to come, and not the very image of the things, can never with those sacrifices which they offered year by year continually make the comers thereunto perfect. For then would they not have ceased to be offered? . . But in those sacrifices there is a remembrance again made of sins every year. For it is not possible that the blood of bulls and of goats should take away sins."—*Hebrews 10:1-3*.

These ceremonial laws were not written on rock, but were contained in ordinances, written on parchment. The rock was to endure, but the ordinances on parchment that foreshadowed the death of Christ were to pass away at His death. It is for this reason that we do not today observe the yearly sabbaths of the Passover and the Wave Sheaf.

"Blotting out the handwriting of ordinances that was against us, which was contrary to us, and took it out of the way, nailing it to His cross . . Let no man therefore judge you in meat, or in drink, or in respect of an holyday, or of the new moon, or of the sabbath days. Which are a shadow of things to come; but the body is of Christ."—*Colossians 2:14,16-17.*

In the Greek it says, "or of the sabbaths." The weekly Sabbath comes down to us from the Creation of this world and will be kept in the New Earth (Isa 66:22-23). But the yearly sabbaths did not begin until Moses. They typified or explained the coming death of Christ, and at His death were nailed to His cross.

If the ordinances containing the yearly sabbaths had not been set aside at Calvary we would need now to sacrifice animals on various occasions throughout the year. But we are not now to slay lambs, for Christ our Passover and Lamb has been sacrificed for us.

"Behold the Lamb of God, which taketh away the sin of the world."—*John 1:29*

"For even Christ our passover is sacrificed for us."—*1 Corinthians 5:7.*

"Ye were not redeemed with corruptible things, as silver and gold, from your vain conversation received by tradition from your fathers; But with the precious blood of Christ, as of a lamb without blemish and without spot."—*1 Peter 1:18-19.*

PILLAR NUMBER SIX — Repeatedly, in Holy Scripture, God gave warnings of dire consequences if those who professed to worship Him did not keep His holy Sabbath. Examples of this can be found in Numbers 15:32-36 and 2 Chronicles 36:11-21 (with Jeremiah 17:19-27 and 52:7-14).

God also gave warning against professed Sabbath observers who at the same time engaged in falsehood and wrongdoing. An example of the problem is given in Isaiah 1:2-20. An example of the solution is to be found in Isaiah 58:1-14. The answers are clear, aren't they? If we will seek God with all our heart and by the grace of Christ put away our darling sins, He will remold us into loving, obedient children. He will place His Holy Spirit within us and write His laws upon our heart. And then it will be heart-work to obey Him—an act of genuine, unfeigned love.

Repeatedly, during the earthly life of Christ, we see that the Jewish rabbis had bound heavy burdens upon the people that God had never asked of them. Jesus ignored these man-made restrictions. For example, on one occasion He ate a meal with His disciples as they walked along. But according to man-made rules this was wrong to do (Matt 12:1-2). On several occasions He healed people on the Sabbath, but the Jews thought it a terrible thing to be kind and helpful to God's suffering creatures on the Sabbath day (Luke 6:7-11; John 5:16; Mark 2:24; Luke 13:14-17; Matt 12:11-12; Luke 14:5-6; John 9:16). Never imagine that because others do not obey God according to His requirements, that therefore you need not do so. Just because the Rabbis would not keep the Sabbath properly, many imagine that they need not do so either. But the Sabbath was not given because of the Rabbis or the Jews. It was given at Creation to all the world.

"And the scribes and Pharisees watched Him, whether He would heal on the Sabbath day; that they might find an accusation against Him . . and they were filled with madness; and communed one with another what they might do to Jesus."—*Luke 6:7, 11.*

"Jesus said unto him, Rise, take up thy bed, and walk . . The man departed and told the Jews that it was Jesus, which had made him whole. And therefore did the Jews persecute Jesus, and sought to slay Him, because He had done these things on the Sabbath day."—*John 5:8, 15-16.*

PILLAR NUMBER SEVEN — Throughout His earthly life, Jesus always kept the Ten Commandments. And by so doing, He gave us an example to follow. And His example we are to follow:

"It is written of Me, I delight to do Thy will, O My God; yea, Thy law is within My heart."—*Psalm 40:7-8.*

"Who did no sin, neither was guile found in His mouth."—*1 Peter 2:22.*

"[He] was in all points tempted like as we are, yet without sin."—*Hebrews 4:15.*

"Wherefore in all things it behooved Him to be made like unto His brethren, that He might be a merciful and faithful High Priest in things pertaining to God, to make reconciliation for the sins of the people."—*Hebrews 4:17.*

"For I came down from heaven, not to do Mine own will, but the will of Him that sent Me."—*John 6:38.*

"For even hereunto were ye called: because Christ also

suffered for us, leaving us an example, that ye should follow His steps."—*1 Peter 2:21*.

"He that saith He abideth in Him ought himself also so to walk, even as He walked."—*1 John 2:6*.

"As ye therefore have received Christ, so walk in Him." —*Colossians 2:6*.

"Let this mind be in you which was also in Christ Jesus."—*Philippians 2:5*.

"I seek not Mine own will, but the will of Him who sent Me."—*John 5:30 (6:38)*.

There were those who feared that Jesus intended to overthrow the Law of God. But He definitely stated His belief in its eternity. The Law of God will never pass away. Its moral precepts are for all men through all time to come. And would we want it any other way?

"Think not that I am come to destroy the law, or the prophets: I am not come to destroy, but to fulfill. For verily I say unto you, Till heaven and earth pass, one jot or one tittle shall in no wise pass from the law, till all be fulfilled."—*Matthew 5:17-19*.

PILLAR NUMBER EIGHT — There is no doubt but that the actions and attitudes of the disciples of Jesus at the time of His death on Calvary, clearly revealed that which He had been teaching them for the preceding three-and-a-half years. The sacred importance of the Seventh-day Sabbath was of such concern to them that they would not even prepare the body of Jesus properly for burial on Friday, lest they transgress the Fourth Commandment.

"And now when the even was come, because it was the preparation, that is, the day before the Sabbath . . Mary Magdalene and Mary the mother of Joses beheld where He was laid.

"And when the Sabbath was past, Mary Magdalene, and Mary the mother of James, and Salome, had bought sweet spices, that they might come and anoint Him. And very early in the morning the first day of the week, they came unto the sepulchre at the rising of the sun. And they said among themselves, Who shall roll us away the stone from the door of the sepulchre?"—*Mark 15:42,47-16:3*.

"And he took it down, and wrapped it in linen, and laid it in a sepulchre that was hewn in stone, wherein never man before was laid. And that day was the preparation, and the

Sabbath drew on. And the women also, which came with Him from Galilee, followed after, and beheld the sepulchre, and how His body was laid. And they returned, and prepared spices and ointments; and rested the Sabbath day according to the commandment.

"Now upon the first day of the week, very early in the morning, they came unto the sepulchre, bringing the spices which they had prepared, and certain others with them. And they found the stone rolled away from the sepulchre."—*Luke 23:53-24:2.*

But there were others who did not so regard the Bible Sabbath. But we would not wish to be reckoned among that company. These were the murderers of Jesus, who cared neither for His life of obedience to the Ten Commandments, nor for His teachings to obey the Ten Commandments:

"And there was Mary Magdalene, and the other Mary, sitting over against the sepulchre.

"Now the next day [Sabbath], that followed the day of preparation, the chief priests and Pharisees came together unto Pilate. Saying, Sir, we remember that that deceiver said, while He was yet alive, After three days I will rise again. Command therefore that the sepulchre be made sure until the third day, lest His disciples come by night, and steal Him away, and say unto the people, He is risen from the dead: so the last error shall be worse than the first. Pilate said unto them, Ye have a watch [of Roman guards] : go your way, make it as sure as ye can. So they went, and made the sepulchre sure, sealing the stone, and setting a watch.

"In the end of the Sabbath, as it began to dawn toward the first day of the week, came Mary Magdalene and the other Mary to see the sepulchre. And, behold, there was a great earthquake: for the angel of the Lord descended from heaven, and came and rolled back the stone from the door, and sat upon it."—*Matthew 27:61-28:2.*

On Friday, in the presence of the people, the Jewish rulers refused to enter Pilate's Judgment Hall, lest they be "defiled." And so he had to come outside and speak with them (John 18:28-29, 33, 38). But on the Holy Sabbath, they secretly did business on the Sabbath—and went into the Judgment Hall of Pilate to conduct it! While the evil priests and scribes did weekday business upon the hours of the Sabbath, those who had daily listened to the teachings of Jesus and loved and obeyed His beliefs, carefully refrained from working on those holy hours—even though it would lead them to the impossible situation of how to anoint His body two days later after the tomb had been closed.

And what did Jesus do during those holy hours of that Sabbath? This is also very revealing. God, in His great time clock, had arranged for the exact time when Christ should be born and when He should die. His death took place in A.D. 31, in accordance with the prophecy of Daniel 9:25-27. And it came in the spring of the year—at the Passover time when the lamb prefiguring His death was to be slain. And when did the death come? On a Friday afternoon, so that He could keep the Sabbath rest, free from enemies, in the tomb all through those sacred hours. And then, on the first day of the week, He arose and began working again: He went all the way to heaven and presented His great sacrifice to His Father and received assurance that it had been accepted on behalf of His faithful ones on earth. Prior to this, He asked Mary not to touch Him for He had not yet ascended to the Father (John 20:17). When He returned to earth that evening, He walked with two disciples to Emmaus (Luke 24:13-31), and then spoke with many of the others in the upper room (John 20:19; Luke 24:36). And now He invited them to touch and handle Him, that they might be assured that it was He (Luke 24:39-43; John 20:20). That was a busy first day. But then, it was just another working day, as Scripture tells us.

At the Creation, God used the first day of the week as a working day: Genesis 1:3-5.

On Mount Sinai, He commanded that it be nothing more than a working day: Exodus 20:8-9.

Our God considers it nothing more than a "working day:" Ezekiel 46:1.

Should we consider it anything more than this?

But there is no such example of Sundaykeeping by the Apostles. The talk that Paul gave on the first day of the week at Troas was on Saturday night (because a night meeting on the first day would have to be on Saturday night, since according to the Biblical pattern the day begins and ends at sunset), and the next day—Sunday—he chose to walk 28 miles to

Assos, while his companions journeyed by ship. This was not Sabbathkeeping. Sunday was just another workday for Paul. And that "first day passage" in 1 Corinthians 16:1-2 is only a statement by Paul that the faithful set aside at home each Sunday morning, as they do their weekly accounts and budget-keeping, a donation for the poor in Jerusalem. Paul wanted to obtain it when he later passed through town. They were to set it aside "without gatherings." Modern translations show that this means to set aside the money at home. —And Acts 20:6-14 and 1 Corinthians 16:1-2 are the only two first-day passages mentioned in Paul's travels or writings.

PILLAR NUMBER NINE — According to all of the records that we have in the New Testament, the Apostles of Jesus always kept the Bible Sabbath, and never kept Sunday sacred.

"They came to Antioch in Pisidia, and went into the synagogue on the Sabbath day."—*Acts 13:14.*

"And when the Jews were gone out of the synagogue, the Gentiles besought that these words might be preached to them the next Sabbath."—*Acts 13:42.*

"And on the Sabbath we went out of the city by a river side, where prayer was wont to be made; and we sat down, and spake unto the women which resorted thither."—*Acts 16:13.*

"They came to Thessalonica, where was a synagogue of the Jews: and Paul, as his manner was, went in unto them, and three Sabbath days reasoned with them out of the Scriptures." —*Acts 17:1-2.*

Paul supported himself by tentmaking, and then on the Sabbath, he would preach the gospel.

"Because he was of the same craft, he abode with them, and wrought: for by their occupation, they were tentmakers . . And he reasoned in the synagogue every Sabbath, and persuaded the Jews and the Greeks . . He continued there a year and six months, teaching the Word of God among them."—*Acts 18:3,4,11.*

Paul's manner was the same as Christ's custom: to keep the Bible Sabbath (Acts 17:1; Luke 4:16).

Paul never taught that the Moral Law was or could be set aside. Ever will it govern the conduct of mankind:

"Do we then make void the law through faith? God forbid: yea, we establish the law."—*Romans 3:31.*

"What shall we say then? Shall we continue in sin, that grace may abound? God forbid. How shall we, that are dead to sin, live any longer therein?"—*Romans 6:1-2.*

"What shall we say then? Is the law sin? God forbid. Nay, I had not known sin, but by the law: for I had not known lust, except the law had said, Thou shalt not covet."—*Romans 7:7.*

Paul clearly saw that the problem was that we needed to obey the law; there was nothing wrong with the requirements of the law itself.

"Wherefore the law is holy, and the commandment holy, and just, and good."—*Romans 7:12.*

"Circumcision is nothing, and uncircumcision is nothing, but [that which is important is] the keeping of the commandments of God."—*1 Corinthians 7:19.*

The moral standard that governs mankind was not relaxed or destroyed by the death of Christ, for, indeed, it is through the merits of Christ's sacrifice that we can be empowered to keep that law.

"Thou shalt call His name Jesus, for He shall save His people from their sins."—*Matthew 1:21.*

Jesus saves us from our sins, not in our sins. And since sin is the breaking of the Ten Commandments, it is obvious that He saves us by enabling—strengthening—us to keep that law.

"Whosoever committeth sin transgresseth also the law: for sin is the transgression of the law."—*1 John 3:4.*

The other Apostles saw this same great truth that the moral standard that governs mankind was not relaxed or destroyed by the death of Christ:

"But be ye doers of the Word, and not hearers only, deceiving your own selves. For if any be a hearer of the Word, and not a doer, he is like unto a man beholding his natural face in a glass; For he beholdeth himself, and goeth his way, and straightway forgetteth what manner of man he was.

"But whoso looketh into the perfect law of liberty, and continueth therein, he being not a forgetful hearer, but a doer of the work, this man shall be blessed in his deed . . For whosoever shall keep the whole law, and yet offend in one point, he is guilty of all. For He that saith, Do not commit adultery, said also, Do not kill. Now if thou commit no adultery, yet if

thou kill, thou art become a transgressor of the law. So speak
ye, and so do, as they that shall be judged by the law of liberty . . Faith, if it hath not works, is dead, being alone. Yea, a
man may say, Thou hast faith, and I have works; shew me thy
faith without thy works, and I will shew thee my faith by my
works."—*James 1:22-25; 2:10-12, 17-18.*

"By this we know that we love the children of God,
when we love God, and keep His commandments. For this is
the love of God, that we keep His commandments: and His
commandments are not grievous."—*1 John 5:2-3.*

PILLAR NUMBER TEN — God predicted in Scripture
that men would later try to change the Law of God—and the
"time law" in particular. And we can understand that such a
prophecy would be told us, for the Bible Sabbath is very important (it is the very center of our worship of God!), and if
men were later to try to change it—we could surely expect a
warning of what was to come.

"And he [the little horn power] shall speak great words
against the most High, and shall wear out the saints of the
most High, and think to change times and laws: and they shall
be given into His hand until a time and times and the dividing
of time."—*Daniel 7:25.*

Papal Rome was to rule the world for 1260 years, and
during this time would try to tear out God's holy Time Law,
and put a counterfeit in its place. Oh, what blasphemy men
can dream up, when they are tempted by Satan to gain religious control of their fellow men!

"For that day [the Second Coming of Christ] shall not
come, except there come a falling away first, and that man of
sin be revealed, the son of perdition; who opposeth and exalteth himself above all that is called God, or that is worshiped."
—*2 Thessalonians 2:3-4.*

God said: "And hallow My Sabbaths; and they shall be a
sign between Me and you, that ye may know that I am the
Lord your God." (Ezekiel 20:20). But the papacy said, "No,
you shall trample upon the Bible Sabbath, and in its place you
shall honor my counterfeit, and on it alone you shall have
your weekly holy day."

"Know ye not, that to whom ye yield yourselves servants to obey, his servants ye are to whom ye obey?"—*Romans 6:16.*

"It is written, Thou shalt worship the Lord thy God, and Him only shalt thou serve."—*Matthew 4:10*.

"But in vain they do worship Me, teaching for doctrines the commandments of men."—*Matthew 15:9*.

"How long halt ye between two opinions? If the Lord be God, follow Him; but if Baal, then follow him."—*1 Kings 18:21*.

PILLAR NUMBER ELEVEN — The Seventh-day Sabbath, instituted by God at the Creation of this world is the seal of His governmental authority, for it alone identifies Him in His basic governmental code for mankind: the Ten Commandments.

Of all the commandments in the Decalogue, only the Fourth Commandment reveals the (1) name, (2) authority, and (3) dominion of the Author of this Law:

In six days, (1) the Lord (name) (2) made (office—the Creator) (3) heaven and earth (dominion or territory over which He rules). This commandment alone contains the seal of God.

Examine the notary seal of a notary public, or any other legal seal. They will always contain the above three identifying marks.

"Remember the Sabbath day, to keep it holy . . for in six days the Lord made heaven and earth, the sea, and all that in them is, and rested the Seventh day: wherefore the Lord blessed the Sabbath day, and hallowed it."—*Exodus 20:8-11*.

The Sabbath commandment contains the seal of God, and the Sabbath itself—given in this commandment—is inseperably connected with this seal. For the Sabbath is the basis of all true worship of our Creator. And this worship lies at the heart of all our acknowledgement of His authority as our Creator and our God. The Sabbath is ever to be kept as a sign that we belong to Him. And the keeping of it brings us within the circle of this seal.

The seal is impressed in order that all may know the authority from whence it comes—and that all may know that it is not to be changed. The Seventh-day Sabbath comes from God. Let no man dare to tamper with it—for the seal of God is upon it.

204   *Beyond Pitcairn*

"Now, O king, establish the decree, and sign the writing, that it be not changed."—*Daniel 6:8.*

"Bind up the testimony, seal the law among My disciples."—*Isaiah 8:16.*

"It [the Sabbath] is a sign between Me and the children of Israel for ever: for in six days the Lord made heaven and earth, and on the Seventh day He rested, and was refreshed."—*Exodus 31:17.*

"And hallow My Sabbaths; and they shall be a sign between Me and you, that ye may know that I am the Lord your God."—*Ezekiel 20:20.*

The Sabbath is a vivid sign of God's creative power—not only of this earth, but in our lives as well. It requires the same power to clean our lives and redeem us as it did to create us in the first place.

"Create in me a clean heart, O God."—*Psalm 51:10.*

"We are . . created in Christ Jesus unto good works."—*Ephesians 2:10.*

But there is to be a special sealing work in these last days, just before the return of Jesus in the clouds of heaven:

"And I saw another angel ascending from the east, having the seal of the living God: and he cried with a loud voice to the four angels, . . saying, Hurt not the earth, neither the sea, or the trees, till we have sealed the servants of our God in their foreheads."—*Revelation 7:2-4. (Ezekiel 9:1-6)*

"And I looked, and, lo, a Lamb stood on the mount Sion, and with Him an hundred forty and four thousand, having His Father's name written in their foreheads."—*Revelation 14:1.*

The name of the Father is expressive of His character. When Moses asked to see the glory of God, the Lord passed by and told His name—that which He was like: "The Lord, the Lord God, merciful and gracious, longsuffering, and abundant in goodness and truth." (Exodus 33:18-19; 34:6) And as we look at God's holy law, we see another view of His character. It is a transcript of that character—God's characteristics written out.

When God writes His name on your forehead and right hand—He has written His law on your heart. This is the work of the new covenant (Heb 8:10; 10:16; Jer 31:33), and that work reaches its climax when God "seals in" His own just before He returns the second time in the clouds of heaven.

What are those sealed ones like? They are fully obedient to the Law of God:

"And in their mouth was found no guile: for they are without fault before the throne of God."—*Revelation 14:5*.

But in the final crisis before His return, there will be those who will yield obedience to the beast instead of to God.

"And the third angel followed them, saying with a loud voice, If any man worship the beast and his image, and receive his mark in his forehead, or in his hand, the same shall drink of the wine of the wrath of God."—*Revelation 14:9-10*.

"And he [the beast] causeth all, both small and great, rich and poor, free and bond, to receive a mark in their right hand, or in their foreheads."—*Revelation 13:6*.

In contrast with those who serve the beast and receive his mark, are those who in the last days will serve God and receive His seal. How can they be identified? God has told us in His Word. Here is a description of God's remnant people at the end of time:

"And the dragon [Satan, working through his agents] was wroth with the woman [the true church], and went to make war with the remnant of her seed, which keep the commandments of God, and have the testimony of Jesus Christ."—*Revelation 12:17*.

And the third angel of Revelation 14, which warns men to not receive the mark of the beast, at the same time tells them how to avoid receiving it—by keeping the commandments of God through the faith of Jesus Christ:

"And the third angel followed them, saying with a loud voice, If any man worship the beast and his image, and receive his mark in his forehead, or in his hand, The same shall drink of the wine of the wrath of God, which is poured out without mixture . . Here is the patience of the saints: here are they that keep the commandments of God, and the faith of Jesus."—*Revelation 14:9-10,12*.

The final crisis will come over a decree by the beast that all men must disobey a commandment of the law of God. The nations and churches of the world will not require men to steal or lie or commit adultery. The growing movement toward national Sunday laws is growing stronger every passing year. It is seen that in this point, and in this alone, will be found the heart of the crisis of Revelation 13 and 14.

The first angel of Revelation 14 calls on all men everywhere today to reverence God—by returning to the worship of the Creator of all things.

"And I saw another angel fly in the midst of heaven, having the everlasting gospel to preach unto them that dwell on the earth, and to every nation, and kindred, and tongue, and people:

"Saying with a loud voice, Fear God, and give glory to Him; for the hour of His judgment is come: and worship Him that made heaven, and earth, and the sea, and the fountains of waters."—*Revelation 14:6-7.*

As the crisis nears, we must prepare for it.

"The observance of Sunday by the Protestants is an homage they pay, in spite of themselves, to the authority of the [Catholic] Church."—*Monsignor Louis Segur, "Plain Talk About the Protestantism of Today," page 213.*

Already we are facing Sunday closing laws on local levels. Men are prohibited from doing business on the first working day of the week, lest they be fined or imprisoned. And the situation will grow worse in the days just ahead.

"That the image of the beast should both speak, and cause [decree] that as many as would not worship the image of the beast should be killed. And he causeth all, both small and great, rich and poor, free and bond, to receive a mark in their right hand, or in their foreheads: and that no man might buy or sell, save he that had the mark."—*Revelation 13:15-17.*

But there is victory for those who will stand true to the God of heaven. There is overcoming power for those who will "keep the commandments of God and the faith of Jesus" (Rev 14:12).

"And I saw . . them that had gotten the victory over the beast, and over his image, and over his mark, and over the number of his name, stand on the sea of glass, having the harps of God."—*Revelation 15:2.*

PILLAR NUMBER TWELVE — And it is a double-strength pillar:

(1) Even though there are over two thousand denominations today, the remnant people of God, living at the end of time, can be identified. God has identified them for us. After

speaking about how the antichrist power (especially papal Rome) has tried to destroy the people of God for long ages of time, we are told how to identify them in these last days, just before Christ returns in the clouds for His own:

"And the dragon was wroth with the woman, and went to make war with the remnant of her seed, which keep the commandments of God, and have the testimony of Jesus Christ."—*Revelation 12:17.*

And the third angel, after warning all men against receiving the mark of the beast, tells us clearly who will be the little group that will stand apart from this almost universal apostasy:

"Here is the patience of the saints: here are they that keep the commandments of God, and the faith of Jesus."—*Revelation 14:12.*

And it will be an almost universal apostasy. All around us can be seen a rising tide of rebellion against the Ten Commandments. The colleges and universities teach, in their science, history, psychology—that man is but an animal descended from worms and amoeba. The churches teach that God destroyed the Ten Commandments at Calvary, and that Jesus died to take sinners to heaven just as they are. Governmental agencies are relaxing moral restrictions, and permitting gambling, abortion, homosexuality, and other vices.

This world is becoming a curse, but soon God will intervene. Prophecy tells us that before the end there will be a small company who will stand true to the commandments of God, by faith in Jesus Christ.

(2) And soon this present evil world will be ended suddenly by the return of Jesus Christ—and heaven will begin for the faithful.

And in that heaven the Seventh-day Sabbath will be kept forever. God's people suffered and died for it down here; they will worship God on that holy day through all ages to come.

Revelation 21 and 22 tells us about this new life with Jesus, when sin has come to an end and the wicked are no longer alive.

"And I saw a new heaven and a new earth: for the first heaven and the first earth were passed away; and there was no

more sea . . And he shewed me a pure river of water of life, clear as crystal, proceeding out of the throne of God and of the Lamb."—*Revelation 21:1; 22:1.*

And then we are told who will enter that beautiful new world:

"Blessed are they that do His commandments, that they may have right to the tree of life, and may enter in through the gates into the city."—*Revelation 22:14.*

But more: there is the promise that they will keep the holy Sabbath through all eternity:

"For, behold, I create a new heavens and a new earth: and the former shall not be remembered, nor come into mind . . And they shall build houses, and inhabit them; and they shall plant vineyards, and eat the fruit of them. They shall not build, and another inhabit; they shall not plant, and another eat: for as the days of a tree are the days of My people, and Mine elect shall long enjoy the work of their hands . . The wolf and the lamb shall feed together, and the lion shall eat straw like the bullock; and dust shall be the serpent's meat. They shall not hurt nor destroy in all My holy mountain, saith the Lord . .

"For as the new heavens and the new earth, which I make, shall remain before Me, saith the Lord, so shall your seed and your name remain. And it shall come to pass, that from one new moon to another, and from one Sabbath to another, shall all flesh come to worship before Me, saith the Lord."—*Isaiah 65:17,21-22,25; 66:22-23.*

Now you have seen God's plan for His people. And it is a wonderful one. It can begin for you right now. And it will continue on throughout eternity. Why not begin today—this very week? Ask God to forgive you for the past, and tell Him that by His grace you will worship your Creator on His day.

And next Sabbath—begin that holy walk with God on His day, the holy day of Isaiah 58. Read that chapter and see the blessings He will add if you will but let Him take over your life.

But do not think that there will be no problems or trials. Satan will bring many upon you. He hates the Sabbath and all who will stand loyal to it. But if you will determine to be true to God and His Word, you will have strength from above to go through all that lies ahead.

And one day soon, if faithful, you with the redeemed of all ages will rejoice on the sea of glass and will receive from the hand of Jesus the overcomer's crown. And you will be given that new name, expressive of a new character. And you will begin a walk with Jesus that will last through all eternity to come.

"And one of the elders answered, saying unto me, What are these which are arrayed in white robes? and whence come they?

"And I said unto him, Sir, thou knowest. And he said unto me, These are they which came out of great tribulation, and have washed their robes, and made them white in the blood of the Lamb.

"Therefore are they before the throne of God, and serve Him day and night in His temple: and He that sitteth on the throne shall dwell among them.

"They shall hunger no more, neither thirst any more; neither shall the sun light on them, nor any heat.

"For the Lamb which is in the midst of the throne shall feed them, and shall lead them unto living fountains of waters: and God shall wipe away all tears from their eyes."—*Revelation 7:13-17.*

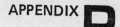

We all like to receive mail. Here is a letter from the Roman Catholic Church. And it is a thought-provoking one. The message is forceful and to-the-point, with lots of Scriptural proofs for its position.

And what is the message from Rome? Simply this: Protestants are half-baptized Catholics and ought to return to the Mother Church of Rome—unless they are going to become genuine Protestants and keep the Bible Sabbath—the Seventh-day Sabbath! Protestantism finds its basis in the Bible; Roman Catholicism is founded on the traditions and sayings of Roman Catholic Church leaders in times past. The Bible Sabbath has no reason for existence apart from definite commands of God given in the Holy Bible. Sunday has no reason for sacredness—except for earlier Roman Catholic official decrees.

Yes, the message is a clear one: either come back to Rome and stop calling yourself a "Protestant," or obey the commands of the God of Heaven and return to His worship on His day—the Lord's Day—the Seventh-day Sabbath.

Be thankful every day that you have the precious Scriptures. Let them guide you to the end of your earthly days. On the next page begins this Letter from Rome:

THIS APPENDIX, "A LETTER FROM ROME," IS NOT IN-CLUDED IN THE INDEX LISTINGS THAT CONCLUDE THIS BOOK.

I am going to propose a very plain and serious question, to those who follow 'the Bible and the Bible only' to give their most earnest attention. It is this: *Why do you not keep holy the Sabbath Day?*

The command of Almighty God stands clearly written in the Bible in these words: 'Remember the Sabbath day, to keep it holy. *Six days shalt thou labor, and do all thy work; but the Seventh day is the Sabbath* of the Lord thy God; in it thou shalt not do any work' (Exodus xx 8, 9). And again, 'Six days shall work be done; but on the Seventh day there shall be unto you an holy day, a Sabbath of rest to the Lord; whosoever doeth work therein shall be put to death. (Exodus xxxv 2, 3). *How strict and precise is God's commandment* upon this head! [In this matter!] No work whatever was to be done on the day which He had chosen to set apart for Himself and to make holy. And, accordingly, when the children of Israel 'found a man that gathered sticks upon the Sabbath day,' 'the Lord said unto Moses, The man shall surely be put to death; all the congregation shall stone him with stones without the camp' (Numbers xv.35). *Such being God's command then, I ask again, Why do you not obey it? Why do you not keep holy the Sabbath day?*

You will answer me, perhaps, that you do keep holy the Sabbath day; for that you abstain from all worldly business and diligently go to church, and say your prayers, and read your Bible at home, every Sunday of your lives.

But Sunday is not the Sabbath day. Sunday is the first day of the week; the Sabbath day is the seventh day of the week. Almighty God did not give a commandment that men should keep holy one day in seven; but He named His own day, and said distinctly: 'Thou shalt keep holy the seventh day;' and He assigned a reason for choosing this day rather than any other—a reason which belongs only to the seventh day of the week, and cannot be applied to the rest. He says, 'For in six days the Lord made heaven and earth, the sea and all that in them is, and rested the seventh day; *wherefore* the Lord blessed the Sabbath day and hallowed it' [Genesis2:1-3]. Almighty God ordered that all men should rest from their labor on the seventh day, because He too had rested on that day: *He did not rest on Sunday, but on Saturday. On Sunday, which is the first day of the week, He began the work of crea-*

tion, He did not finish it; it was on Saturday that He 'ended His work which He had made; and He rested on the seventh day from all His work which He had made; and God blessed the seventh day, and sanctified it, because that in it He had rested from all His work which God created and made' (Genesis ii. 2, 3). *Nothing can be more plain and easy to understand than all this; and there is nobody who attempts to deny it; it is acknowledged by everybody that the day which Almighty God appointed to be kept holy was Saturday, not Sunday. Why do you then keep holy the Sunday, and not Saturday?*

You will tell me that Saturday was the Jewish Sabbath, but that the Christian Sabbath has been changed to Sunday; Changed! but by whom? Who has authority to change an express commandment of Almighty God? When God has spoken and said, Thou shalt keep holy the seventh day, who shall dare to say, Nay, thou mayest work and do all manner of worldly business on the seventh day; but thou shalt keep holy the first day in its stead? This is a most important question, which I know not how you can answer.

You are a Protestant, and you profess to go by the Bible and the Bible only; and yet in so important a matter as the observance of one day in seven as a holy day, you go against the plain letter of the Bible, and put another day in the place of that day which the Bible has commanded. The command to keep holy the seventh day is one of the Ten Commandments; you believe that the other nine are still binding; who gave you authority to tamper with the fourth? If you are consistent with your own principles, if you really follow the Bible and the Bible only, you ought to be able to produce some portion of the New Testament in which this fourth commandment is expressly altered. *Let us see whether any such passages can be found. I will look for them in the writings of your own champions,* who have attempted to defend your practice in this matter.

1. *The first text* which I find quoted upon the subject is this: 'Let no man judge you in respect of an holy day, or of the new moon, or of the sabbath days' (Colossians ii. 16) [the ceremonial—sacrificial—yearly sabbaths of Leviticus 23, which were done away at the Cross]. I could understand a Bible Christian arguing from this passage, that we ought to

make no difference between Saturday, Sunday, and every other day of the week; that under the Christian dispensation all such distinctions of days were done away with; one day was as good and as holy as another; there were to be no Sabbaths, no holy days at all. *But not one syllable does it say about the obligation of the Sabbath being transferred from one day to another.*

2. *Secondly,* the words of St. John are quoted, 'I was in the Spirit on Lord's day (Apocalypse [Revelation] i.10). *Is it possible that anybody can for a moment imagine that here is a safe and clear rule for changing the weekly feast from the seventh to the first day?* This passage is utterly silent upon such a subject; it does not but [only] give us Scriptural authority for calling some one day in particular (it does not even say *which* day) 'the Lord's day.'

3. *Next* we are reminded that St. Paul bade his Corinthian converts, 'upon the first day of the week, lay by them in store, that there might be no gatherings' when he himself came (1Corinthians xvi. 2). *How is this supposed to affect the law of the Jewish Sabbath?* It commands a certain act of alms-giving [at home] to be done on the first day of the week. *It says absolutely nothing about not doing certain other acts of prayer and public worship on the seventh day.*

4. But it was 'on the first day of the week' when the disciples were assembled *with closed doors for fear of the Jews,* and Jesus stood in the midst of them' (John xx.19). *What is there in these facts to do away with the obligation of keeping holy the seventh day?* Our Lord rose from the dead on the first day of the week, and on the same day at evening He appears to many of His disciples. Let Protestants, if they will, keep holy the first day of the week in grateful commemoration of that stupendous mystery, the Resurrection of Christ, and of the evidences which He vouchsafed to give of it to His doubting disciples; *but this is no scriptural authority for ceasing to keep holy another day of the week which God had expressly commanded to be kept holy for another and altogether different reason.*

5. *But lastly,* we have the example of the Apostles themselves. 'Upon the first day of the week, when the disciples came together to break bread, Paul preached unto them,

ready to depart on the morrow; and continued his speech until midnight' (Acts xx.7). Here we have clear proof that the disciples heard a sermon on a Sunday. *But is that not proof they had not done the same on the Saturdays also?* [Acts 13: 14,42-44,16:12-13, 17:1-2, 18:1-4,11]. Is it not expressly written concerning those early Christians, that they 'continued daily with one accord in the temple, breaking bread from house to house?' (Acts ii.46). As a matter of fact, do we not know from other sources that, in many parts of the Church, the ancient Christians were in the habit of meeting together for public worship, to receive Holy Communion, and to perform the other offices, on Saturdays? Again, then, I say, let Protestants keep holy, if they will their first day of the week, in order that they may resemble those Christians who were gathered together on that day in an upper room in Troas; [a Troas meeting on Sunday in Acts 20:7, just prior to a Miletus meeting on Tuesday in Acts 20:17-38—although no one today keeps Tuesday sacred because of it] ; *but let them remember that this cannot possibly release them from the obligation of keeping holy another day which Almighty God has ordered to be kept holy, because on that day He 'rested from all His work.'*

I do not know of any other passages of holy Scripture which protestants are in the habit of quoting to defend their practice of keeping holy the first day of the week instead of the seventh; yet, surely those which I have quoted are not such as should satisfy any reasonable man, who looks upon the written word of God *as they profess to look upon it, namely, as the only appointed means of learning God's will,* and who really desires to learn and to obey that will in all things with humbleness and simplicity of heart. *For in spite of all that anyone might say to the contrary, it is fully and absolutely impossible that a reasonable and thoughtful person should be satisfied, by the texts that I have quoted, that Almighty God intended the obligation of Saturday to be transferred to Sunday.* And yet Protestants do so transfer it, and never seem to have the slightest misgivings lest, in doing so, they should be guilty of breaking one of God's commandments. *Why is this? Because, although they talk so largely about following the Bible and the Bible only, they are really guided in this matter by the voice of [Roman Catholic] tradition.* Yes, much as they may hate and denounce the word [tradition], *they have in fact no other authority to allege for this most important change.* The present generation of Protestants keep Sunday holy instead of Saturday, because they received it as part of the Christian religion from the last generation, and that generation received it from the generation before, and so on backwards from one generation to another, by a continual succession, *until we come to the time of the (so-called) Reformation, when it so happened that those who conducted the change of religion [from Catholicism to Protestantism] left this particular portion of Catholic faith and practice untouched.*

But, had it happened otherwise,—had some one or other of the 'Reformers taken it into his head to denouce the observance of Sunday as a Popish corruption and superstition, *and to insist upon it that Saturday was the day which God had appointed to be kept holy, and that He had never authorized the observance of any other,*—all Protestants would have been obliged, in obedience to their *professed principle of following the Bible and the Bible only,* either to acknowledge this teaching as true, and to return to the observance of the ancient Jewish Sabbath [the Bible Sabbath given by God at the Creation, Genesis 2:1-3,—2000 years before there was a Jew], or else to deny that there is any Sabbath at all. And so, in like manner, any one at the present day who should set about, *honestly and without prejudice,* to draw up for himself a form of religious belief and practice out of the written Word of God, must needs come to the same conclusion: *he must either believe that the seventh-day Sabbath is still binding upon men's consciences, because of the Divine command,* 'Thou shalt keep holy the seventh day.' or he must believe that no Sabbath at all is binding upon them. Either one of these conclusions he might honestly come to;—*but he would know nothing whatever of a 'Christian sabbath' distinct from the Biblical Sabbath, [that is] celebrated on a different day, and observed in a different manner,*—simply because Holy Scripture itself nowhere speaks of such a thing.

Now, mind, in all this you would greatly misunderstand me if you supposed I was quarrelling with you for acting in this matter on a true and right principle,—*in other words, a Catholic principle (*viz., the acceptance, without hesitation, of that which has been handed down to you by an unbroken tradition). I would not [then] tear from you a single one of those shreds and fragments of Divine truth [Catholic truth] which you have retained. God forbid! They are the most precious things you possess, and by God's blessing may serve as clues to bring you out of that labyrinth of [Protestant] error in which you find yourselves involved, far more by the fault of your forefathers three centuries ago [when in the Reformation they left Rome] than by your own. *What I do quarrel with you for, is not your inconsistency in occasionally acting on a true principle [such as Roman Catholic Sundaykeeping], but your adoption, as a general rule of a false one [your Protestant refusal to accept the rest of Roman traditional teachings].* You keep the Sunday, and not the Saturday; and you do so rightly, *for this was the practice of all Christians when Protestantism began [in the sixteenth century, as Catholics think]; but you have abandoned other Catholic observances which were equally universal at that day,* preferring the novelties introduced by the men who invented Protestantism, to the unvarying tradition of above 1500 years [of Catholic teaching]. We blame you not for making Sunday your weekly holyday instead of Saturday, *but for rejecting tradition [the sayings of Rome], which is the only safe and clear rule by which this observance [of Sunday] can be justified.* In outward act we do the same as yourselves in this matter; we too no longer observe the Sabbath, but Sunday in its stead; *but then there is this important difference between us, that we do not pretend—as you do—to derive our authority for so doing from a book [the Bible],* but we [Catholics] derive it from a living teacher, and that teacher is the [Roman Catholic] church. Moreover, we believe that not everything which God would have us to know and to do is written in the Bible, but that there is also an unwritten word of God [the sayings of popes and councils and saints], which we are bound to believe and to obey...

We Catholics, then, have precisely the same authority for keeping Sunday holy instead of Saturday as we have for every other article of our creed, namely, the authority of 'the Church of the living God, and ground of truth' (1Timothy iii. 15); whereas you who are Protestants have really no authority for it whatever; for there is no authority for it in the Bible, and you will not allow that there can be authority for it anywhere else. Both you and we do, in fact, follow [Catholic] tradition in this matter; but we follow it, believing it to be a part of God's word, and the [Catholic] Church to be its divinely appointed guardian and interpreter. You follow it, denouncing it all the time as a fallible and treacherous guide which often 'makes the commandment of God of none effect' (Matthew 15:6).

—*"Why Don't You Keep Holy the Sabbath Day?"* pages 3-15, in *The Clifton Tracts, Volume 4,* published by the Roman Catholic Church. Originally released in North America in 1869 through the T.W. Strong Publishing Company of New York City, so that those outside the papal fold might know the pathway back to the authority of the Mother Church of the Vatican.

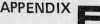

"For He spake in a certain place of the Seventh day on this wise, And God did rest the Seventh day from all His works . . There remaineth therefore a rest to the people of God. For he that is entered into His rest, he also hath ceased from his own works, as God did from His. Let us labour therefore to enter into that rest."—Hebrews 4:4, 9-11.

The Sabbath rest is something special between you and your God. And if kept faithfully now, you will continue to worship Him on it through all eternity to come. He is faithful who hath promised. And the blessing you will realize by obeying His command to keep His Sabbath—will be yours through all time to come.

Keeping the Sabbath changes us. For so our heavenly Father intended it. "Six days shalt thou labour, and do all thy work: But the Seventh day is the Sabbath of the Lord thy God: in it thou shalt not do any work . . for . . the Lord blessed the Sabbath day, and hallowed it."—Exodus 20:9-10, 11.

All through the first six days of the week, we work and rest; buy and sell. But the Seventh day is special. On that day we cease from our worldly cares and labors, that we may have more time to visit with God, to study His Word and pray, and to fellowship with like believers.

It is a day to live the Enoch life more fully. Enoch lived to draw closer to God, and to tell others how they might experience that closer walk also. And that is what we want, is it not? What is life for—if all we do is work seven days a week like the beasts and fish?

But our Father, knowing our deeper needs, says: "Come ye apart and rest."

We prepare for the Sabbath all week long. But the most preparation takes place just before it begins. In the Bible, Friday is called the "preparation day" (Matt 27:62; Mk 15:42; Luke 23:54; John 19:41, 31, 42). The house is cleaned, and the cooking and baking for the Sabbath is completed. (Some mothers tidy their homes on Thursday afternoon, in order to simplify the Friday activities.)

Baths are taken, boots and shoes are polished, and the children's Sabbath clothes are laid out. All of Friday's work should be planned with reference to the Sabbath.

"Oh, Mama," said the little boy, as he helped her in the kitchen on Friday. "Someone special must be coming tomorrow." "Yes, my son," answered Mother, "We will be visiting with God."

The holy hours of the Sabbath begin and end at sunset. For it is at sunset that each day begins and ends, according to the Bible. We first learn this in the first chapter of Genesis, where we discover that each day of Creation Week began and ended at sunset (Gen 1:5, 8, 13, etc.). "From even unto even shall ye celebrate your Sabbaths."—Leviticus 23:32. The evening begins with the setting of the sun.

Late Friday afternoon, as sunset draws near, the family gathers together to sing hymns, to pray, and to read from His Inspired Word. The time of Sabbath evening worship has come. Also called Vespers, it is a time in which we receive far more than we give. The peace of the Sabbath is a blessing, known and felt all through its holy hours.

There will be those who find it necessary to worship God alone each Sabbath. This is unfortunate, but we realize that many things will not be perfect in this life. But God's wonderful tomorrow will be glorious indeed—when we enter the golden gates of heaven and rejoice in all that He has prepared for us. At that time every tear will be wiped away and the trials and perplexities of this earthly life will be seen to have been preparing us for the happier life above.

In the winter months, Friday evening supper often comes after the sun sets. One family that we know, frequently eat the Friday evening meal by subdued lighting, for their children are thus reminded that the special hours of the Sabbath have begun.

Friday evening is also a good time to retire to sleep a little earlier than usual, so that all will be bright and fresh the next morning.

So much has been prepared the day before, that soon the family is ready to leave for Sabbath school, and the church service that follows it. A precious experience may be found in fellowship with like believers in the God of the Sabbath—the Creator God.

After the Church service, the dinner is quickly prepared. It was made the day before and now only a brief reheating is needed in order to be placed on the table. Often a little "Sabbath treat" has been made: something at the noon meal that the children will see as special.

And then comes the Sabbath afternoon. This can be a most interesting and happy part of the day.

Some ask, "What is there to do on the Sabbath?" Here are some thoughts and suggestions:

First, the Sabbath (including the Friday evening that began it) provides time to be with God. And those who love Him will be thankful for such an opportunity. Time to leave the cares of the workaday week and quietly commune with their Father in the study of His Written Word. And time to walk with Him out amid the scenes of nature.

Second, the Sabbath provides time to be with your family. Throughout the week, many children hardly see the face of their father. So many are the duties, the perplexities, the necessities. But God's hand is over the Sabbath. To the work of the week, He says, "Thus far shalt thou come, and no farther."

The Sabbath affords an opportunity for the father and mother to be with their children. It is a day to shut out the world and read God's Word together. There is time to read

Bible stories and mission stories with the children, and to study the deeper truths of Scripture.

And the Sabbath provides time for the family to walk together out in nature, and find "nature nuggets"—little discoveries in nature—to share with one another. The Sabbath began at Creation, and it is when we are out amid His created works that we can best return to the Garden of Eden experience.

The Sabbath is a day to visit shut-ins, the elderly, and those who would appreciate a visit filled with encouragement and words about Jesus. This is a day for heavenly things. Read to or with one another from Scripture or other spiritual books.

If there is no one in your family to share the Sabbath blessing with, then read and pray alone. And go out and visit with those who desire encouragement, Scripture reading, and prayer. And so many need it. Or, if you cannot easily leave the house, write a letter filled with encouragement, cheer and heavenly things to a loved one. Telling them about God's care for His children will rebound with renewed courage to your own heart.

Many years ago I knew a saint of God—an elderly lady—who was, herself, a shut-in. She was not only alone nearly all of the week, but she was alone most of the Sabbath also. But she sang her little songs of gladness, read in her Father's book, and tried to scatter sunshine on the paths of those around her.

But how can that be done—when one is a shut-in, alone most of the day in the house by himself? This humble Sabbathkeeper solved that problem: She wrote letters to encourage others. Who did she write to? Oh, there was always someone who needed a letter. —And frequently she would open the phone book at random and select a name she did not know—and write them a letter of encouragment!

This went on for years. Eventually Mrs. Bell died, and I, her pastor, preached her funeral sermon. She was deeply missed when she was gone. Many attended her funeral and they seemed to be crying for themselves more than for her.

Never imagine that you are all alone, or that you are not needed, or that you are in such a circumstance that you cannot help and encourage another. The world is filled with people who need your help. You are not a shut-in.

And if you are, now, or if you later may become one: Remember Mrs. Bell, and set to work. You have people to help. Your best days are just ahead.

Here are some more Sabbath pointers: Driving long distances in cars is a poor way to spend the Sabbath. Try not to keep yourself and your children within the four walls of meeting houses all through the Sabbath. And do not think your duty is done when you spend all Sabbath afternoon visiting with friends, while your children are outside running and playing. If you have children or youth in your home, center a big part of your Sabbath around them. Remember Jacob: "I will lead on softly, according as the . . children be able to endure."—Genesis 33:14. Find interesting Sabbath afternoon activities that you can do with your little ones, and those in your home who are older.

Do not use the Sabbath hours to plan, discuss or carry out weekly activities. There will be time enough for the six working days—and its many cares—in a few hours. Must you return to it prematurely? Follow God's plan for your life, and you will always be happier.

Acts of mercy are in perfect harmony with the intent of the Sabbath. And there are necessary things that must be done during its hours; we do not crawl into a cocoon and stay there until it is past. "The Sabbath was made for man; not man for the Sabbath."—Mark 2:27. God tests people on how they keep the Sabbath, for there are so many ways in which we can keep it better—or worse.

Sabbath is not for business transactions—or for planning them. And it is not for regular school studies or attendance. We should not converse on common or worldly topics during its holy hours. Do not crowd into the Sabbath the work that could be done earlier. If your own work could not be done before Sabbath began; then wait till the Sabbath is past to do it. Whether it be harvest time or any other time: Give God the special time He asks of you. Give Him the Sabbath hours, and He will give you a lot more than that in return.

Be especially careful to guard the edges of the Sabbath—those hours that usher it in and that mark its departure. Many are lax at such times.

Friday Evening Vespers opened the Sabbath, and now as the Sabbath draws near its end, another vesper service (evening worship) concludes it. Like a beloved friend it departs, but we are thankful that within a week it will be back again.

At this point, it would be well to mention Saturday evening: Many err in so centering their Sabbath afternoon thoughts on the recreation of Saturday night, that they really lose much of the Sabbath blessing. Not only the edges, but the middle of the Sabbath needs to be guarded. And, of course, we should avoid Saturday night activities that require preparations on the Sabbath itself.

Many wonder what to do with their young people on Saturday night, after the Sabbath is past. I recall one place we lived, in which there were four or five Sabbathkeeping families with teenage youth. What to do with them on Saturday night? They solved the problem beautifully: They gathered together in one home, finished the supper off with popcorn, and then, standing by the piano, they sang Christian songs together. Time to sing and time to talk, and they never tired of it.

And so we have come to the end of a Sabbath with God. You have given one day out of seven to Him. Now you will have additional strength to meet the stern duties of life and the harrassments of Satan, to be contended with in the coming days. But you can know that in just a few more, and it will be another strengthening Sabbath.

The idea that we should keep the Seventh-day Sabbath was His plan. Never forget that. And in spite of all that the devil can do to disrupt our efforts to obey God, we must cling to God's plans—all of them—as the best for our lives. Don't let Satan steal your crown.

Cling to God and to His precious Sabbath, more than to any earthly treasure or companion,—and you will be safe throughout the coming years—and the eternity of years that will follow it.

If you would like, I can send you more information on

living a life close to God. And tell me that it was because you were reading this book that you wrote. May our heavenly Father bless and keep you in the days ahead.   —*Vance Ferrell*

Indexes

TOPICAL INDEX

SCRIPTURE INDEX

MAP INDEX

Nine maps are included in this book. Every place name mentioned in the body of the text is shown on them, with the exception of: (1) modern nations, the location of which most people already know, and (2) locations mentioned in non-Biblical quotation references (such as Baltimore, where the "Catholic Mirror" citations were published).

Here are the names and locations of the nine maps:

MAP 1 - Page 6 - "To the Other Side of the World"
MAP 2 - Page 14 - "The Mutineers Return to the Islands"
                    "Tahiti"
MAP 3 - Page 20 - "Pitcairn Island"
MAP 4 - Page 28 - "Into the Holocaust"
MAP 5 - Page 32 - "Rome on its Seven Hills"
MAP 6 - Page 44 - "Europe in the First Century"
MAP 7 - Page 64 - "Fulfilling a Prophecy"
MAP 8 - Page 72 - "From Babylon to Jerusalem"
                    "The City of Babylon"
MAP 9 - Page 84 - "The Exodus"

The first map index that follows is the Main Map Index. It includes an alphabetical listing of all locations (place names) that are given in this book, with one exception. This exception is the local place names in Rome, Babylon, and on Pitcairn. The local place names on these three maps are given on three separate map indexes following the Main Map Index.

MAIN MAP INDEX

PITCAIRN MAP INDEX

ROME MAP INDEX

SOURCE INDEX

Abbott, Dr. Layman, in "The Christian Union," June 26, 1890. (124)

"Albertan," The [Calgary] , News Item, October 28, 1949. (185)

Andrews, John N., "The History of the Sabbath," chapter 27. (142)

Acquinas, Thomas, Statement by. (58)

Augsburg Confession, quoted in "Library of Original Sources," Volume 5, pp. 173-174. (135)

Baillaud, Edouard, "The League of Nations Report on the Reform of the Calendar," p. 52. (168)

Bellarmine, Robert Cardinal, "De Conciliorum Auctoriatate ("On the Authority of the Councils"), Book 2, chap. 17. (118)

Binney, Amos, "Theological Compendium," pp. 180-181, 171. (125)

"Bishop's Pastoral," 1874 editio. (124)

Brady, Priest, address at Elizabeth, N.J., March 17, 1903: reported in "Elizabeth News," March 18, 1903. (116, 135)

Brerewood, E., of Gresham College, London: sermon excerpt. (125)

Brotherhood of St. Paul, "The Clifton Tracts," Vol. 4, tract 4, p. 15. (120)

Buck, Charles, "A Theological Dictionary," art. "Sabbath," p. 403. (124)

Butler, Francis J., "Holy Catechism," No. 3, p. 63. (118, 133)

Cafferata, H., "The Catholic Canon: The Catechism Simply Explained," p. 80. (120)

Campbell, Alexander, "Address to the Readers of the 'Christian Baptists'," Part 1, February 2, 1824, pp. 44-45. (124)

Campbell, Alexander, "The Christian Baptist," February 2, 1824, Vol. 1, No. 7. (101)

Campbell, W.W., Lick Observatory: statement. (169)

Chalmers, E.M., "How Sunday Came into the Christian Church," p. 3. (59)

"Chamber's Encyclopedia," article: "Sabbath." (55)

Clarke, Adam, "The New Testament of our Lord and Saviour Jesus Christ," Vol. 2, p. 524. (126)

Carver, William Owen, "Sabbath Observance," pp. 40, 41, 49, 52, 54. (126, 126)

"Catholic Mirror," September 2, 23, 1893. (116, 117, 152)

Hackett, Horatio B., "Commentary on Acts," pp. 221-222. (103)

Heggtveit, H.G., "Illustreret Kirkehistorie," 1895, p. 202. (57)

Hinckley, Dr., "The Watchman," July, 1926. (169)

Hiscox, E.R., Notarized statement, dated 1893. (123)

Hiscox, E.R., Report of his sermon at Baptist Minister's Convention, "New York Examiner," November 16, 1893. (125)

"Hobart Church News," July 2, 1894. (126)

Holtzman, J.H., "Kanon und Tradition," ("Canon and Tradition,"), p. 263. (134)

"Horne's Introduction," Vol. 1, p. 69. (168)

Hyde, Walter Woodburn, "Paganism to Christianity in the Roman Empire," pp. 60, 261. (54, 55)

Jeffries, Frank, Statement. (170)

Jones, William Mead, "Chart of the Week." (167)

Josephus, "Wars of the Jews." (67)

Keenan, Stephan, "A Doctrinal Catachism," pp. 176, 252, 254. (115, 117)

Kelly, Vincent J., "Forbidden Sunday and Feast-Day Occupations," 1943, p. 2, 29 (55, 116)

Killan, William D., "The Ancient Church," preface, p. xvi. (56)

Labbe, Philippe, and Gabriel Cossart, "The Most Holy Councils," Vol. 13, col. 1167, on "The Council of Trent." (118)

Labbe, Philippe, and Gabriel Cossart, "The Most Holy Councils," "Epistles of Gregory I," Book 13, Epis. 1, in Vol. 5, col. 1511. (58)

Lamar, H., "Mithras," Wurterbuch der Antike, 2nd ed., 1933. (55)

Laux, John, "A Course in Religion for Catholic High Schools and Academies," 1936 edition, Vol. 1, p. 51. (117)

Lentz, F.G., "The Question Box," 1900, p. 98-99. (120, 136, 152)

Leo XIII, "Encyclical Letter," dated June 20, 1894. (119)

Lucas, D.H., art. in "Christian Oracle," January 23, 1890. (124)

"Manual of Christian Doctrine," p. 127. (123)

Millman, Henry Hart, "The History of Christianity," Book 2, chap. 8. (57)

Milton, John, "A Posthumous Treatise on the Christian Doctrine," Book 2, chap. 7. (100)

Mitchell, O.M., "Astronomy of the Bible," p. 235. (169)

"Nature" Magazine, art. in "Our Astronomical Column," London, No. 127, June 6, 1931, p. 869. (169)

Neander, Augustus, "The History of the Christian Religion and Church," Rose's translation of the first German edition, p. 186.

HOW THE SABBATH WAS CHANGED TO SUNDAY

"There is scarcely anything which strikes the mind of the careful student of ancient ecclesiastical history with greater surprise than the comparatively early period at which many of the corruptions of Christianity, which are embodied in the Roman system, took their rise; yet it is not to be supposed that when the first originators of many of these unscriptural notions and practices planted those germs of corruption, they anticipated or even imagined they would ever grow into such a vast and hideous system of superstitution and error as is that of popery."—*John Dowling, "History of Romanism," 13th Edition, p. 65.*

"It would be an error to attribute ['the sanctification of Sunday'] to a definite decision of the Apostles. There is no such decision mentioned in the Apostolic documents [that is, the New Testament]."—*Antoine Villien, "A History of the Commandments of the Church," 1915, p. 23.*

"It must be confessed that there is no law in the New Testament concerning the first day."—*McClintock and Strong, "Cyclopedia of Biblical, Theological and Ecclesiastical Literature," Vol. 9, p. 196.*

"Rites and ceremonies, of which neither Paul nor Peter ever heard, crept silently into use, and then claimed the rank of divine institutions. [Church] officers for whom the primitive disciples could have found no place, and titles which to them would have been altogether unintelligible, began to challenge attention, and to be named apostolic."—*William D. Killen, "The Ancient Church," p. xvi.*

"Until well into the second century [a hundred years after Christ] we do not find the slightest indication in our sources that Christians marked Sunday by any kind of abstention from work."—*W. Rordorf, "Sunday," p. 157.*

"The ancient Sabbath did remain and was observed . . by the Christians of the Eastern Church [in the area near Palestine] above three hundred years after our Saviour's death."—*"A Learned Treatise of the Sabbath," p. 77.*

"Modern Christians who talk of keeping Sunday as a 'holy' day, as in the still extant 'Blue Laws,' of colonial America, should know that as a 'holy' day of rest and cessation from labor and amusements Sunday was unknown to Jesus . . It formed no tenet [teaching] of the primitive Church and became 'sacred' only in the course of time. Outside the Church its observance was legalized for the Roman Empire through a series of decrees starting with the famous one of Constantine in 321, an edict due to his political and social ideas."—*W. W. Hyde, "Paganism to Christianity in the Roman Empire," 1946, p. 257.*

"The festival of Sunday, like all other festivals, was always only a human ordinance, and it was far from the intentions of the apostles to establish a Divine command in this respect, far from them, and from the early apostolic Church, to transfer the laws of the Sabbath to Sunday."—*Augustus Neander, "The History of the Christian Religion and Church," 1843, p. 186.*

"The [Catholic] Church took the pagan buckler of faith against the heathen. She took the pagan Roman Pantheon, [the Roman] temple to all the gods, and made it sacred to all the martyrs; so it stands to this day. She took the pagan Sunday and made it the Christian Sunday .. The Sun was a foremost god with heathendom. Balder the beautiful: the White God, the old Scandinavians called him. The sun has worshipers at this very hour in Persia and other lands .. Hence the Church would seem to have said, 'Keep that old, pagan name. It shall remain consecrated, sanctified.' And thus the pagan Sunday, dedicated to Balder, became the Christian Sunday, sacred to Jesus. The sun is a fitting emblem of Jesus. The Fathers often compared Jesus to the sun; as they compared Mary to the moon."—*William L. Gildea, "Paschale Gaudium," in "The Catholic World," 58, March, 1894.*

"The Church made a sacred day of Sunday .. largely because it was the weekly festival of the sun;—for it was a definite Christian policy to take over the pagan festivals endeared to the people by tradition, and to give them a Christian significance."—*Arthur Weigall, "The Paganism in Our Christianity," 1928, p. 145.*

"Remains of the struggle [between the religion of Christianity and the religion of Mithraism] are found in two institutions adopted from its rival by Christianity in the fourth century, the two Mithraic sacred days: December 25, 'dies natalis solis' [birthday of the sun], as the birthday of Jesus,—and Sunday, 'the venerable day of the Sun,' as Constantine called it in his edict of 321."—*Walter Woodburn Hyde, "Paganism to Christianity in the Roman Empire," p. 60.*

"Is it not strange that Sunday is almost universally observed when the Sacred Writings do not endorse it? Satan, the great counterfeiter, worked through the 'mystery of iniquity' to introduce a counterfeit Sabbath to take the place of the true Sabbath of God. Sunday stands side by side with Ash Wednesday, Palm Sunday, Holy (or Maundy) Thursday, Good Friday, Easter Sunday, Whitsunday, Corpus Christi, Assumption Day, All Soul's Day, Christmas Day, and a host of other ecclesiastical feast days too numerous to mention. This array of Roman Catholic feasts and fast days are all man made. None of them bears the divine credentials of the Author of the Inspired Word."—*M. E. Walsh.*

"Sun worship was the earliest idolatry."—*A.R. Fausset, "Bible Dictionary," p. 666.*

Sun worship was "one of the oldest components of the Roman

religion."—Gaston H. Halsberghe, "The Cult of Sol Invictus," 1972, p. 26.

" 'Babylon, the mother of harlots,' derived much of her teaching from pagan Rome and thence from Babylon. Sun worship—that led her to Sundaykeeping,—was one of those choice bits of paganism that sprang originally from the heathen lore of ancient Babylon: 'The solar theology of the "Chaldeans" had a decisive effect upon the final development of Semitic paganism . . [It led to their] seeing the sun the directing power of the cosmic system. All the Baals were thence forward turned into suns; the sun itself being the mover of the other stars—like it eternal and 'unconquerable.' . . Such was the final form reached by the religion of the pagan Semites, and, following them, by that of the Romans . . when they raised 'Sol Invictus' [the Invincible Sun] to the rank of supreme divinity in the Empire."—Franz V.M. Cumont, "The Frontier Provinces of the East," in "The Cambridge Ancient History," Vol. 11, pp. 643, 646-647.

"With [Constantine's father] Constantius Cholorus (A.D. 305) there ascended the throne [of the Roman Empire] a solar dynasty which . . professed to have 'Sol Invictus' as its special protector and ancestor. Even the Christian emperors, Constantine and Constantius, did not altogether forget the pretensions which they could derive from so illustrious a descent."—Franz F.V.M. Cumont, "Astrology and Religion Among the Greeks and Romans," p. 55.

"When Christianity conquered Rome, the ecclesiastical structure of the pagan church, the title and the vestments of the 'pontifex maximus,' the worship of the 'Great Mother' goddess and a multitude of comforting divinities, . . the joy or solemnity of old festivals, and the pageantry of immemorial ceremony, passed like material blood into the new religion,—and captive Rome conquered her conqueror. The reins and skills of government were handed down by a dying empire to a virile papacy."—Will Durant, "Caesar and Christ," p. 672.

"The power of the Caesars lived again in the universal dominion of the popes."—H.G. Guiness, "Romanism and the Reformation."

"From simple beginnings, the church developed a distinct priesthood and an elaborate service. In this way, Christianity and the higher forms of paganism tended to come nearer and nearer to each other as time went on. In one sense, it is true, they met like armies in mortal conflict, but at the same time they tended to merge into one another like streams which had been following converging courses."—J.H. Robinson, "Introduction to the History of Western Europe," p. 31.

"Like two sacred rivers flowing from paradise, the Bible and divine Tradition contain the Word of God, the precious gems of revealed truth. Though these two divine streams are in themselves, on account of their divine origin, of equal sacredness, and are both full of revealed truths, still, of the two, Tradition [the sayings of popes and councils] is to us more clear and safe."—*Di Bruno, "Catholic Belief," p. 33.*

"Unquestionably the first law, either ecclesiastical or civil, by which the Sabbatical observance of that day is known to have been ordained, is the edict of Constantine, 321 A.D."—*"Chamber's Encyclopedia," article, "Sabbath."*

Here is the first Sunday Law in history, a legal enactment by Constantine I (reigned 306-337): "On the Venerable Day of the Sun ["venerabili die Solis"—the sacred day of the Sun] let the magistrates and people residing in cities rest, and let all workshops be closed. In the country, however, persons engaged in agriculture may freely and lawfully continue their pursuits; because it often happens that another day is not so suitable for grain-sowing or for vine-planting; lest by neglecting the proper moment for such operations the bounty of heaven should be lost—Given the 7th day of March, [A.D. 321], Crispus and Constantine being consuls each of them for the second time."—*The First Sunday Law of Constantine I, in "Codex Justinianus," lib. 3, tit. 12, 3; trans. in Phillip Schaff, "History of the Christian Church," Vol. 3, p. 380.*

"This [Constantine's Sunday decree of March, 321] is the 'parent' Sunday law making it a day of rest and release from labor. For from that time to the present there have been decrees about the observance of Sunday which have profoundly influenced European and American society. When the Church became a part of State under the Christian emperors, Sunday observance was enforced by civil statutes, and later when the Empire was past, the Church in the hands of the papacy enforced it by ecclesiastical and also by civil enactments."—*Walter W. Hyde, "Paganism to Christianity in the Roman Empire," 1946, p. 261.*

"Constantine's decree marked the beginning of a long, though intermittent series of imperial decrees in support of Sunday rest." —*Vincent J. Kelly, "Forbidden Sunday and Feast-Day Occupations," 1943, p. 29.*

"Constantine labored at this time untiringly to unite the worshipers of the old and the new into one religion. All his laws and contrivances are aimed at promoting this amalgamation of religions. He would by all lawful and peaceable means melt together a purified heathenism and a moderated Christianity . . Of all his blending and melting together of Christianity and heathenism, none is more easy to see through than this making of his Sunday law: The Christians worshiped their Christ, the heathen their Sun-god . . [so they should now be combined]."—*H.G. Heggtveit, "Illustreret Kirkehistorie," 1895, p. 202.*

"If every Sunday is to be observed joyfully by the Christians on account of the resurrection, then every Sabbath on account of the burial is to be regarded in execration [cursing] of the Jews."—*Pope Sylvester, quoted by S.R.E. Humbert, "Adversus Graecorum Calumnias," in J.P. Migne, "Patrologie," p. 143. [Sylvester (A.D. 314-337) was the pope at the time Constantine I was Emperor.]*

"All things whatsoever that were prescribed for the [Bible] Sabbath, we have transferred them to the Lord's day, as being more authoritative and more highly regarded and first in rank, and more honorable than the Jewish Sabbath."—*Bishop Eusebius, quoted in J.P. Migne, "Patrologie," p. 23, 1169-1172. [Eusebius of Caesarea was a high-ranking Catholic leader during Constantine's lifetime.]*

"As we have already noted, excepting for the Roman and Alexandrian Christians, the majority of Christians were observing the seventh-day Sabbath at least as late as the middle of the fifth century [A.D. 450]. The Roman and Alexandrian Christians were among those converted from heathenism. They began observing Sunday as a merry religious festival in honor of the Lord's resurrection, about the latter half of the second century A.D. However, they did not try to teach that the Lord or His apostles commanded it. In fact, no ecclesiastical writer before Eusebius of Caesarea in the fourth century even suggested that either Christ or His apostles instituted the observance of the first day of the week.

"These Gentile Christians of Rome and Alexandria began calling the first day of the week 'the Lord's day.' This was not difficult for the pagans of the Roman Empire who were steeped in sun worship to accept, because they [the pagans] referred to their sun-god as their 'Lord.' "—*E.M. Chalmers, "How Sunday Came Into the Christian Church," p. 3.*

The following statement was made 100 years after Constantine's Sunday Law was passed: "Although almost all churches throughout the world celebrate the sacred mysteries on the Sabbath every week, yet the Christians of Alexandria and at Rome, on account of some ancient tradition, have ceased to do this."—*Socrates Scholasticus, quoted in "Ecclesiastical History," Book 5, chap. 22. [Written shortly after A.D. 439.]*

"The people of Constantinople, and almost everywhere, assemble together on the Sabbath, as well as on the first day of the week, which custom is never observed at Rome or at Alexandria."—*Hermias Sozomen, quoted in "Ecclesiastical History," vii, 19, in "A Select Library of Nicene and Post-Nicene Fathers," 2nd Series, Vol. 2, p. 390. [Written soon after A.D. 415.]*

"Down even to the fifth century the observance of the Jewish Sabbath was continued in the Christian church, but with a rigor and solemnity gradually diminishing until it was wholly discontinued."—*Lyman Coleman, "Ancient Christianity Exemplified," chap. 26, sec. 2, p. 527.*

"Constantine's [five Sunday Law] decrees marked the beginning of a long though intermittent series of imperial decrees in support of Sunday rest."—*"A History of the Councils of the Church," Vol. 2, p. 316.*

"What began, however, as a pagan ordinance, ended as a Christian regulation; and a long series of imperial decrees, during the fourth, fifth, and sixth centuries, enjoined with increasing stringency abstinence from labor on Sunday."—*Hutton Webster, "Rest Days," pp. 122-123, 270.*

Here is the first Sunday Law decree of a Christian council. It was given about 16 years after Constantine's first Sunday Law of A.D. 321: "Christians shall not Judaize and be idle on Saturday [in the original: "sabbato"—shall not be idle on the Sabbath], but shall work on that day; but the Lord's day they shall especially honour, and as being Christians, shall, if possible, do no work on that day. If, however, they are found Judaizing, they shall be shut out ["anathema,"—excommunicated] from Christ."—*Council of Laodicea, c. A.D. 337, Canon 29, quoted in C.J. Hefele, "A History of the Councils of the Church," Vol. 2, p. 316.*

"The keeping of the Sunday rest arose from the custom of the people and the constitution of the [Catholic] Church . . Tertullian was probably the first to refer to a cessation of affairs on the Sun day; the Council of Laodicea issued the first counciliar legislation for that day; Constantine 1 issued the first civil legislation."—*Priest Vincent J. Kelly, "Forbidden Sunday and Feast-Day Occupations," p. 203. [a thesis presented to the Catholic University of America.]*

"About 590, Pope Gregory, in a letter to the Roman people, denounced as the prophets of Antichrist those who maintained that work ought not to be done on the seventh day."—*James T. Ringgold, "The Law of Sunday," p. 267.*

In the centuries that followed, persecution against believers in the Bible Sabbath intensified until very few were left alive. When the Reformation began, the true Sabbath was almost unknown.

"Now the [Catholic] Church . . instituted, by God's authority, Sunday as the day of worship. This same Church, by the same divine authority, taught the doctrine of Purgatory . . We have, therefore, the same authority for Purgatory as we have for Sunday."—*Martin J. Scott, "Things Catholics Are Asked About," 1927, p. 236.*

"Of course the Catholic Church claims that the change [of the Sabbath to Sunday] was her act . . AND THE ACT IS A MARK of her ecclesiastical power."—*from the office of Cardinal Gibbons, through Chancellor H.F. Thomas, November 11, 1895.*

THE LAW OF GOD

I

Thou shalt have no other gods before Me.

II

Thou shalt not make unto thee any graven image, or any likeness of anything that is in heaven above, or that is in the earth beneath, or that is in the water under the earth. Thou shalt not bow down thyself to them, nor serve them, for I the Lord thy God am a jealous God, visiting the iniquity of the fathers upon the children unto the third and fourth generation of them that hate Me; and showing mercy unto thousands of them that love Me, and keep My commandments.

III

Thou shalt not take the name of the Lord thy God in vain; for the Lord will not hold him guiltless that taketh His name in vain.

IV

Remember the Sabbath day, to keep it holy. Six days shalt thou labor, and do all thy work; but the Seventh day is the Sabbath of the Lord thy God. In it thou shalt not do any work, thou, nor thy son, nor thy daughter, thy manservant, nor thy maidservant nor thy cattle, nor thy stranger that is within thy gates. For in six days the Lord made heaven and earth, the sea, and all that in them is, and rested the Seventh day: Wherefore the Lord blessed the Sabbath day, and hallowed it.

V

Honor thy father and thy mother, that thy days may be long upon the land which the Lord thy God giveth thee.

VI

Thou shalt not kill.

VII

Thou shalt not commit adultery.

VIII

Thou shalt not steal.

IX

Thou shalt not bear false witness against thy neighbor.

X

Thou shalt not covet thy neighbor's house; thou shalt not covet thy neighbor's wife, nor his manservant, nor his maidservant, nor his ox, nor his ass, nor anything that is thy neighbor's.

—Exodus 20:3-17.

THE LAW OF GOD AS CHANGED BY MAN

I

I am the Lord thy God. Thou shalt not have strange gods before me.

[The Second Commandment has been left out]

II *[actually III]*

Thou shalt not take the name of the Lord thy God in vain.

III *[IV]*

Remember that thou keep holy the Sabbath day.

[The Sabbath Commandment has been changed]

IV *[V]*

Honor thy father and thy mother.

V *[VI]*

Thou shalt not kill.

VI *[VII]*

Thou shalt not commit adultery.

VII *[VIII]*

Thou shalt not steal.

VIII *[IX]*

Thou shalt not bear false witness against thy neighbor.

IX *[X - First Part]*

Thou shalt not covet thy neighbor's wife.

X *[X - Second Part]*

Thou shalt not covet thy neighbor's goods.

—*The General Catholic Catechism.*

"Q.—Have you any other way of proving that the [Catholic] Church has power to institute festivals of precept?

"A.—Had she not such power .. she could not have substituted the observance of Sunday, the first day of the week for Saturday, the seventh day, a change for which there is no scriptural authority."—Doctrinal Catechism, p. 174 [Roman Catholic].

"Prove to me from the Bible alone that I am bound to keep Sunday holy. There is no such law in the Bible. It is a law of the holy Catholic Church alone. The Bible says 'Remember the Sabbath day to keep it holy.' The Catholic Church says, No. By my divine power I abolish the Sabbath day and command you to keep holy the first day of the week. And lo! The entire civilized world bows down in reverent obedience to the command of the Holy Catholic Church."—Thomas Enright, CSSR, President, Redemptorist College, Kansas City, Mo., Feb. 18, 1884. [Roman Catholic].

THE LAW OF GOD IN THE NEW TESTAMENT

I

"Thou shalt worship the Lord thy God, and Him only shalt thou serve."—*Matthew 4:10.*

II

"Little children, keep yourselves from idols." "Forasmuch then as we are the offspring of God, we ought not to think that the Godhead is like unto gold, or silver, or stone, graven by art and man's device."—*1 John 5:21; Acts 17:29.*

III

"That the name of God and His doctrine be not blasphemed."—*1 Timothy 6:1.*

IV

"Pray ye that your flight be not in the winter, neither on the Sabbath day." "The Sabbath was made for man, and not man for the Sabbath: therefore the Son of man is Lord also of the Sabbath." "For He spake in a certain place of the seventh day on this wise, And God did rest the seventh day from all His works." "There remaineth therefore a keeping of a Sabbath to the people of God. For he that is entered into His rest, he also hath ceased from his own works, as God did from His." "For by Him were all things created that are in heaven, and that are in earth."—*Matthew 24:20; Mark 2:27-28; Hebrews 4:4, 9, 10 margin; Colossians 1:16.*

V

"Honor thy father and thy mother."—*Matthew 19:19.*

VI

"Thou shalt not kill."—*Romans 13:9.*

VII

"Thou shalt not commit adultery."—*Matthew 19:18.*

VIII

"Thou shalt not steal."—*Romans 13:9.*

IX

"Thou shalt not bear false witness."—*Romans 13:9.*

X

"Thou shalt not covet."—*Romans 7:7.*

A BOOK WORTH READING

What happened when the Bible ended? What happened to the people of God and to the Bible? What were the forces at work that tried to destroy both?

In the book, GREAT CONTROVERSY, by Ellen White, this story is told. For, you see, although four thousand years of history are given to us in the Bible,—a powerful story began when the Bible ended. A story that would affect the people of God down to the end of time.

In the last week before His death, Jesus predicted the holocaust that was coming, and in urgent words He foretold the massive destruction of Jerusalem, the ages of persecution that were to follow, and the crisis of our own time.

And then, in the centuries that followed, the powers of earth and hell arrayed themselves against Christ in the person of His followers. A systematic effort to blot out Bible truth—and the true church along with it—began. But in vain were Satan's efforts to destroy God's people by violence. For even in death they conquered.

You may kill us, torture us, condemn us . . Your injustice is the proof that we are innocent . . Nor does your cruelty avail you . . The oftener we are mown down by you, the more in number we grow,—the blood of Christians is seed!"
—Tertullian, to the emperor Semtimius Severus, c. A.D. 206,
Quoted in chapter two of "Great Controversy."

But a century later, Satan introduced a new tactic to devastate the church of God. And it is still destroying churches and Christian families today.

Read what happened when the churches united with the world.

Read it in GREAT CONTROVERSY.

Read about the Waldenses, who loved God and their Bibles, and as a result were persecuted and hunted for their faith. What caused it all? How did they survive? DID they survive?

Read about John Wycliff—who determined to give the Bible back to the people. Read about John Huss—who revealed Christ to an entire nation—even though it meant imprisonment and death.

Read about the Protestant Reformation of the Sixteenth Century—and what it means to you today. Martin Luther, Ulric Zwingli, John Calvin, and others. Read about men and women who dared to take the Bible as it reads—no matter what the cost.

Read about the English Reformation: William Tyndale who gave the first printed Bible to England; John and Charles Wesley who brought Christ to two continents; George Whitfield who could speak to 100,000 people in a field as if they were but two.

Read about the crisis in our own day—and what is ahead. We who live at the end-time of history need to know what is coming.

In this book, the issues are made very, very clear. The story is traced so vividly that this book has become one of the most widely-distributed best-sellers of modern times—with editions currently on sale in a score of languages.

GREAT CONTROVERSY—A panorama of men and women who determined to cling to Christ, no matter what the outcome. Powerful encouragement is to be found here—to help you weather the storms in your own life.

GREAT CONTROVERSY—A gripping drama of 2,000 years of time—as it selects out fascinating stories and incidents that explain why we are on the edge of a holocaust today.

GREAT CONTROVERSY—The book that explains the crisis we are rapidly headed toward in our time—and the reasons behind it.

GREAT CONTROVERSY —
— PAPERBACK EDITION · 752 PAGES —
— US 5.00, postpaid

HARVESTIME BOOKS · ALTAMONT, TN 37301 USA

LISTENING FOR LIFE

THE VOICE OF PROPHECY –

Few religious radio broadcasts have survived the turbulent years since the 1930s. But the Voice of Prophecy with its personal messages has done so. It is the oldest religious radio broadcast in America, and is currently aired on over 500 radio stations, many of them daily broadcasts.

Over the years, the Voice of Prophecy has developed a number of provocative Bible correspondence courses that have brought courage to millions. You may well find here just what you, or a loved one, needs.

The Voice of Prophecy
Box 55
Los Angeles, California 90053

THE QUIET HOUR –

The Quiet Hour has over forty years of continuous radio broadcasting. This is due to the message it brings: a calm, assured confidence in God, in the midst of a troubled world in need of help.

This is another broadcast that has a deeply satisfying Bible correspondence course. Keeping God's Word before our thoughts—keeps God in our thoughts.

The Quiet Hour
630 Brookside Drive
Redlands California 92373

AMAZING FACTS –

This broadcast demands attention—and gets it. Hard-hitting, yet solidly in the Word. Few religious broadcasts can equal Amazing Facts. And a different kind of correspondence course is available.

Amazing Facts
P.O. Box 680
Frederick, Maryland 21701

LOOKING FOR SOMETHING BETTER

IT IS WRITTEN –

George Vandeman has an unusual approach that has kept his television broadcast in homes throughout North America for over 25 years. Write for a TV log and tune in. You will be glad that you did.

We understand that an excellent set of video cassettes and accompanying lessons is available from It Is Written. You would need to write for prices.

It Is Written
Box 0
Thousand Oaks, California 91360

BREATH OF LIFE –

A television broadcast with punch is this weekly production by Charles D. Brooks. Originally designed for minority groups, it has gained a wide acceptance in many homes throughout the country.

A complete Bible correspondence course is available from Breath of Life. We can be thankful that there are those who are determined that Christ will be proclaimed, in spite of the terrible times in which we live.

Breath of Life
P.O. Box 744
Newbury Park, California 91320

SEARCH TELECAST –

Practical, down to earth; trying to help people right where they are: This is "Search." And it is something you will not want to miss.

An intriguing correspondence course that you will appreciate is available. The more we study God's Word, the more we benefit.

Search Telecast
630 Brookside Drive
Redlands, California 92373

AN OPEN DOOR
—INTO A VAST TREASURE HOUSE

Yes, open the doors to a treasure.

For the treasure is already there; now just open the door to it.

And the key is Bible study helps that you can use and enjoy—simple guides to open before you the treasures of God's Word.

These are the *Bible Study Guides:* Scripture lesson helps that you and your loved ones can use in the privacy of your own home.

What is more important than a personal knowledge of the most important book in the whole world? What is more important than studying it?

No book can change your life for the better— as this one can. No book can bring you peace and happiness and self-control as can the Bible. For it is God's own book of messages to you. Over the centuries, millions have testified to the creative power to be found within its pages.

The Bible has the power to bring us back to our Maker. Through the words of Scripture we can find peace in Him! Forgiveness of sin, and strength to live in obedience to God's laws—all this is ours through a personal daily relationship with our Creator. Find Him in the morning through prayer and study of His Word. Walk with Him all day long through prayerful dependence upon Him. This is the secret that millions have found. And it is a way of life that can bring you a peace of heart you may never have known before.

Just now, fill out and mail the slip below—and the *Bible Study Guides* will be sent to you without charge or obligation.

And you can begin that definite program of Bible study that you have so long wanted.

MAIL TO — The Voice of Prophecy · Box 55 · Los Angeles CA 90053

Please send me the free Bible Study Guides.

Name . . . .

Address . . . .

City, State, Zip . . . .

WORTHWHILE BOOKS FOR YOUR HOME

Here is an outstanding set of books that will help your entire family:

BIBLE READINGS—For nearly a century, this book has helped millions of people in their study of the Bible. It contains 180 chapters in 18 major sections, and will provide you with hours of reading.

CHRIST'S OBJECT LESSONS—Here you will find the parables of Christ masterfully told. The best stories in all the world are the stories that Jesus told while here on earth.

THE DESIRE OF AGES—This book carefully explains the life and lessons of Christ during His earthly life. Millions of copies have been printed in recent decades.

THE GREAT CONTROVERSY—Here is the story of a planet in crisis. Thinking men everywhere recognize that we are on the edge of a crisis; but few understand its exact nature. Here you will find the events leading up to it.

THE MINISTRY OF HEALING—Over a million copies published, and now for the first time in large-print paperback. Within its pages you will find principles dealing with natural healing, disease prevention, conquering stress, mental health, answers to depression, prayer for the sick, successful families, and child training.

PATRIARCHS AND PROPHETS—In this book you will find a major part of the Old Testament clearly explained, powerfully written: from the Creation on down to the end of David's reign. Here is a book your entire family will value.

SHELTER IN THE STORM—In everyone's life a storm is coming. In these pages you will learn how to come back to God and ask Him for forgiveness; the New Birth, what it is and how to receive it; how His love can change your life.

FOR ADDITIONAL INFORMATION on how you can obtain these books, write to the publisher. The address is given on the second page of this book.